AN ONLY CHILD

BOOKS BY LES ROBERTS

Milan Jacovich Mysteries
Pepper Pike
Full Cleveland
Deep Shakeer'
The Cleveland Connection
The Lake Effect
The Duke of Cleveland
Collision Bend
The Cleveland Local
A Shoot in Cleveland
The Best-Kept Secret
The Indian Sign
The Dutch
The Irish Sports Pages
King of the Holly Hop
The Cleveland Creep
Whiskey Island
Win, Place or Die
(with Dan S. Kennedy)
The Ashtabula Hat Trick
Speaking of Murder
(with Dan S. Kennedy)

Dominic Candiotti Novels
*The Strange Death of
Father Candy*
Wet Work

Saxon Mysteries
*An Infinite Number
of Monkeys*
Not Enough Horses
A Carrot for the Donkey
Snake Oil
Seeing the Elephant
The Lemon Chicken Jones

Stand-Alones
The Chinese Fire Drill
Sheehan's Dog
The C.I.
An Only Child

Novella
A Carol for Cleveland
(later made into a play by
Eric Coble for the Cleveland
Play House holiday season)

Short Stories
The Scent of Spiced Oranges

Non-Fiction Memoir
We'll Always Have Cleveland

LES ROBERTS

AN ONLY CHILD

Down & Out Books
3959 Van Dyke Road, Suite 265
Lutz, FL 33558
DownAndOutBooks.com

The characters and events in this book are fictitious. Any similarity to real persons, living or dead, is coincidental and not intended by the author.

Cover design by JT Lindroos

ISBN: 1-64396-355-4
ISBN-13: 978-1-64396-355-6

To My Parents, who welcomed me as an only child,
And to Chicagoans, who helped make me who I am.

CHAPTER ONE

I am an only child.

That title describes me as well as anything else—and there are several other descriptive phrases I have to live with, whether I like them or not. I have no brothers, sisters, or second cousins once removed, either. Whether that's a good thing or bad thing depends entirely on your point of view.

My parents—the middle-aged couple who adopted me when I was four weeks old—are long gone. They were David and Dorothy Reinert, so the monicker they bestowed upon me is Russell Arthur Reinert, which is on my birth certificate. Nobody knows the names of my biological parents, and I've never had the urge to find out who they were, as they dumped my ass on the steps of a Methodist church on Berwyn Avenue, one block west of Sheridan Road on the North Side of Chicago, before I even got my eyes open, so to hell with them.

My one living aunt—my adoptive father's sister—hates my guts because I'm not a blood-red member of the family. She looked at me only as an interloper who had the effrontery to take over the last name. She was coldly nasty to me while I was growing up and has not spoken to me since I turned twenty-one. She lives somewhere in Maine; I'm not sure in what community and I don't give a damn. Everyone bitches how COVID-19 didn't allow family to visit virus victims in hospital, but that's one thing about the pandemic that didn't disturb me, because I have no family at all.

There is a happy side to being without a big family. An only child never feels ignored because there's no other relative in the home to have even a sliver of attention. No squabbles about who gets the bigger slice of cake, or the turkey drumstick at Thanksgiving, because the single child is always at the front of the line. No fighting over who sleeps in the top bunk and who gets stuck in the lower one, because I never slept in a bunk bed. No lifelong resentments as to which sibling is bigger, smarter, stronger, sexier, better looking, more successful. In adulthood, a fortune is saved at Christmastime—no buying gifts for brothers or sisters who have your last name, too, and whom you detest in the first place.

I'm too young—late thirties—to have grown up with the legendary magazine cover paintings of one Norman Rockwell on the now-defunct *Saturday Evening Post*, but I've seen copies of them. In many of his artistic masterpieces, there are kids running around doing things older viewers found adorable. My generation considers them weird and cumbersome. We didn't grow up playing outside until dinnertime, because someone figured out there are murderous pedophiles walking the streets. No magazine covers of us getting our tearful first haircut for all the world to see or doing a nine-year-old boy-girl first cheek kiss. We hung out in our own rooms—if we had our own rooms—and played Donkey Kong, listened to Selena, Britney Spears, and Smashing Pumpkins, or watched endless TV re-runs of *The Brady Bunch*.

Now here comes the bad news: Every "only child" suffers from loneliness. No one to play with on a cold rainy day when you're stuck in the house and can't go outside to have fun. No one shares the bedroom to whisper private kid thoughts before you close your eyes, or to soothe you when you sleep with your bedclothes over your head because you're terrified of the monsters in the closet. No one to ask for advice. Absent any adult human being who can put away a bottle of wine on a quiet afternoon and hear about the fears and frights of a marriage which is never, *ever,* perfect and will never make judgments no matter how much you ask them to. Nobody with whom to trade baseball cards—or secrets.

You can boast to the world how in your family, you are the "special one," the one who got all the parental attention and didn't have to share it with brothers and sisters—but you probably never believed it, and no one else did, either. The hollow yaw of loneliness lies in dark readiness each night. Bereft and abandonment were your terrifying roommates when the lights went out.

And oh yes—no family relative to pick you up and take you home when you're finally released from a sprawling prison in downstate Illinois in which you spent seven years without ever sticking your nose out and taking a big deep breath of fresh air. That's what happened to me.

The only one who could rescue me on my release day and drive me back to Chicago was my lawyer, Tana Phillips. She came on board when my first published novel surprised the crap out of me and became an overnight hit, Number Two or Number Three on the New York Times best-selling book list for nine weeks, an award from the Mystery Writers of America for "Best First Novel," and then a high-budget Hollywood movie which starred a giganticallytalented actor who grows old right along with me growing old, all of which made me comfortably rich. Before that, in my twenties, I never had money with which to hire a lawyer.

It was an amazing eight-year rush. My publishers even put me on television to flog book sales. I was a bigger deal than usual because I was younger than most debut authors. I was invited to appear on *Good Morning America, Entertainment Tonight,* and several local talk shows in Chicago, Cleveland, Denver, and even in Los Angeles. I got booked as a cameo actor—an actor, for crysakes—playing myself on that old TV show about a guy who writes mystery novels and hangs out with New York cops, and every so often I was paid handsomely to fly to Los Angeles and appear in a scene playing poker with the star and other real-life mystery writers like me who don't spend their days in police precincts and fall in love with gorgeous New York cops.

I traveled around the country for book signings, and got paid more than I ever imagined to give speeches to clubs and organizations. Not many people recognized me on the street as they would Morgan Freeman or Tom Hanks, and I never cottoned to the idea of being a "celebrity," but I did enjoy my success all over the world—been published in several different languages—French, German, Spanish, Italian, Japanese, Slovenian, Serbo-Croatian, and Hebrew. The foreign countries often changed my book titles, and now, all these years later, I can't even remember them, though I have foreign language translations of them in my bookcase.

Tana Phillips, an African American attorney eighteen years my senior, with a husband and a thriving business, turned out to be the best lawyer in the world, even though when I went on criminal trial, we were fucked from the beginning by an impossible judge who hated all creative people and everyone else who made less than seven figures per year, a stubborn-as-hell jury who despised me because I wrote books they either never read or had consumed the first twenty pages and then returned to the library and bitched about it, and a prosecutor who had in his mind to become the District Attorney and eventually the governor of the state by winning a case against someone relatively famous.

"Famous" is a strange word I never truly accepted about myself. The President of the United States is famous—or infamous, depending on one's political preferences. Athletes and movie stars are famous only for a while before they fade from sight like teen-age acne, chicken pox, or that passionate nymphomaniac who, for a short time, makes your life worth living. Writers—big ones who get millions of dollars for an advance on each book—are famous only to those who read them, and they damn well better churn out at least one book per year before they, too, are forgotten.

When I was found guilty, sentenced, and put away, Tana Phillips gathered all my assets together in a trust no one could touch but me, and kept them safe and secure, even allowing my supply of money to draw interest. When the powers that be caved in to Tana's relentless pleading, it was announced I would get out after seven, she rented me a beautiful (and expensive) second-floor apartment in a brownstone on East Oak Street in Chicago, less than half a block from Lake Michigan and a sprawling beach, and she and her husband, Jack, were on hand outside the Joliet Correctional Institution to drive me there from my incarceration.

Husband Jack, by the way, who is a hugely successful hedge fund manager on Wells Avenue and one of the rare, frighteningly bright NFL football players, used to be a defensive end for the Chicago Bears—another once-famous sort-of celebrity. Rich, handsome guy with a record of tackles, take-downs and a Super Bowl ring marries rich, beautiful lawyer. As Humphrey Bogart said as he handled a Maltese falcon statue at the end of a classic private-eye movie, "This is the stuff that dreams are made of."

That's really a Shakespeare quote—but I prefer Bogart.

On a table near the doorway were keys to the apartment and to a new Toyota Prius Hybrid——no, not keys, as new cars have remote-control buttons instead. The Prius, I was told, was dark blue in color and parked in a private garage just around the corner, all paid for from my stash and registered to me—and the damn thing ran mostly on water. A pantry off the kitchen was stocked with the snack foods I'd always loved, like chips, pretzels, pita, several family-sized jars of peanut butter and a box of super-fresh bagels the Phillips family bought that morning before motoring down to Joliet to get me.

Jesus Christ, I thought as I looked around the pantry. Seven prison years without one single bagel with cream cheese. *Seven years!*

Attached to the main bedroom was a glorious sprawling closet big enough for a family of eight to live in. Hanging there in plastic covers were three brand new expensive suits, one gray, one blue and one beige, decent enough that I would throw away the ghastly, shapeless getting-out suit issued to me the day I left "the joint." Tana had visited me shortly before I got out and asked me what size suit I wore. I had to guess. I'd lost fifteen or more pounds in the past seven years, mostly because I had little to do inside besides exercising, but once I got settled as a released civilian, I'd buy my own suits, tailored to fit.

There were also several sports jackets, hanging slacks, and too many dress and informal shirts to count. The drawers in the main bedroom were filled with socks, T-shirts, and ten folded ties, plus twelve pairs of briefs in various dark colors—none white, as I hadn't owned whitey-tighties since childhood, not counting white boxers the state of Illinois had issued to Joliet inmates for the past seven years.

How did Tana know what kind of underwear I preferred, as she'd never seen me in undies before? I had no clue, but there were lots of things I didn't know since first being imprisoned. The world changes so fast no one is able to catch up. Most private citizens gave up laptops for iPads, but I couldn't imagine myself writing a book on a cell phone approximately the size of a pack of cigarettes.

There were also three pairs of carefully folded designer jeans, half a dozen sweatshirts, one with the logo of the University of Illinois on its chest to remind me of where I'd attended twenty years earlier, three Calvin Klein sweaters for when the air turned chilly, and a multi-colored Australian sweater which a decade earlier had sold for five hundred dollars. I had no idea what it cost now—probably the price of a used car.

The bed was queen-sized, with several extra pillows and a

subtly attractive blue bedspread. Before getting used to a prison cot, I'd always slept in a king-sized bed, but at the moment I had no one with whom to share sleeping space. Tana picked out the bedsheets, light blue, Egyptian-made with a high-number thread count, as she'd picked out everything else in the apartment.

They had set the second bedroom up as my office. A large desk with a throne-like leather executive chair, a matching wood file cabinet, and a large TV set mounted on the wall, approximately the size of a movie screen in one of the old-fashioned cinema palaces. The windows faced north. If I kept the drapes open, as I'd love to be able to look out as I had not been able to for seven years, I'd get a face full of bright, blinding sun late in the afternoon, meaning I could spend almost every minute of the day actually writing. The laptop was shiny, new and gold-colored, a MacBookAir. Tana had confiscated my old one and had the Geek Squad at Best Buy transfer everything to the present one.

I was luckier than hell, I suppose. Most people who walk out of prison don't own a damn thing, and unless they had to report to their parole officers every week, no one really knew what they were supposed to do with their newfound freedom, as it was difficult as hell for a felon to get a decent job. When they began their sentence, they were not as financially comfortable as I was, so they had nothing waiting for them in the real world.

However, they could get away with where they'd been, and why. Many had families waiting with open arms.

Not me. Not by a long shot. No family.

Now free again, I wondered who my real biological parents were, on the off-chance they were criminally insane serial killers. It was possible. Anything is possible, but highly unlikely. And I don't think I was anywhere near insanity.

Neither of my adoptive parents had survived my imprisonment to point me in the right direction. They were nowhere near religious, which is why I grew up agnostic-slash-atheist, and the only time my mother had seen the inside of a jail was watching "Orange is the New Black." They were quiet, middle-class Cook County Democrats with no scandal that linked them to me.

I couldn't get away quietly with that kind of untold tale because I was already a big-time author.Anyone who ever read my books or saw any of the film versions knew all about my so-called criminal past and wouldn't trust me as far as they could throw me.

A few of my fellow convicts *could* throw me—clear across a room—and sometimes did so during my enforced residency. But most who got to know me held me in their own kind of respect because I actually wrote books. So I was untormented during my prison years. Nobody wanted to force-rape a celebrity.

Some prison buddies, especially the lifers, talked the warden into starting a reading class with me teaching literature, which made me even more safe. Thanks to our well-stocked prison library, most were turned on by *Huckleberry Finn* and the strength and courage of the escaped black slave, Jim, and even cheerfully ignored the repetitive use of the N-word, as that reflected the sign of the times a hundred fifty years ago.

The warden refused to allow me to teach them any books about criminals, which shot hell out of the Dashiell Hammett-Raymond Chandler classics I love. But they all enjoyed *Moby Dick*, and the exciting and eventual tragedy of chasing a big white whale all over the world. The young inmates of color were highly amused one main character was named Queequeg. None had ever met or even heard of anyone called Queequeg before.

Let's face it. *No one* wants to take up permanent residency at the Graybar Hotel, but if they're clever enough, they could get through their sentence with brain, skills, and an infinite amount of patience. I possessed the first two, and fought daily to live with the third.

Knowing I'd be in this new apartment for some time, it took me half an hour to explore the new set-up, while Tana and Jack sat in the living room, nervous I'd hate the whole thing. They were needlessly on edge. It was a pretty neat place, and Tana's taste in tailoring and interior decorating was impeccable. Naturally I'd had a large, elegant home in the suburb of Winnetka before I got arrested and shut away. After only a few hours of freedom I was not yet ready to deal with an estate, swooping lawns, an oyster-shell driveway, a three-car garage, and a housekeeper who made sure the place shimmered with clean-and-neat.

Eventually, I returned to the living room and sat in a recliner I later learned was electric, with buttons to raise and lower the seat so I didn't struggle getting my ass up or down without great effort. Aches and pains did not yet torment me when I awoke every morning, but for a while I found myself playing with the lift-and-lower whenever I was bored.

Tana and Jack were side-by-side on a three-piece sofa when I finally returned to them. I took only a moment to decide that as soon as they left, I would rearrange the sofa sections and the rest of the living room furniture to how I wanted them.

"So," Tana said, voice quivering with uncertain nerves, "what do you think, Russ?"

"It's pretty amazing," I said with as much gratitude as I could muster. "I always wanted to live on the Near North Side. All the work you did, picking everything out and making this almost feel like home. How can I thank you?"

"Thank Tana," Jack rumbled. "She did ninety percent," he grinned, then cleared his throat. "I picked out the bedspread, though."

"Very macho, Jack."

"Don't thank me yet," Tana warned. "We have to talk a little business."

"I stink at talking business, since I never had to think about it in prison. I write books. That's what I do."

"Will you do it some more, Russ? After I sold your house and car, I put all your money in a trust except for about eighty thousand dollars, most of which is still in your checking account. I made some insignificant purchases with each of your credit cards and kept them up to date." She pointed to one of several large manila envelopes on the coffee table. "Those cards are in here, ready to use whenever you want them. We can get the rest of your money out of trust and you can put it wherever you want it."

Jack added, "Keep all that money under your mattress, Russ, or roll it up in a pair of socks where no one would look for it."

"I have to consider the socks option," I said. Then I turned directly to Tana. "Talk about this trust for a minute. How much is in there?"

"Royalty checks for all your books went directly into that trust," she said. "Of course, the royalties have grown smaller because you haven't come out with anything new in seven years, but they're still pretty substantial."

"What's the rough total?"

"I don't have the exact numbers in my head, Russ, but I figure it's about eleven million dollars."

"Give or take a few bucks," I said, but it set my head spinning. I knew I'd made a lot of money from my books and the movie versions. But eleven million dollars? She spent my money buying me a car and signing a year-long apartment rental lease. As my attorney, my money paid for all the work she did for me and managed to increase the total up to eleven mil while I spent seven years mopping floors and cleaning prison toilets to earn just enough to purchase my own toothpaste every month.

And I *still* had eleven million fucking dollars!

"You can buy yourself a yacht," Tana reminded me.

"Too expensive," I said. "How much money does a rowboat cost?"

They hung around for another hour, mostly for Jack to explain how to change that eleven million into twenty million with hedge funds, but I wasn't listening. What would I do with all that money, anyway? After you bought everything in the world you want, why do you need another twenty million?

As much as I adore Tana, I found myself wishing the Phillips to say goodbye and go home. Other than accustoming myself to my new apartment, there were only two things I looked forward to.

With the exception of hugging Tana in front of her husband when I walked through the Stony Lonesome gates earlier that day, I had not touched another woman for seven years.

Touched.

No hugging, no kissing, not even a handshake with any female person until I walked out to meet Tana and Jack outside the iron gates. *No touching* was the big rule.

And sex? As the mob guys say in Brooklyn, *Fuhgeddaboudit*.

No past ex-girlfriends would renew a relationship with a convicted killer, so there's no one I could call. And though in the old days there were too many places to count where one could strike up a relationship—bars, mostly, and lectures about whatever you gave a damn—COVID-19 had made it generally impossible to meet strangers at all, much less touch.

Sex with a hooker didn't interest me—never did. It's not that I ever expected a virgin, but I realized most prostitutes had already fucked the entire United States Navy and didn't give a shit about me. As long as I paid in advance.

There was something else which was even more important to me.

Writing another book.

The State of Illinois refused my right to compose anything I chose to while I was incarcerated. I was not allowed to use a laptop or even a typewriter, and my cursive handwriting is so ghastly even I can't read it. Before going to prison, I would actually type out my shopping lists before cruising the aisles of a supermarket.

I can't remember how many legal-sized notepads I bought

from the prison gift shop whenever I needed them. I jotted ideas down every day, using large, almost childish printing——maybe just a snippet of conversation I'd overheard between convicts, often in the prison yard. Sometimes during quiet evening hours, we'd tell each other stories about our lives, not because they were dying to get their biographies published but because, like most other human beings, they needed to talk.

No one spoke of the crimes that got them locked up in the first place. In Joliet, the one question one inmate never asks another is, "What are you in for?" We all knew everyone was guilty—including ourselves—and we mostly stayed away from the whiners.

I haven't seriously mentioned what crime I did to get myself imprisoned. Let's just say it wasn't premeditated, but when it happened, I wasn't wracked with guilt about it, either.

I'd mailed all those notes off to Tana Phillips during my incarceration, and she had her assistant decipher the handwriting, then type them up and put them all in the many stuffed manila envelopes she made sure were now piled at the side of my new desk. After seven years, I don't recall most of my scribbled ideas, but having been unencumbered by prison cells and tough guards with guns for several hours, this was not the time.

I changed into one pair of jeans, which fit me pretty well, though a bit loose around the waist—and a sweatshirt, the one with the Illini logo. Then I looked into the full-length mirror on the closet door and gave myself a good once-over. A first-time-in-seven-years look wearing decent civilian clothing. Not bad—but did I look seven years older? A few more lines around the corners of my eyes, an unhappy downward sloop to my mouth, and even some gray hair at my temples where dark brown used to be.

I was as pale as a three-day-old corpse. Should I go to a tanning salon to pick up more color? Probably not, as it had never occurred to me before. Maybe the grayish-white skin would make me look menacing.

I put on more comfortable shoes, made sure the apartment key was in my pocket, and went downstairs and out onto Oak Street. Some old businesses had folded their tents and stolen away, and others had taken their place, but the row of brownstones had changed very little, and I loved that. The more my surroundings are the same, the more comfortable I am.

Loping along across the street was a youngish kid with a long, curly black beard. Rastafarian braids covered his ears and his Caucasian cheeks, and he wore a three-cornered hat and an ankle-length black coat that looked like a cape. Blackbeard the Pirate? North Side, in Chicago, had not changed much at all while I was gone.

I crossed over to the Michigan Avenue Beach. The waves were medium-high, active in the blasts of Lake Michigan wind. It's no mistake Chicago is nicknamed "The Windy City," but on this day the chilly gusts were not yet angry, and I sucked in the waterfront fresh air so deeply it made me dizzy. My blood moved a bit faster. It made my heart stop hurting. It nudged my inactive brain to wake the hell up and go on with my life. It made me free.

Free.

CHAPTER TWO

Most people sleep in a bed, don't they? For me, that bed Tana Phillips bought for me was a high point of my existence so far. I'd almost forgotten I'd slept in a bed for my entire life before trading it in for a lumpy mattress, one tired, saggy pillow, and a cellmate named Merle Dupree, who constantly hummed "It Had to Be You" for hours and hours, and masturbated every morning in his cot. I was fortunate to be assigned the upper bunk and not the lower one.

Merle never told me why he was in prison, so I didn't know if he was a purse-snatcher, a pickpocket, or a serial murderer who cooked and ate his victims for lunch. However, he spoke often—at least three times per week—about a bimbo he picked up in a bar one night. When they got back to her apartment, it startled him to find though she was a relatively dark brunette, her pubic hair was that of a redhead. When Merle asked her if she dyed it, she said no, that she grew up that way. One of those stories one never grows tired of hearing.

I was awakened at six thirty each day and marched down to the dining hall with a few hundred other grumpy, sleepy-eyed convicts, where I was fed egg substitutes, white toast already buttered, a serving of orange juice in a shot glass, a mini-carton of milk, and a bowl of Cheerios—or rather, a Cheerios rip-off. I never heard of it before. The morning meal in the calaboose made Denny's Breakfast Special seem like a gourmet feast at the Four Seasons.

Ah, but my new bed! Blue sheets, three fluffy pillows, and a warm electric blanket. I luxuriated in them, especially on that first morning on which I slept until half-past eight. The sheets felt amazing, sensuous, soft against my skin—all my skin, as this was my first sleep completely naked in seven years.

I rolled around. I stretched. I snuggled. I buried my face in the pillows, fantasizing things I'd forced myself to not think about while in prison, and wondered how long it will be and under what circumstances I can make that hallucination come to life.

Staying abed all day was a fabulous thought, but if I did, it would feel too good for me to not get up the next day, and the day after that, which will make me a lazy-ass ex-con. I dislike that label even more than plain old "ex-con."

I dressed quickly and casually, made a pot of coffee from a large tin of Folger's, which I looked forward to drinking, black. When I got around to it, I'd shop for a more expensive coffee at Trader Joe's, but at the moment, one sip was like ambrosia.

Then I checked the grocery items. Real bacon! Bagels—with cream cheese! The kitchen inmates made Sunday bacon on Sundays, not cooked long enough—half-raw and dripping fat. And oh my god—real eggs!

Sure, in prison we got real eggs for breakfast twice a week or so, instead of egg substitutes, but they were scrambled. Always scrambled. There's no point in arguing with the cook, because scrambled eggs were quicker and easier to cook than any other way. I was a sunny side up guy, have been all my life. I choked those scrambled eggs down each time, pushed the half-raw bacon aside, chewed the already-buttered toast, and drank lousy coffee purchased by fifty-pound sacks from Costco—what you get for committing a crime and getting your ass caught.

I rinsed everything off and put the breakfast detritus into the dishwasher.

Dishwasher—a little slice of heaven. For the past seven years I'd eaten with dishes and utensils I wasn't certain had been washed thoroughly by the guys who worked at the gigantic sink in the prison kitchen—guys who probably never washed their hands after using the sink and toilet in their cells.

I yearned for another day strolling aimlessly around, maybe dropping into one of the Miracle Mile stores to buy something for myself—just for the opportunity to use my credit cards once more. This was my first full day of complete freedom. But the itch within me, the positive need to begin doing things again overwhelmed everything else.

I shaved, showered, and shampooed my hair. I stayed under the hot water until it ran out. In prison, they only let us shower twice per week, and beard control was done with electric shavers; prisoners running around with razor blades in prison were frowned upon by the guards. Also, our prison showers were automatically timed—ten minutes and out.

One of my first trips to get clean in Joliet, about two weeks after I entered, took more than ten minutes, because three inmates propositioned me. They had been straight all their lives, but endless years without a woman had turned them temporarily gay. My refusal led to an attack, and though I fought back as hard as I could—I knew I'd be beaten to a pulp, and then gang-raped.

One eye was already swollen shut and my nose was bleeding, but I managed to stay on my feet and got a few good licks in. Before I collapsed, Denver Tolliver was there. How he found out a new inmate was being readied for pulling a train and desperately needed his help, I had no idea. But that giant black man I'd never seen before spent a good five minutes physically destroying the bad guys, and from then on, I felt relatively safe, even in a hardcore prison.

I loved staying in my apartment shower for more than half an hour and spent another fifteen minutes deciding what to wear. Jeans and a sweatshirt won't cut it where I was heading, so I first picked out the gray suit. Black was too formidable, and tan was too summery, so the gray was perfect. I chose an off-white dress shirt with buttons, no cufflinks—and one of the many Jerry Garcia ties Tana had chosen for me. I always liked Garcia ties, even though after seven years they were somewhat out of date. But they were colorful, and they were different.

I suppose I'm different, too. Richer than ninety-nine percent of all writers, my name was recognized by everyone who reads my books—even some cons. I ran in different circles, and never really met an ex-con before.

Now I am one.

I walked a block to the garage where Tana left my car, and introduced myself to the valet, who was on duty six days a week. His name was Rollo Jackson. He was somewhere in his middle sixties, and he had a full head of kinky hair that was pure white, a lovely addition to his dark brown skin. He was tall, over six feet, though he hunched over, making him look shorter—and older. A very pleasant guy, he must have paid more attention to me than usual. His handshake was extra firm and warm, both hands holding mine, making me think he somehow knew who I was. Perhaps he'd spent a stretch of time inside the way I did. He'd picked me a permanent parking spot, and promised to wash my car once a week, even in winter when it snowed.

I fired up the car, sitting there for a while, enjoying the luxurious soft purr of the new engine. Then I drove up onto the busy street and headed south. Anyone living north of the towering Wrigley Building *must* drive across one of the many bridges spanning the Chicago River if they want to get downtown. I was looking for an old office building on Wabash Avenue, the elevated trains running beside it, that particular transportation known far and wide as "The L."

I'd visited this fifteenth floor office many times, but now, somehow, the building itself looked strange to me. When I walked in, I recognized many book jacket covers mounted on the wall, mostly thriller and suspense. Six of them were mine.

The young woman in the reception room was pretty, coffee tan, and smiling. Damn young, too. I figured when I got arrested, she was in middle school. I introduced myself.

"Hi. I'm Russell Reinert, here to see Owen Fullmer."

"Did you have an appointment?"

"I've never needed an appointment. I'm one of Owen's clients." I moved to the wall and pointed at two of my titles. "Russell Reinert. See?"

She got just a tad flustered. "I'm so sorry, Mr. Reinert. I should have recognized you."

"That's okay," I shrugged. "I haven't been up here in a long, long time."

"Oh? Out of the country?"

"Not exactly. Is he in?"

"Hang on," she said. She picked up her phone, punched two keys, and waited. Then she said with more eagerness than usual, "Mr. Russell Reinert is here." She waited, listened, her beaming happy smile slowly fading away as if into a strong wind. Then, with a completely different tone, she said, "Mr. Fullmer will see you," and pointed to an inner door.

"I know where it is," I said, and marched into Owen Fullmer's inner sanctum.

He stood as I entered, dressed almost as expensively as I was. Ever since I began writing best-selling novels, he took fifteen percent of whatever money I made, as he did to all the other famous authors whose book jackets hung in his reception room. All but two of us were male—he didn't relate to female mystery writers. In fact, he didn't relate to women in any other way, either. But it was only after he'd had two or three drinks could anyone tell he was a bit light in his loafers.

Owen was a literary agent. In stir, I realized I'd take a year or more to write a novel and give it to him.One phone call to my publisher that takes no more than five minutes, and I was sold. Owen took that bite out of my royalties while I was in prison. I wonder why any successful author needs him, or someone like him. I guess that's just the way the business works.

"Russ," Owen said, and reached across the big desk to shake. His smile didn't make it to his eyes. "I heard you were out. Congratulations. It's good to see you."

"It's good to be back in Chicago," I said.

"You're looking good. Nice suit. You lost some weight?"

"Some. Not by design."

"Now you can pack the weight back on again."

"I had a good breakfast for the first time in years, if that means anything."

"Sit down, sit down, be comfortable," he urged. "Should I have the girl get you some coffee?"

"The girl?" I sat on one of his visitor chairs. "I thought people stopped saying 'girl 'about anyone over the age of twelve."

"Jesus," Owen said, "you jailbirds are getting politically correct?"

"Jailbird? Is that what I am now, Owen? A jailbird? Let me explain something to you. Jail is where people spend the night when they got caught driving drunk. It's where they put in thirty days for a misdemeanor. It's where they stay before they go to trial and get sentenced to ten or twenty years, or life. I wasn't in jail, Owen. I was in prison."

"Well, whatever." He waved his hand in front of his face as though shooing away a gnat. "So—tell me, Russ. What are your plans now?"

"To write another book. What did you think? I have seven years of notes and a new laptop, so I'm ready to go."

"A novel about prison?"

"Probably not. I've had more than enough time thinking about prison."

He frowned, wrinkling up his forehead, making him look twenty years older. "Maybe you should give that some more thought."

The backs of my hands tingled, as if they'd fallen asleep. Oversensitive nerves. The first time that ever happened was when all the lights went out on my first night inside and I could hear the screaming and the singing and the sound of raped gay sex. It was not the last. "Explain," I ordered.

He humphed, wriggled in his chair, pressed down his right eyebrow with his finger. He finally said, "You haven't published a book in seven years."

"Harper Lee hadn't published a book in forty-five years, Owen, but her second book reached a hell of a lot of people,"

"Yeah, but she wrote *To Kill a Mockingbird*. You didn't."

"Nobody else did, either. But I can name you a dozen popular authors who took several years off between books."

"They weren't convicted criminals—not convicted of murder."

My upper body turned in on itself, making me feel smaller and very weak. I recalled the first moment they wrapped a chain around my waist and cuffs around my wrists and ankles, so it was difficult for me to walk. I felt those chains again, dragging me down. I hadn't expected that last remark from someone with whom I worked for fifteen years. My mouth was dry, but I managed to say, "It wasn't murder, Owen. It was involuntary manslaughter."

He shook his head. "Words, words, words," he cribbed from Shakespeare. "You took the life of another human being."

"That's a fucking lie!"

"The jury didn't think so."

The next few words fought to come out of my mouth. Finally, quietly: "You don't think so, either. Do you?"

Fullmer sighed, putting both hands atop his desk. "Russ, we were never what you call *friends*. I was your agent, and you were one of my writers. I admired your talent. I still do. But I don't think your publisher wants you back because he thinks like I do. People won't spend thirty bucks to read a book by somebody who's been imprisoned for seven years with nothing but yellow foolscap and a two-dollar ballpoint pen."

"You astonish me, Owen," I said.

"I was fine with you all the good times because you made a hell of a lot of money you can live off forever—or get even richer if you invest. Relax, for crysakes. You had a shitty seven years, now you can have great years for the rest of your life."

"Relax? I'm thirty-seven years old. I won't relax, sitting in a rocking chair and waiting to die. I need to get back to work."

"Maybe." He fiddled in his outbox on the desk and pulled out a pink message slip. "By the way, I got a call for you this morning. If you haven't read the *Chicago Tribune*, your return to your city has been noted. This guy wanted to know where you'd be living. I figured you'd show up, so I wrote his number down if you're interested." He slid the message slip across the desk. A strange name was scrawled beneath mine. *Cole Cabot.*

"I have no idea who he is," I said, shoving the message into a jacket pocket. "He probably he wants to collaborate with me. You know that bullshit game, don't you? A complete stranger takes ten minutes to tell me some cockamamie story, I take a year turning it into a book, and he expects half the advance and the royalties. Sure."

"Is he an ex-con buddy, and you deliberately forgot his name?"

That was like an ice water shock. I said, "I don't know this Cole Cabot, nor do I care. I want my feet back on free land again and get to the work I love."

"Good luck, then, Russ. But I can't handle you anymore—and I'm pretty sure most big-time agents can't handle you either."

I gave him no answer. I couldn't. I just stared at my knees, thinking, as Owen warned, my work, my talent, my life as I knew it, had disappeared, never to be seen again.

"You'll get royalties," he continued, "but long time no book from you, so they slowed down. That will get worse. Maybe you can teach writing at some marginal company who sells classes on damn near everything." He offered me a phony smile.

"You won't die of hunger, Russ Reinert."

I inhaled deeply, held it for a while. Then I let the air rush out and pushed myself out of my chair. "No, I won't starve. But if I get real hungry, I know where my next meal will come from."

"Where's that?"

"I'll find you wherever you are, Owen—-and chew out your fucking throat."

It felt like a surprising divorce from a long-time marriage. Despite my lengthy confinement, I thought Fuller, who represented me from the beginning, would be on my side, no matter what. That's why he was my first visit the day after I walked free.

He threw me under the bus.

So—no publisher and no agent. They really doubted I was innocent of the crime for which I was convicted. No romance in my personal liberty. No friends except for Tana Phillips, who was a very busy attorney. While she did an astonishing job taking care of me when I was away and set me up with a great apartment, a classy car and a terrific wardrobe, Tana forgot a few things which were once important to me. No season tickets to Bears football games. No more membership with the Chicago Athletic Club. I've probably been scrubbed from the lists of the Mystery Writers of America and Sisters in Crime, who all write about violent death, but haven't been within a thousand miles of someone who actually got convicted of one.

Another book, then. I itched to begin, as soon as I figured out how to use my new laptop.

What else would I do with my life? Sit around watching daytime television? Judge Judy? Divorce Court? Endless re-runs of the Andy Griffith Show? No. The Joliet warden forbidding me a laptop on which to write and create, or even an old clanky typewriter was to me like kicking heroin cold turkey. My writing is an addiction, just like tobacco, alcohol, gambling, drugs or sex. I got hooked on all of them at one time or another, except gambling. Now, turning a new page in my life, I'm only guilty of one of those addictions. But I can't just write another book every year, slap it between leather covers and present it to my adoring children, as I don't have any children. I *had* to find a publisher.

Friends. I don't have any. I have many acquaintances from the old days, like bookstore owners and fans and other writers who show up to mystery conventions like Bouchercon, held in a different city every year. It was a lot of fun, until I was arrested for manslaughter, convicted by a jury of my peers, whatever the hell peers are, and tossed in a big ugly building with razor wire along the walls and guards with rifles on every tower.

Maybe I should start socializing more, in case no one ever heard of me or knew where I've been. It won't be easy. Knock on my new neighbor's door, whoever the hell he or she or they are, and hope they're not pain pill addicts or serial killers or morons who shoot stray cats for the fun of it? Should I hang out at a bar——a habit that went out thirty years ago? Maybe start going to lectures about things I don't give a shit, in hopes some pretty girl is sitting next to me and breathing heavily?

I went home, made myself a sausage sandwich and opened a bag of potato chips to go with it. Kettle Chips, which Tana remembered I loved. There's no chip as good as a Kettle Chip. Poured myself a dollop of Scotch, energized my sound system and listened to classical music. I was lost, because there was no classical music in prison.

I figured to sit in the recliner and read myself to sleep, but when I came home, I tossed my jacket onto the back of one of the dining room chairs. Figuring to get it out of the way, I grabbed it to hang it up and heard a crinkle coming from my pocket. What could that be?

It was the message slip from Owen Fullmer's office with the name and phone number of someone I never heard of. Cole Cabot. Young guy? Old guy?

Maybe he just wants to be my friend—-and pigs fly, because you don't make friends with a total stranger convicted of killing another human being. He has something to sell me. Collaborate with me on my next book? Or maybe he's been waiting seven years for me to autograph all the books I've written.

In my head, I played out all the different ways I should tell him to go fuck himself. They bored me.

I figured I might as well call him back. Whatever his deal was, he'd be a hell of a lot nicer than that jag-off agent of mine who cut me off at the knees. I poured myself another Scotch, but I had to be careful. I hadn't touched alcohol in seven years and my sobriety wasn't what it used to be. Then I curled myself up in my recliner and dialed his number.

"Mr. Cabot?" I said after he answered. "This is Russ Reinert."

"I'm surprised you'd call me back so soon." He sounded excited, nervous. "I didn't think you'd call at all."

Not sounding old. Not young, either, but his voice was that of an adult.

"I'm not buying anything," I said, "no matter what you're selling."

"I'm hardly a salesman."

"A religious fanatic? Save your breath, I'm an atheist."

"Nothing like that."

"Then what can I do for you, Mr. Cabot?"

"Call me Cole, please. We share an acquaintance." He sighed. "It's Aubrey Sinden. I'm—I'm married to her."

Aubrey Sinden. The most recent woman in my life—and that ended seven years ago. She was a knock-out. Dirty blond hair, as she referred to it—long, down past her waist. Big blue eyes, the windows to her soul, and when I looked into them, a soaring symphony rose and fell with each breath. The softest, sweetest lips in my memory. She's quiet until you got to know her—-not shy, just a private person. I loved her—-seriously and for the first time ever.

It's not easy to talk about Aubrey now, because I was married at the time.

Not to her.

We were lovers for more than a year. We were discreet, but if we'd been seen together in some small, obscure romantic restaurant, or walking hand in hand through the Lincoln Park Zoo, I wouldn't have given a damn. I could leave my wife in a New York minute and marry Aubrey the next day, but my novels had been quite successful and made me rich. But a divorce, the forced pre-nup, and the rapacious revenge-seeker I was married to would leave me flat-on-my-ass broke.

Aubrey stuck by me when I was on trial. She was in the courtroom every day until her own name came up, and a subpoena forced her to testify for the prosecution. She was a young woman who I knew couldn't hold out for ten years without even being touched. She was honest with me, so we mutually decided to end our relationship without even hugging goodbye because we were in a barred room with several other inmates and their visiting wives or lovers. Armed guards were present and watchful, too. No touching.

I never heard from her again. I sent her a letter which was returned, no forwarding address. I phoned, something I could only do every two weeks. Disconnected. As far as I knew, she'd disappeared into the mist.

And married Cole Cabot.

"I haven't seen or spoken to her since right after I—went away," I told him. "I didn't know she got married, but I'm not surprised. She always hoped for that one very special guy, and I guess she found one. Congratulations." I attempted a hard swallow of saliva that wasn't there. "You have kids?"

"No," Cabot said. "Can we get together and talk?"

Red flag—cross at your peril. "What do you want to talk about?"

"Not over the phone. Somewhere private, where nobody could hear us. Do you have an apartment?"

My tone took on a razor-sharp edge. "Nobody comes to my apartment! Shall we just sit in a car in some parking lot?" I shook my head, though he couldn't see it. "I don't even know you."

Cabot said, "Do you know where the old Viking ship is, near the zoo?"

"Everyone in Chicago knows where the Viking ship is."

"There are benches, but usually no one sits in them. We can talk privately."

"Mr. Cabot, this is weird."

"Trust me," he said.

Trust me? That stopped being believable back in the 1950s. I just asked, "When is this secret meeting going to happen?"

"Tomorrow," he said. "Two o'clock in the afternoon, if that's all right. We can just meet on the bench."

"How will I know you?"

"Don't worry, I know what you look like. Your picture was on the back cover of all your books." His voice became sullen. "Aubrey has all of them, signed by you with a lot of goony romantic shit. I begged her to throw them out after our wedding, but she refused."

All of a sudden, I was on top of the world. Aubrey had moved on, but she kept my books with her.

"That was very nice of Aubrey after all these years. Did you read any of them, Mr. Cabot?"

I heard him suck in air quickly, and waited for about fifteen seconds before finally saying, "Are you out of your fucking mind?"

CHAPTER THREE

Very mysterious. Cole Cabot, a complete stranger, calls my former agent the day I'm released from prison because he desired contact with me, and like a dumb-ass, I return his call. He's married to my ex-girlfriend and wants to talk privately, but won't tell me why on the phone. Is his phone bugged so that someone with electronic skills hears every word? Is *my* phone bugged? And if so, how come he knows that?

Maybe Cabot has a story of his own, preferably about a murder, he wants me to turn into a novel. Doubtful he'd want to work with me, considering my past relationship with his wife. Does he possibly hate my guts because she was once my mistress? Does he just want a look at me, the man who'd fucked his wife before he did? Is he planning to kill me, or only beat the crap out of me because of Aubrey? Not likely at a park bench in the middle of the afternoon. Is he a criminal himself whom I never met or heard about? Was his brother a fellow convict, or his employer or his best friend, and he thinks I know the secret to a buried treasure?

No.

Unless he was brainwashed by a Nicolas Cage film, that last thought was too ridiculous. And he sure as hell didn't want my autograph.

Me, of all people? I crossed the threshold from the Joliet

Hilton less than forty-eight hours earlier, and hardly yearned to share it with some stranger. I toyed with the idea of telling him to pound sand, but the name of Aubrey Sinden stayed my hand.

Aubrey Sinden, now Aubrey Sinden Cabot. If she coaxed her husband into calling me, her reason wasn't really important. Our romance was good seven years ago. Not great, but damn good. I couldn't ignore Cole Cabot if she was behind this meeting.

I have no one else on my side except Tana and Jack. I knew I should find new ones, making pals with whom I could have a drink or watch Bears football games together. The man married to the woman I once loved was absent from my hopeful to-be-buddies list. Yet he knew I was out , and called my ex-agent to leave his phone number and make sure I call him. Urgent.

I slept fitfully that night. I kept waking up every few minutes, staring at the ceiling and thinking about Cole Cabot. Was he tall? Short? Fat? Skinny? Ugly? Bald? Gay? Straight?

He said he'd recognize me from my author photos. I don't resemble those pictures anymore, taken eight or ten years ago. I suppose we all look in the mirror and see what we want to see, until one morning we accidentally catch a glimpse of our reflection and think, "Oh my god! How did my grandfather get into my bathroom?"

I spent the morning studying my behind-bars writing notes transferred to my laptop. Seven years of relative loneliness had given birth to a ton of ideas, characters, plots. Two jumped out at me, possible novel-length stories to which I'd give a great deal of study. Yet many more notebook pages had to be exposed before I could really get going on my career.

If I still *had* a career. No more agent, no more publisher. I'd turned once more into a wannabe writer.

When I went to prison, the prosecutor's office took away a laptop computer that was then about five years old. Add another seven years, and the new laptop Tana had bought for me, a MacBookAir, had many changes, additions and subtractions from the old one. I'd never been an Apple production freak, and I was lost trying to learn what they were and how I can use them. It makes me wonder. You buy an iron with which to press your clothes, and even the inexpensive ones from China come with a whole set of instructions, like the manual that says "Don't iron clothes while you are wearing them." Same with vacuums, sound systems, coffeemakers, toasters, firearms, baby cribs or anything else more complex than a T-shirt. But today when you buy a computer, there are no instructions enclosed at all.

Hopefully, when you acquire a laptop, you have a youngish parent or older sibling or, god help you, a six-year-old techno-logical genius grandchild to help you out—but I'm on my own.

I dressed casually and started north toward Lincoln Park on foot. An eight-minute drive would have delivered me to the Cole Cabot meeting, but a hike near the lake would do me good, as fresh air walks of the last seven years were twice around the prison yard, while sharpshooter guards with guns followed my every move.

Lake Shore Drive is amazing, as it's always been—mostly century-old houses and buildings. I have millions in the bank, but I still could not afford to live on Lake Shore Drive.

Twenty minutes later, in Lincoln Park, the hulk of the Viking Ship loomed ahead of me. I'd seen it often before, even as a child when my parents took me to the zoo, but this time it looked different to me. It used to be romantic, adventuresome, mysterious, a thick slice of history. Now it just looked tacky.

It sailed to the USA from Norway in 1893 for the World's Columbia Exposition. After that, it bopped around this country until it wound up in Chicago in 1920. One hundred years later, it's still there, though somewhat blighted. They—whoever in hell *they* are, probably the Chicago Parks Department—have removed the decorative dragon head of the ship, and its tail, too, and built a barbed wire fence around it to keep vandals from setting it aflame or chopping it up for firewood. They also have not cleaned it in decades, if ever, and it is now well-encrusted with more than a century of rain, snow, wind, and pigeon shit. Yet it remains a Chicago landmark.

I found a bench at which to wait. On a cloudy pewter-gray weekday there were few pedestrians. At one point a young woman came by pushing her whining toddler in a stroller and gave me one of those I'm-sorry-but-he's-making-noise-not-me looks and walked a little bit faster, but otherwise that area of Lincoln Park was practically deserted.

After about five minutes, I saw him coming toward me, or at least I guessed it was him. Cole Cabot. He was a smidgin taller than I, but walked hunched over, so if we stood side by side, I'd appear taller. His receding hairline he'd done nothing about made him seem older. His face was ordinary—not ugly nor handsome. Ordinary. His gray suit was wrinkled, two sizes too large and hanging loose on him, as if he'd bought it off the rack at Kohl's and didn't try it on until he got home. He was one of those people who could invade a crowded bank with a loaded tommy gun, unmasked, abscond with thousands of dollars, and not one person would remember what he looked like when questioned later by the police.

"Mr. Reinert," he said, and sat down next to me—but not too close. There must have been six feet between us on the bench. No handshake. Likely he loathed touching the hand that had once touched his wife in certain private places, even though it happened years before he met her.

"You chose a strange place to meet, Mr. Cabot."

"I wanted our conversation to be private," he said. "But I picked a place outdoors where there are sometimes people, in case you were thinking I wanted to kill you."

"I doubt you're carrying heat. If you have a knife—well, I've been in prison for many years, so I can take it away from you with one hand tied behind my back and remove your left lung with it, not even breaking a sweat."

"I don't have any desire to kill you. In fact, just the opposite."

"What opposite?"

"I'm hoping you'll help me."

"There are a million other people in Chicago you can turn to."

He shook his head almost sadly. "This is—this is about Aubrey."

Not surprised, I nodded. "How is Aubrey? I haven't seen or heard from her for years. I was unaware she was married until I talked to you yesterday."

His chin almost touched his chest, a visual portrait of mortification. He whispered, "There's a problem, Mr. Reinert."

"I'm no marriage counselor."

"You *are* a mystery writer, aren't you? You write stories about crime and punishment?"

"I was," I said, "and hope to be one again."

"Well, I believe a crime has been committed."

"What crime?"

His speech was halting. "Aubrey—my wife Aubrey is missing. She's been missing for six days now."

"Missing? How? Did she walk out on you? Did she just take off?"

His eyes filled with tears that looked ready to run down his face, and he blinked hard to keep them from flowing. "She took nothing, not her clothes or make-up or anything else belonging to her except her purse. And she left her car at home. She didn't run out on me."

"Are you sure?" I asked.

"Would any woman deliberately leave her husband with only the clothes she was wearing and be gone for more than a week?"

"Probably not."

He shook his head slowly. "There was a short mention in the *Tribune* about you getting out of prison. I called your agent. His name was in the paper that day, too."

"I guess nobody cared about it, because you've been my only call. My question, I suppose, is—why me?"

He closed his eyes and leaned his head back, his body supported by the back of the bench. "Listen to me—just for a minute." Then he turned his face toward me. "She was with you for a little more than a year, right?"

"How could we be together after I got locked up downstate?"

"I mean, before you went to prison, you were married to someone else?"

I ground my teeth together. "I was."

"And Aubrey knew that?"

"Naturally. We couldn't be together very much. Every time we met, I thought we might get caught. But my wife never knew about her."

He licked his lips as if he desperately wanted a swig of mouthwash. "And then you got arrested for killing your wife. Her name was Dyana, wasn't it?"?

"It was Dayna. Not Dyana. Dayna. I'm no murderer, I was just nailed for manslaughter. I'm getting pissed off at you, Cabot. Dangerously pissed off."

"There was a gas leak in your basement, no?" He straightened up and leaned toward me like an assistant district attorney. "When an explosion and then a fire took her life, the police found that a gas hose had been deliberately cut, and decided you killed her."

"I didn't kill her. I wouldn't, not in a million years. And I never got near enough to see it, but I don't think anyone cut that hose. I didn't love her anymore, but I'd do nothing to hurt her—or anyone else. I was out of town that day and evening, in Milwaukee. I heard about the fire just after my speech—and her death."

Cabot said, "Did you know much about Aubrey when the affair started?"

"Immediate mutual attraction. We learned more about each other as the relationship progressed."

He tilted his head to one side, and his mouth turned into a

smug sneer. "You never knew she was seeing someone else at the same time, did you?"

A shocking kick in the balls. It was seven years ago, but it was still a kick in the balls. "I don't believe that."

"You should, Mr. Reinert. Because her other lover was a very rich and powerful man. And he was married, too."

I said nothing for almost a minute. Then: "Was she seeing this person after you got married?"

"She was still with him when we started dating, but I guess she cut him loose right before our wedding. Or maybe he cut her loose. I don't know."

I stayed quiet again, just staring at the rotting seventy-three-foot mess of the Viking ship and thinking her connection with some other man marred my togetherness with Aubrey. I knew when I was hauled into stir our love story would not stand the length of my sentence, and I was not jealous of Cole Cabot. He helped her move on. But I was jarred right down to my toes that, during those fifteen months we were together, I was sharing her with another man. That hurt.

Pain slicing through my heart meant she could have gone off with him again, and Cabot was shattered. I eventually got my act together enough to say, "I still don't understand why you called me. How can I help you?"

"You research when you write your books. You know all about mystery and crimes. I want you—I *beg* you, Mr. Reinert—help me. *Find her*!"

I slumped forward, my arms on my thighs, staring at the sidewalk in front of me. "I don't find missing people for a living. I never have. I'm a writer, for crysakes. I've been in the slammer for the last seven years, so I couldn't even find a drugstore without written instructions. Where the hell could I look for *your* wife I haven't seen for almost a decade?"

Cabot sniffed. "What about the man who shared her with you? That's a place to start."

"Still a long time ago."

"He's around. He's famous—almost as famous in Chicago as Ernie Banks."

I tried not to laugh. "This guy plays shortstop for the Cubs, too?"

"He's too rich to play sports, Mr. Reinert. He's Gaylord Ogilvy."

I rubbed my forehead, trying to think. At length, the name clicked. Gaylord Ogilvy is a multi-billionaire businessman. He has built several skyscrapers in downtown Chicago, several elegant residential properties, two high-end golf clubs in the suburbs, and even a Miracle Mile retail store called "Gaylord." I don't know what they sell inside it, but considering its location, it had to be pretty damn expensive.

Thinking more on it, on his name plastered all over the buildings—Gaylord Retreat, Gaylord Arms, Gaylord Condos, Gaylord Tower. I recall he was once referred to as "Gay," back when that word just meant *happy*. When that shortening became embarrassing, he ordered everyone to call him by his given name, or preferably just "Mr. Ogilvy."

So—nights or weekends I didn't see Aubrey, she was probably with him and not working, not hanging out with her girlfriends, not seeing her aunt and her nieces who lived on the west side, near what used to be the enormous Union Stockyards, the largest slaughterhouse in the country. The stockyards closed in the 1960s, but the community is still blue-collar industrial and home to scores of immigrants, and is still referred to as the Back-of-the-Yards neighborhood. Famous twentieth century Chicago authors like Studs Terkel and Nelson Algren wrote about it constantly.

The Gaylord Citadel was built right on Halsted Street in the mid-fifties address, and I began wondering if he kept a penthouse apartment there for evenings when he entertained Aubrey Sinden.

"I know who Gaylord Ogilvy is," I told Cabot. "What makes you think Aubrey is back with him?"

"I don't know," he answered. "She never told me much about him. I'm wondering if she's somehow involved with him business-wise."

I said, "if Aubrey left you with nothing but the clothes on her back, her car in the garage, and not a word from her, she didn't just run away from you. I could be wrong."

"Then help me," he pleaded.

"I'm no detective, or a finder of missing persons. But I knew several Chicago private investigators. Still, I haven't spoken to most of them in more than a decade. I can text you their phone numbers."

"I couldn't afford them. I'm an actuary at an insurance company and don't make much money."

That possibly explained the ill-fitting suit. It might also explain why Aubrey left. She was a money-oriented young woman shared between a million-dollar best-selling author and a multibillionaire who built huge buildings wherever there wasn't a tree in his way and stuck his name on the outside. "Where do you live?"

"In a two-bedroom apartment just off Lincoln," he said. "You've got to get her back for me. I can't pay you anything." For a scant moment, he turned bitter. "You probably don't need it anyway—but helping me will save my life." He chewed on his lower lip. "I love her so much, Mr. Reinert. So much."

And then he started to cry.

CHAPTER FOUR

How I got into this mess, I'll never understand. I've gone through several different existences, but being a private detective wasn't one of them. I'll forever be an unlicensed P.I., too. The state of Illinois wouldn't license a former felon to poke into the private lives, loves and illegal doings of ordinary people.

A former felon? I never lived in a ghetto, I never ran with a gang, the most dangerous weapon I ever carried was a Swiss Army knife, and I don't recall stealing the smallest thing from a local drugstore, like a candy bar or a cheap keychain or a comic book.

A little bit of auto-bio here. Looking back on my childhood, it was at best peculiar. I was brought up as an only child of Caucasian entitlement by adoptive parents who weren't all that rich but who loved me beyond belief, and frankly I loved them right back. Anything I say about them that is not idolatry kind of shines a light on who I became, not on them. My father would hear nothing less than I spend ten college years being educated and trained as a highly paid doctor, probably a surgeon. He was half-assed about it because he never had the money for a long, financially draining medical education, but he would have forced me to do it, too, if he hadn't died when I was only thirteen.

He had his first major heart attack when I was two years old.

I was allowed only to tiptoe into his bedroom for about fifteen minutes, twice a day. [Mother?] warned me, on pain of being skinned alive, to be a good, quiet little kid and not get him excited over anything, In the remaining years together, when he was more or less in good physical shape, if I even hinted I didn't want to be a doctor, or if my mother disagreed with him on damn near anything, he would grab his chest and sink down on the sofa, gasping, faking another heart seizure until I changed my mind. I was terrified that decade of medical school and internship at a hospital possibly as far away as Fairbanks, Alaska to become a doctor at a job that frightened and disgusted me. I thought then, and still do, that my dad's early life— very different than cracking people's necks—was high-speed adventure, worthy of a high budget movie.

If it were true. I only heard these colorful stories from him, many times, and then, as now, I chose to believe them.

When he was a teenager in London, the fourth of six siblings, he wanted to be rid of the torturous behavior towards him of his two older brothers and an older sister. At sixteen, he ran away from home and joined a circus. He was no performer— no trapeze flyer, no high-wire walker, and certainly no lion tamer. He was just a punk kid who hung around to sweep up elephant shit and help the roustabouts put up tents. He never admitted it, but he probably lost his virginity to a young woman who rode at top speed around the center ring standing barefoot on the back of a white horse.

After touring the British Isles for a year, he returned to London to discover his rattletrap apartment empty and his family gone—-moved, as he learned from a neighbor, to America. Flat broke and homeless, he decided to become a boxer—a featherweight, as he was only five foot five but brave and fiery. His touring circus life had been peppered with several fistfights, many of which he won, so he was pretty successful in the ring for several bouts. Then he was matched against the number one featherweight contender for the championship, and got his ass knocked off in the third round. His retirement from pugilistic challenges was immediate.

Still, he loved boxing, and when I was about seven years old, he'd take me every Friday night to local boxing matches. I quickly became the darling of the habitual fight fans who hung out at these contests, and I shouted and cheered with the rest of them. Most of the combatants were African American, even thirty-some years ago, and I always rooted for them because my father was super-liberal, a white member of the NAACP, a years-long subscriber to Ebony Magazine, and an admirer of most things black, whether in sports or entertainment. I've stuck with his belief about that ever since.

What never occurred to me the two men flailing at each other up in the ring might have been good friends in normal life, but now bent on destroying each other. I learned that a "knockout" was actually a brain concussion, so I grew up with that knowledge, too, and never struck anyone in anger since the age of eleven.

My victim then, as I recall, was Milton Glasser. Whatever happened to him in the last thirty years, anyway? And why exactly did I punch him in the head during recess? Too long ago. What's up, Milton, wherever you are?

It wasn't until after my father died I realized he never lost the Cockney accent he grew up with in the East End of London. As a kid, I assumed everybody's father talked like that.

My mother developed a stiff neck from some ballroom dancing lessons, went to a chiropractor for help, and wound up marrying him when she and my dad were twenty-one years apart in age. She had worked for the Cunard Shipping Line, though she never left the downtown office in Chicago, but as I grew, she would tell me of the romantic and adventurous cruises they took in their imaginations, including *Titanic*'s only voyage. Her marriage, naturally, ended her business career forever.

Pretty much a coward, mom ruled after my birth there would

be no more children. She had an extremely low tolerance for pain, and her fear from having never being anywhere near an infant made the full-time presence of my helpless, pissing self difficult for her. They hired a nanny caretaker for me when I was newly born because Mom was afraid to hold me unless she was sitting down, fearing she'd drop me. I was a unique celebrity in my own home, and was endlessly told I was a beautiful infant with a full head of shockingly curly hair—which never stopped, despite my hair straightening out completely after the first haircut.

Side story that might make you smile: I was around eighteen months old, with a head full of bushy hair that had never been cut. I was out shopping with my mother in the Diversey and Clark neighborhood on Chicago's north side. My stroller was parked near the door of an old-time drugstore—-soda fountain and all—-while my mother poked around somewhere else in the aisles. Another woman came into the store, saw me, squatted down and said, "Hello, you beautiful little doll," and I replied, "Hello, you son of a bitch." I learned it from my father, who used that expression at least twice weekly, though I certainly didn't know what it meant. It became part of my vocabulary and never went away.

Between her terror of dropping me on my head and my father's unshakeable insistence this weeks-old creature was going to grow up to be a world-famous surgeon, the pressure was on me before I could sit up. From the time I could understand speech, it was hammered into my head to be a good boy, because I was so very special.

I made few friends in high school, as I was not into social, not into sports, and thank god, not into mathematics. Because of his heart attack, my father came home from his office early—-and expected me to be there to be with him, rather than my staying outside in the neighborhood playing, like all the other kids. Not a real problem for me, because I stayed busy wanting to be a writer, starting when I was only six years old.

My parents had an old, beat-up Royal portable typewriter around the house, and I began writing one-page stories, mostly about a boy and his dog. All imagination, I confess, because I was never allowed to have any pet other than goldfish, who always died within a month of coming to live with me. My mother didn't like dogs and treated cats as if they were sewer rats who found their way into the house.

In kindergarten, my school principal was amazed I could read very well, and the tests they put me through proved my word-perusing ability was that of a high school senior. I have no idea why, other than both Mom and Dad would read kiddy books aloud to me while I was on their laps and I somehow got used to looking at the words and figuring out what they meant.

I guess that's why I was treated by my parents as being entitled, being a genius and all that, except I was certain I was no genius. The entitlements, especially to my father, meant I was not allowed to play anything rough, not even *Red Rover, Red Rover, Let Russell come over.*

Softball was okay, but never hardball, as a pitcher could split my skull open with a wild pitch. I wasn't allowed to roller-skate because I might fall and hurt myself, like a skinned knee. If I ice-skated, he warned someone would run me over with their sharp skates and kill or disfigure me. They forbade me to ride a bicycle because of an unlikely accident happening that might break my arm or leg.

To this day, I don't know how to ride a bicycle.

When I was fifteen, I wrote a novel. Of course, it was ghastly, since I didn't know a goddamn thing about anything, but my English teacher, Mr. Chamberlain, told me I was an excellent writer. The subject I chose, though, was far beyond my reach. It was all about whores and villains, believe it or not, though I'd never known any villains other than those on TV cop shows and, to my knowledge, never even seen a whore at a distance. A lot of violence went along with the story and characters, but my writing, Mr. Chamberlin said, was just about perfect. He even worked with me twice a week for half an hour before school started. I never stopped writing after that, even while stumbling through four difficult years at the University of Illinois in the twin cities of Champaign and Urbana. Frankly, the only things I learned during that awkward period were the university was part of the Big Ten football conference despite having horrible losing teams each year, in the 1990s it was easier to get laid than learning to tie your shoes, and Champaign was a lot more fun than Urbana.

After graduation, though, everything became fun. My father was gone, and my mother remarried. My stepfather was never really unkind to me, but from the day after their wedding, he pretty much ignored me. I no longer had to bust my ass every day trying to be a good boy and not get into trouble—-and I sure as hell would never become a doctor. I hate the sight of blood, especially if it's not mine. If I had to touch naked people all over their bodies, I prefer to make the choice which people I touched—and when. That hasn't changed.

Even though I'd majored in Literature, the world wasn't hiring writers hand over fist, and I wouldn't start teaching book-reading at the U of I, which at the time was full of nerds, geeks, jocks, and jag-offs who couldn't get admitted anywhere else. Instead, I got a dynamic job at an ad agency downtown, but didn't take the accounts that seriously. Deadly important advertising featuring slogans like "Where's the beef?," "Do you have any Grey Poupon?" and "This is your brain on drugs" just made me giggle.

But because I'd turned into a fun guy, the company mavens figured my sociability overrode my advertising knowledge, so they assigned me to take clients out to dinner, the theater, ballgames, or wherever else they'd have a good enough time to keep us on as their ad agency. I confess quite often they ordered me to find a willing, attractive, and highly expensive woman to entertain them for the evening.

I tried hard not to think of myself as a high-paid pimp, because women were lots of fun for me, too. Lots of non-professional women fulfilled my fondest dreams when I was a teenager or in my twenties, and those of that age were, for the most, part floozies. I was pretty much a floozy as well. I drove a shiny black Chevy Impala, and had it washed gleamingly clean at least once a week, usually on Fridays.

I rented a high-rise apartment right next to the Wrigley Building, complete with doorman, twice-a-week housekeeper who came with the rent, and a three-block walk from my ad office. When I wasn't out partying, I was writing. At night when I sat at my desk by the picture window, looking south, the lights of Chicago made me love my city all over again. Writing was enjoyable, too, especially when a particular piece was finished and bought by a newspaper or magazine. But while I was bent over that laptop, coffee always at my right hand, I took my writing as serious as hell.

A quote attributed to Red Smith, one of the all-time great sports journalists for the *New York Times* assured me, "There's nothing to writing. You just sit down at a typewriter and open a vein." I opened that vein at least once a day, seven days a week. Christmas, my birthday, Valentine's Day, Rosh Hashanah, Ash Wednesday and Arbor Day—they didn't matter to me. If I were well enough to sit up straight, I'd write.

Chicago literary agent, Owen Fullmer, got his hands on my manuscript. It was so long ago, I can't remember how it happened, but he liked it, shipped it off to a top New York publisher, and the next thing I knew, I received a sixty-thousand-dollar advance, a huge promotional push, two weeks at Number Two on the New York Times best-seller list and a twelve-week run altogether.

The publisher came back with a six-figure advance for the next two books I hadn't even written yet. Royalties began pouring in.

Hollywood called, too, begging to do a big, splashy autumn-released movie version of the first one. They eventually produced it with a popular star whose career had begun to run out of steam. This one put him back on top, and the opening credits listed me as the novelist and one of six executive producers. I didn't know why, as I was ignorant of what executive producers do, though I pocketed extra money for it. Other than writing the novel, I didn't do one damn thing except attend a meeting with the director and the screenwriter before the film went into production. The first purchase check I received from the studio was more money than I'd made in my lifetime.

The original story, goosed up a bit by the producers, was indeed a crime film, but filled with sensual lovemaking, nudity included, between the two leading players who, in real life couldn't stand each other, as he was thirty years older than she. There was some violence, one gruesome murder (both actor and actress were naked in the scene, but I won't give away who killed who. Rent the movie, now—I get a percentage), and the strained psychological relationship between the protagonist and his wife. Lots of neuroses just below the surface, which I am told had audiences talking.

Movie-goers loved it, and it also became a big hit movie in Japan, Italy and Greece. Not *"The Godfather,"* of course, but it made its money back and an amazing dividend for all concerned. It still shows up several times a year on TV's Turner Classic Movies and on Netflix.

There I was, a Nobody who became a Somebody. Sure, I had— no, I have talent. I write pretty good books. Some literary critics were mentioning me in the same sentence as Nelson Algren, a great Chicago writer of the twenties and thirties, but I had nowhere near the genius and skill he possessed. Still, when they rave about you in the papers, you bow your head, shuffle your feet, make a noise that sounds like "Awww…" and pretend it's not the best goddamn praise you've ever heard in your life.

But what really put me over the top was luck. Plain, unadulterated *luck*. I loved it, wallowed in it, luxuriated in it as though it were Piper-Heidsieck Brut champagne filling a great big bathtub.

Shortly after the third book came out, though, the luck in which I delightedly writhed changed. Slowly. It took me a long time to notice it, but by the time I realized it, it was turning into toxic waste water. My work became a sideline and not the reason I woke up in the morning.

I met and fell in love with Dayna Winship.

I'd appeared to speak and sign at an author evening in downtown Chicago—-and was thrilled I sold six hundred books in one night. Afterwards, four friends who attended waited for me and gave me hugs and congratulations afterward. Standing with them was a woman I'd never seen before, but she was obviously part of the group. I turned to her and said, "I have no idea who you are, but if you're part of this crowd, you get a hug, too."

The hug was memorable. Maybe the way her hair smelled, or more probably the feel of her breasts against my chest. We all went out for drinks afterward, and when going-home time arrived, I walked to her car. Hug Number Two turned into Kiss Number One. Not to be forgotten. Was it, I wondered, just one kiss that lasted more than ninety seconds, or was it a bunch of kisses, rapidly repeated without even coming up for air? Six-week stands and one-night stands to the contrary, there are times when you meet someone and the feeling fills you up inside and makes it difficult to talk, to think, to breathe, even to write. Dayna was about five-foot-four, blond hair cut short, so when she got up in the morning, all she had to do was run her fingers through it and it looked astonishing. She was slim, small-busted, with big green eyes that just jumped out at you, full and kissable lips, a beautiful face and a walk that was graceful and sensuous at the same time.

We decided fairly quickly there was no time to waste. After dating for four months, we married, the Chicago mayor reading the love-honor-and-obey rules in front of all the local press. He apparently found my own celebrity one more chance to get his name and face plastered in the local newspapers. The ceremony was witnessed by Dayna's best girlfriend, and by my attorney

Tana Phillips and her husband Jack. After the quick nicety and a few photos from the mayor's official photographer, we had to fight our way through a horde of local and national reporters in the outer hallway to get to my car and drive to the home I'd just purchased in Winnetka, north of the city. Four bedrooms, one of which I turned into my office/writing room, far enough off the beaten track I rarely heard traffic noises, especially when I worked. There was also a roomy backyard on the edge of a beautiful stand of woods, big enough for a child or two.

The child or two never happened.

Right after the wedding Dayna quit her job—-something having to do with office management—-and set about refurnishing my home. Painting replaced by wallpaper I wasn't fond of, a knockdown of an entire wall that put our roomy kitchen right into one end of the living room, two steps up. She proceeded to re-do all the flat surfaces in the kitchen and three bathrooms with granite counters and floors. The smallest of the bedrooms was turned into a huge closet for her clothes alone, and all the wood floors on the first level replaced with very expensive bamboo. Hard for me to write with workers running in and out all day long, knocking things down and pounding and hammering and destroying so I couldn't hear myself think anymore. I spent several days a week huddled up inside a Starbucks, pounding away on my laptop and hoping no one would recognize me.

Finally, though, almost a year later, everything was done. Wonderful news for me—except Dayna had quickly grown bored with it. She was nervous, anxious, often whiny, and smoked pot almost every night, which had never been my thing. Sure, I smoked weed in college like everyone else, but after graduation, I more or less forgot about it.

She was sick of remodeling, especially since we rarely invited company. Her three best girlfriends were all single, and having them over for dinner was awkward. They occasionally brought dates with them, but those guys disappeared after a few weeks, never to be heard from again, so looking back on those evenings was even more uncomfortable.

Now Dayna wanted to travel, as the only foreign places she had visited before I met her were Toronto, Montreal, and Jamaica. On her list for the two of us to visit were Spain, Greece, the Czech Republic, the Taj Mahal, the French Riviera, the Italian Riviera, the Swiss Alps, Rome, Florence, Paris, Hong Kong and the British Isles. All of them. I figured if we stayed married for thirty-five years, we'd get to most of them eventually—-but she wanted a several-month world tour as soon as possible.

Ernest Hemingway and Scott Fitzgerald traveled a lot and wrote wherever they were, but my work, my crime stories, were all set in American places, mostly in Chicago where I'd lived for my entire life, and anything more than a fourteen-day getaway would have made me insane. If we went to Paris, we could rent a roomy apartment near the Moulin Rouge, and I'd stay home all day, writing, while Dayna gallivanted around town and bought more clothes and stuff than I could afford, despite my healthy bank account. However, she was hip deep into traveling, and only yearned to stay in one place for two weeks or less, depending on how the surroundings affected her.

The constant, almost frantic sex we'd enjoyed during courtship quickly slowed down after marriage. I wouldn't say the lovemaking was brilliant and adventurous and even dangerous, though I'd experienced all of that before. It had always been pretty good between us. In any romantic relationship, it takes time to adjust, to try things, even to discuss things, but there was damn little adjusting after matrimony. I never thought I'd be the knight in shining armor because I'm terrified of horses. And it just wasn't that old, corny "the earth moved" shit. I was no missionary, but my marital sex life turned into that rarely changed position and made me feel like one.

I suppose ennui got the best of her, or perhaps she thought every time I left the house I was cheating on her, ridiculous because, in marriage at that time, I was totally faithful. Even if I'd say, "I'm going to pick up my blue suit from the dry cleaners," she'd answer, "Wait, I'll go with you." My dry-cleaners was six minutes away. Why she'd think I got laid on fifteen-minute trips like that baffled me. And since I met her at a book-signing, anyplace I'd go when I was the so-called guest of honor, or even one of several, she was with me as though we were joined at the hip, and frequently spoke up even though the question had been asked of me.

As marital time passed, we were rarely joined anywhere else. My books got more erotic even as my real sex life grew almost forbearing. Lovemaking was down to one or two Saturdays per month, and only at bedtime. I can't recall any sex during those days when the sun had not yet disappeared. She was apparently too tired, too busy, too—-whatever. I never knew if she had affairs, because as the months turned into years, I frankly didn't give a damn.

There was that memorable time, a few years in, when *Newsweek* was doing a story on me. It wasn't a "cover" story, as those were reserved for overbearing politicians, dead or dying movie stars, and giant writers like Stephen King. But I'd probably get a page and a half out of it, plus a picture or two, so I went downtown to a photo shoot, as per requested by the magazine.

I dressed casually. Few, if any, male authors of that era dressed up in a suit and tie to sit by themselves, smoking a pipe, hunching over a laptop. I wore a light blue shirt open at the neck under a darker blue Cardigan sweater, and Dockers, figuring they wouldn't want full-length studies of me (they didn't even try). At the studio, a young woman named Bethany who looked like a neighborhood bowling all-star combed my hair the way she liked it and sprayed it stiff, and slapped lotion and powder all over my face. I really couldn't tell what kind of fancy make-up was required for a black-and-white photograph, though. I took one glance in the mirror before going out into the studio and figured I looked like one of the victims on the autopsy table in TV's *NCIS*. Behind the camera—-adjusting the lights, the angles, suggested sitting, standing, leaning, even putting my head and my hands and the rest of my body in poses that would go well with the pictures—-was Aubrey Sinden.

Much of the time that day, I couldn't see her eyes. One was squinted, and the other was smack behind the camera, looking at me. Her hands and skin were soft as she turned my head one way or the other. When her head was close to mine during the set-ups, her breath smelled like flowers.

There were three assistants on set, too, though I had no idea what they did. I don't even remember their genders. I only had eyes for the camera lady, and I'd swear on a stack of bibles—-or a stack of mystery novels or dictionaries or thesauruses or *"Picture Taking for Dummies"*— she only had eyes for me, too.

"Have lunch with me," I suggested when the shoot ended.

"It's four thirty in the afternoon," she said. "Kind of late for lunch, don't you think?"

"All right then. How about dinner?"

She shook her beautiful head. "I'm afraid I have plans this evening."

"Plans?" I questioned. "Tactics? Strategies? Procedures? Arranging the imminent nuclear bombing of Finland?"

She smiled—a sensuous smile. "How did you know I'm going to bomb Finland?"

"Because gorgeous women named Aubrey-with-a-B are sorcerers of evil when it comes to going to war with Finland. So, when *are* you free?"

"I'll call you up and tell you." Then her eyebrows lifted and her eyes twinkled. "Oh, right. I can't call you, can I? Because you're married."

I wiggled my left hand wearing the wedding ring.

She said, "I've even read two of your books." She airily waving one hand at the rest of the studio so I could realize how spacious it was. "I don't just lie around all day while my slaves fan me with giant palm leaves and feed me peeled grapes.”

“I don’t have slaves, I don’t like peeled grapes, and I don’t do windows.”

“Too bad,” she said, “I’d hire you. When you’re in the grape-peeling business sometime, why don’t you call me?”

“What’s your phone number?”

“You know the name of this office. Look it up.”

“What about your home number?”

She shook her head. “I can’t tell you that, because you’ll warn Finland I’m going to bomb them.”

CHAPTER FIVE

I fell head over heels with Aubrey. My wife Dayna, who had drifted away from me a little bit every day, beginning with the end of our honeymoon, is killed when my house catches fire, and though I'm a hundred and twenty miles from where it happens, I'm arrested for manslaughter, convicted, and imprisoned for seven years. Newspapers, TV news shows, and everyone who hates my books decided I killed her by putting a hole in a gas hose in the basement because I was involved with Aubrey, and wanted my wife dead.

The very day I'm released, Aubrey's husband, Cole Cabot, whom she married while I was still behind bars, approaches me to tell me his wife has been missing for ten days and that her unexplained disappearance probably had something to do with Chicago billionaire Gaylord Ogilvy. Apparently, Aubrey Sinden had been Ogilvy's mistress all the time she was being mine, too. Though I'm in no way a detective or investigator, Cabot demands I put my new life of relative freedom on hold while I go search for her. This, from a guy who looks as if he buys both suits and haircuts at K-Mart.

Did I mention everything in these last two paragraphs? If not, just hang with me. It'll all come out sooner or later.

I spent the evening following my Viking Ship meeting with Cole Cabot, fooling with my new laptop I hadn't yet figured out how to use to its fullest extent. I tried to find out everything I could about Gaylord Ogilvy. I had no idea he had anything to do with Aubrey's disappearance, but he's the only one who was seriously involved with her at one point, as was I, so it seemed the only place to start.

It didn't take long for me to get myself on the Internet to look up Ogilvy's business phone number. Good thing I figured that out on my computer, as there was no such thing as a "phone book" anymore. I used to get an updated thick phone book every year. Had I been in prison that long, or has American society moved so quickly in the past seven years?

"Ogilvy Corporation. Good morning. Where may I direct your call?"

"Good morning," I replied. "Is Mr. Ogilvy in?"

"Your name, sir?"

I told her.

"Is Mr. Ogilvy familiar with you?"

"I don't know," I said, "but I'm a well-known mystery novelist."

"Uh-huh," she said. That was all, in a flat, bored voice; I wasn't as well-known as I thought I was. From the sound of her, I intuited the only books she'd ever read in her life were "Fifty Shades of Gray" and "The Well of Loneliness."

She finally deigned to continue the conversation. "Mr. Ogilvy is in conference, sir, but he rarely accepts calls from people he doesn't know."

"Fair enough," I said. "Will you tell him I phoned and give him my number? If he wants to speak with me, he can call me back. Okay?"

"I'll pass it on to Mr. Ogilvy's second-in-command."

"You aren't Mr. Ogilvy's private secretary?"

"I hardly ever speak to Mr. Ogilvy unless he says good morning when he arrives," she said, "and that doesn't happen often. I'm just a receptionist, sir."

Hanging up, I actually felt sorry for her, whoever she was. I wouldn't get much more out of her about her boss.

I had vague recollections of Ogilvy, but until now, his name and presence never occurred to me. I searched around on Google, trying to learn everything I could about him. There were many mentions, including on Wikipedia. Gaylord Manford Ogilvy was sixty-four years old and a native of Chicago's West Side. Entrepreneur—big word, right? That means a big important guy. Also—realtor, real estate developer, builder, pushy businessman who loved to get on TV or have a great photo in the local papers whenever he could. He also insisted his name being displayed on every building he builds, which, I supposed, was all over Chicago. Most of those edifices I'd never heard of, or even noticed. The Wrigley Building—named along with the Chicago Cubs baseball park after a guy who sold chewing gum—the old Sears Tower, the athletic stadiums, the elegant downtown hotels like the Palmer House, and the Board of Trade Building were familiar to me, but the Ogilvy Buildings were not. He was married for twenty-two years to Lilith Shadburn Ogilvy. Lilith, I thought, a biblical name few people know about. They had no children.

There was no mention of Aubrey Sinden, but those sites never identified mistresses by name unless they were those of Charles II of England. I tried visiting Google sites about me, but most of them spoke only about my work. Only two mentioned I'd been imprisoned for manslaughter—-or still was locked up, if they apparently hadn't heard my good news by then. Some mentions of Dayna, but none at all of Aubrey. I Googled her name, too and didn't find her, but she was a Facebook member. On her profile was her hometown and a mention of her being married to Cole Cabot.

I'd never used the Internet for much before going inside. Emails, naturally, though I deleted most of them without reading because they always asked for money. Facebook, but only to publicize my work, though I got lots of messages and pretty pictures, mostly of kittens. Big-time cleavage from beautiful women who lived in places like Ukraine, Uzbekistan or Bangladesh wanting to marry me, sight unseen, as long as I kicked in for the long trip to Chicago from wherever the hell they were. None of them knew I was a writer, much less a semi-famous one.

I thought about the millions of people all over the world who are never mentioned online for any reason whatsoever. Many lived and died before anyone ever heard of Google or the Internet. They get born, they go to work, they marry, they have children, they die quietly and without incident, and only close friends and acquaintances ever know about it. Many don't own a laptop, iPhone or iPad on which they might choose to leave a few sentences or paragraphs to tell the rest of the planet who they are.

I hadn't been on Facebook since before I went to prison, and I thought about checking my own FB page, but decided against it. My conviction made almost all the papers in the country, and the state of Dayna's death ran on the news for more than a month. I couldn't face reading what people said about me on Facebook. It troubled me, too, as Facebook was an excellent way to let people know about my books. I won't know what to do with the one I was about to write—assuming I'd ever find the time to write it.

I didn't get that far into in when the phone rang.

"Mr. Reinert?" a male voice said. "This is Irvin Greenfield, with the Ogilvy Company."

Irvin Greenfield. Second-in-command? Or just some guy on the payroll who makes phone calls big shtarkers don't want to bother with. Whoever it was, I'd have to get past him to get anywhere near The Big Man.

"I understand," he went on, "you want to talk to Mr. Ogilvy. May I ask what that's in regard to?"

"It's personal," I said.

"You'll have to do better than that."

"I will—when I speak to him."

"I see." Pause. "I know who you are, Mr. Reinert. I also know where you've been."

"Then you must know I'm out now, and a free man, just like you. I told you my business with Ogilvy is personal, and I'm damned if I'll discuss it over the telephone with some guy I've never heard of." Pause. "Like you."

Amusement colored his tone. "I'm beginning to dislike you, I'm afraid."

"I didn't call you, Mr. Greenfield. You called me. I need to talk to your boss, and if I can't get him through you, I can always try another way. Remember, I write private eye novels, and I give my P.I.'s exactly what tricks they need to solve the murder case, especially when they can't just ask someone about it."

"Is there a murder here?"

"I'll find out from Mr. Ogilvy if anyone has been killed."

"I'm damned if you'll do any such thing!" Greenfield exploded, and I heard him slap the top of his desk in a rage. "What are you planning, asshole? Hang out in front of his home and nail him as he drives in? Think again. He has a chauffeur who drives him to and from work every day, and he's twice as big and mean as you are——that's why he gets paid more than other limo drivers. Knock on his door and get him out of bed in the middle of the night? Stalk him in one of the restaurants he frequents and bother him before he can put food in his mouth?" He made a noise that sounded like *Pffft,* and I imagined him shooing away a bothersome gnat. "Who in hell do you think you are? I'm the executive vice president of Ogilvy Inc. I run this company from top to bottom. I make exactly the same salary as the President of the United States. I have lunch with the mayor, I have dinner with the governor, I go hunting on weekends with the senator, and if I happen to pick my nose in public, nobody has the balls to mention it. You, on the other hand, are a fucking nobody! Your books are so old no one knows who the hell you are—and you're such a recent ex-con the prison stink still wafts around you like body odor."

"Nice," I observed.

"You're damn right it's nice. You want to talk with Mr. Ogilvy? Then you talk to me first. I'm not recording this phone call, but if you think I care enough, come into the office to see me personally. Then *I* decide if and when you talk to the boss. Nobody else. You get my meaning, Reinert?"

"I guess I do."

"Good." I heard him flipping some papers. "Be in my office at eleven o'clock tomorrow morning. If you're late, at 11:03, you'll be physically removed and thrown out on your ass."

"If you say so, Mr. Greenfield. Can you give me the address of your office?"

He did. His office, and I assume Ogilvy's office, too, was someplace so famous in Chicago even Helen Keller would have found it without any help at all.

When the Merchandise Mart opened back in 1930, it was called the largest building in the world until the Pentagon in Washington opened a few years later. Twenty-five stories high and covering two entire blocks right at the bank of the Chicago River, it has hosted merchandise shows of all kinds, expositions, meetings and conventions, and has several floors of private offices. Ogilvy International took up all the offices on a higher floor. It surprised me because as far as I know he does *not* own the Merchandise Mart.

That is a hell of a lot of offices, another big hint as to just how huge Ogilvy International is and how many true businesses they have running.

I had to get through the armed guards at an Information Booth in the lobby, and one of the three receptionists hunkered down outside the elevator's doors upstairs. The one I spoke to was older, very serious, with all the warmth of an S.S. storm-trooper, but she sent me way *way* down the long hall to a suite of offices near the end. There was another receptionist there, apparently one who works only for Greenfield. When I introduced myself, she glanced at a clock on the wall. I guess I was three minutes early, saved from forcible removal.

Irvin Greenfield—not Irving with a G, according to the gold name bar on his desk—was in his fifties. About five foot seven, well-barbered dark hair, too many extra pounds, and since he was in shirtsleeves and a boring tie, rather observable love handles. He did not stand up, nor offer a handshake. I, on the other hand, was in no mood to use an ultra-polite Japanese bow.

His greeting was kind, gracious, overly polite. "Siddown," he said.

I saddown.

"My assistant did some fact-searching on you," he said, nodding toward the door. "You've only been out for three days."

I nodded. "Sorry for my prison stink, Mr. Greenfield. I ran out of Dove for Men this morning."

He ignored my pitiful attempt at humor. "You're wearing a new suit and tie. I'm impressed. They didn't give you that suit when you checked out."

"Are you that fascinated with my fashion choices?"

"You're the one who wanted this meeting."

"Not with you," I reminded him.

"Wise guy, eh?"

"I'm wise. I learned wisdom from all my fellow prisoners who were Professors of Philosophy at Harvard."

He opened and scanned a thin file on his desk. "You murdered your wife."

"And you're a prick."

"Not necessarily. I haven't been in prison."

"When you are, don't miss the Jell-O salad on Sundays. And while you're inside, ask around. I didn't commit murder."

He looked at the file again. "Manslaughter. Same thing."

"Not at all. Involuntary manslaughter. When you're tired of playing Imperial Wizard to the king, open up a law book sometime."

"I don't need a law book," Greenfield said. "I have clippings from the Chicago *Tribune* right here. It was believed you killed your wife to be with your mistress." He closed the file. "Aubrey Sinden."

"It's all coming together now," I said. "Aubrey Sinden is why I'm here. Not for you, of course, but for Mr. Ogilvy."

"I thought as much. Well, you're right, Mr. Reinert. Sadly. Because while she was your mistress, at the same time she was also working part time for this company. Now she's married," and he glanced at the top paper on the file he had in front of him, "to this Cole Cabot. Mr. Ogilvy decided enough was enough. He doesn't approve of breaking up marriages."

"Just his own," I said.

Irvin laughed, but there was no amusement behind it. "His marriage is not broken. They've been together for years." He put his hands together in front of him as if he were praying. "What do you want with Aubrey?"

"I'd prefer to discuss it with Mr. Ogilvy."

"And I'd prefer I was six foot one and looked like Brad Pitt, but nobody always get what they prefer. Talk to me first, Reinert, or talk to your mirror. Your choice."

It took me a while to decide. I didn't like Irvin Greenfield, and I was sure I wouldn't like Gaylord Ogilvy—but I promised Cole Cabot I'd look for his wife, and Ogilvy was the only place to start. I gave in.

I hate giving in. I especially hated the jury that sent me away. But as Irvin put it—it's my choice. "Cole Cabot met with me the day after I left prison," I said. "His wife was missing for days, and he asked if I'd look for her."

"Why you? You probably haven't seen her since the day you walked into that hellhole of a prison downstate."

"She visited me a few times," I admitted, "but she didn't

hang around for years, waiting for me. I didn't know she got married until Cabot called me."

"Again, why you, Reinert?"

"I used to write mystery novels," I said. "My protagonists are private investigators. They always investigate murder crimes and solve them." I shook my head sadly. "While I was writing, people would sometimes call me, thinking I was a real private eye, and wanted me to track down their missing husband or son or daughter."

"But you're not. You never knew about her—relationship with Mr. Ogilvy?"

"Not till Cabot told me."

"Are you pissed off about it?"

"Not really," I said. "Too long ago."

"So you show up here, anyway? Mr. O hasn't seen Aubrey since she got married, and that was several years ago."

"I don't know who else to ask."

Now Greenfield put his elbow on the desk and cupped his chin in his hand. "Are you planning to punch him in the mouth because he fucked Aubrey on the days you didn't?"

"Sure," I assured him, "just as soon as I find some Englishman to punch in the mouth because of the War of 1812."

"Suppose he refuses to talk to you? Then what?"

"Then I go home and write my next book."

His laugh was almost genuine. "I should write a book myself. I live on the North Side, in the Diversey area—but I've got a little cabin out in the boondocks near Lombard, in DuPage County."

"I can't ever remember being in DuPage County."

"Probably not the best place in the world for people like you. Residents there are so rich they can buy up successful mystery authors like buying a roll of Life Savers. But I'm right in the middle of the woods. I ought to head up there with my laptop and write a book. It'd be a hell of a lot better than the crap you write."

"Fascinating, Mr. Greenfield. What will you write about?"

"My life's work, which is keeping pushy assholes like you from hassling my boss. I get a shitload of money for that." Apparently using his feet, he slowly moved his chair in a half-circle so he could look out at the river, and further out to the diamond-studded waters of Lake Michigan, remaining quiet for a while. Then he said, without turning around, "Would you mind waiting outside the office for a few minutes?"

"I don't recall seeing an extra chair out there."

"Then lean against the wall so you don't fall over. You're a big boy now."

I went into the outer office and stood there for a while. His secretary glared at me as if I'd been a stranger who just exposed himself on the subway.

"I'm waiting," I explained, which was no explanation at all.

"Good for you," she said. Then she went back to her typing.

Ten minutes later—was it only ten minutes? It felt like an hour—Irvin Greenfield came out of his office quickly. The love handles at his waist bobbled beneath his shirt. "I spoke to Mr. Ogilvy. If you come back at four o'clock, he'll see you then. Again, Reinert—be on time. He hates it if anyone is late."

I looked at the expensive watch Tara got for me. "It's not even noon," I said. "What am I supposed to do for the next four hours."

"Like I give a shit," he answered. "If Mr. O says four o'clock, he doesn't mean right now, or in half an hour. He means four o'clock." He raised one eyebrow. I suspect he practices sneering in front of a mirror. "See a movie. There must be someplace showing 'The Shawshank Redemption.'"

Cute, I thought, to say that to a man freshly out of prison.

Then Irvin Greenfield spun on his heel and went back into his office, perhaps to spend four more hours staring out the window at Lake Michigan.

As he admitted, he earns a shitload of money for that.

CHAPTER SIX

It was a hefty walk from the Merchandise Mart to where I headed for some peace and tranquility before I had to go head-to-head with Gaylord Ogilvy. I was in the mood for some fresh air exercise, and the weather was sunny and pleasant. Grant Park, right downtown and smack against the lake, is one of the most beautiful urban parks in the country, and in my younger times I'd go down there and hang around, attending concerts, sometimes visiting the Shedd Aquarium or the Field Museum of Natural History. I also adored the Art Institute, one of the finest art museums in the world, to check out spectacular paintings by Van Gogh, Monet, Renoir and Degas, amongst many others. It was a great place, too, for starting up a conversation with an attractive female art lover, if that were one's *modus operandi*.

On this day, though, the fearsome blast chilly air off the lake that gave Chicago its most-used nickname, the Windy City, was moderate, so I paid a visit to the amazing Buckingham Fountain. It is huge, even menacing-looking, with dark bricks and stones, and when the water is turned on, the sprays reach skyward and turn to diamonds in the sun. It's glorious to behold. But when I was a kid, for some reason it frightened me terribly and gave me bad dreams.

I'm no kid anymore, and after living a seven-year nightmare, no fountain was going to scare me. The sound of the water, coming from more inlets than I can count, was actually soothing, and gave me time to think about what to say when I presented myself to one of America's wealthiest men later that afternoon.

Ogilvy was a multiple billionaire, and he says so all the time. By reputation, though, he's a tough guy, or that's what everyone says. In the old days, if you wanted to do anything in Chicago, you'd contact "Hizzoner," Mayor Richard J. Daley or one of his minions, all of whom grew up Back of the Yards. The first question put to any hopeful was, *What's In It for Me?*

Now, the rumor goes, if you want a slice of the Chicago pie, you must get in touch with Gaylord Ogilvy, never appointed or elected to anything.

I didn't look forward to this meeting. Awkward at best, because we'd shared the same mistress without knowing about each other. I suppose I would have been jealous had I known seven years ago, but that was in the past. I'd disappeared behind a stone wall with bars, and Aubrey Sinden married someone else. Even in prison, I kept good feelings for her and wished her well, but like many relationships, those feelings flourished, withered, then died. It's the way of things.

Sometimes we read about a couple celebrating their seventy years anniversary, but that's so damn rare it even makes the newspaper.

When I was on trial for Dayna's death, Aubrey got dragged into it publicly by the prosecutor, whose big dream in life was finding and punishing a well-known person, especially a Chicagoan like me. He called her to the stand to cast more blame on me wanting my wife dead so I could marry my mistress. I wondered then, and still do, how the ADA found out about our secret relationship. Whatever it was caught on with the jurors. They huddled together for less than two hours before announcing their verdict.

Involuntary manslaughter.

The fact is, it never happened that way.

I'd stopped loving Dayna some years before, and a divorce

seemed the most logical next step—but it wouldn't work out. During our passionate lovemaking, we never stopped to call our lawyers, mostly because I'd never imagined Dayna turning into a money-grubbing adulteress. For a successful best-selling author, a divorce would have cut my legs off at the knees.

Which would make me look like an idiotic schmuck.

I could live with it, I suppose. We were no longer physically attracted to each other, and hardly got along at all. With many other unhappily married people of either gender, I sometimes took advantage of my physical needs if I could find them, and imagined, never knowing for sure, if Dayna did, also.

That was the time Aubrey Sinden and I found each other.

She was startled at first, but then she smiled. It was a warm smile, a sincere smile—and I couldn't prove it, but it sure as hell looked like a sexy smile to me. "Russell Reinert," she almost breathed. "Oh, my god." She closed the book and turned it over to look at my photo on the back jacket. "By the way, I don't like the open-shirt look for an author photo. You should have worn a tie. Otherwise, you're a pretty handsome writer."

I said, "I'm afraid you're way ahead of me."

"Why is that?"

"Because I don't have a picture of you with your name under it, so I have no idea who you are. Do I get three guesses?"

"As long as one of your guesses isn't Rumpelstiltskin." She put out a soft, cool hand. "I'm Aubrey Sinden," she said. "Aubrey with a B."

"I'm sorry to interrupt your lunch, Aubrey with a B—but I noticed what you're reading. I just wanted to say—"

"Now that you're here in the flesh, you can tell me the ending so I won't have to finish it."

I laughed. "There's no way in hell you can make me tell you the ending. I have a high tolerance for pain."

"We'll see about that," she said.

* * *

Aubrey lived in a nice apartment in the Edgewater neighborhood on the north side, just one block from the lake. Not elegant, of course—that wasn't her thing—but comfortable. I never asked where she got the money to live in such a place. She might have been the daughter of the obscenely rich, taking a year off to see how we lower classes survive. It didn't matter to me. What did matter is whenever we made love while in town, it was always at her place and never at mine in Winnetka, because I never knew when Dayna might come home unexpectedly.

There was no beach within a short stroll, but a long strip of rocky walkways and borders that went from Foster Avenue south for almost two miles, keeping those high lake waves that raged in winter blizzards from flooding the nearby city streets. Aubrey and I walked there in the summertime, but I used to go there as a kid, too, with my adopted father, usually to fish off the edge of the rocks for perch. I rarely got one, which was fine because I hated the taste of perch. I still do.

Good news, if you can call it that: seven years in prison and they never served perch. Tuna only occasionally, usually as tuna salad. Incarcerated hardboiled criminals like me were never crazy about eating fish.

Aubrey and I went out to dinner two nights after we met— some nice but very obscure restaurant on the west side, as neither of us wanted to be seen. That reaction from her made me wonder if there were other men in her life. We wound up at her apartment after that first dinner date and left one of those quickly discarded clothing trails from the front door to the bedroom. I never asked her about her other sexual experiences, though, past or current—not that first night and not a hundred times afterward. At that dinner, I told her I was married, but it didn't hold back either of us. I'm also one of the few people who never snooped around in her bureau drawers or her laptop, never checked her mail. I'm an honest guy, or I was before spending seven years with a bunch of men who'd have to look up the meaning of "honest" in the dictionary, assuming they knew how to read. But if anyone invaded the privacy of *my* home to unearth secrets that had nothing to do with them, I'd lash back with high dudgeon, uncontrolled rage, and razor-sharp sarcasm that would disembowel them where they stood.

Our adulterous playtime was fun and exciting, and keeping it secret from everyone else made it an adventure. Sex was more than amazing, winding up with both of us being sweaty and blissfully exhausted. Post-cuddles were even more so. Laughs were boisterous, exhilarating. The walks at the beach or through the parks or occasionally a trip out of town, probably up to somewhere in Wisconsin were moments of great good feelings and emotional healing.

The times we did not spend together, I figured, we were each with someone else. It bothered me, naturally, but I wasn't going to get hysterical about it. I didn't ask, never leaned on her for a name. She knew I was married to Dayna, but neither of us ever mentioned her. I guess the old horseshoe saying fit: Close but No Cigar. I knew, though, whether or not Dayna would stay in my life, I had no desire to get married again.

Those who write full time for a living usually crave alone-ness. If they make good money, as I do, they generally have a space in their home in which no one dares to invade during the writing hours. Nothing shoots the hell out of a writing day like an unwanted interruption during a period of furious creation. Dayna and I lived in a four-bedroom home, and I worked in one of the bedrooms—the one that looked out on a heavily wooded area with tall swaying trees like oaks and black walnuts, full of birds, squirrels, deer, and other non-rapacious creatures. I labored in there at least six hours per day,

Then came the famous two days, the ones that changed my existence forever. As I was packed to drive to Milwaukee to give a speech the next day—and be compensated generously as well—Dayna told me she'd gone to the basement to put in a load of laundry and thought she smelled gas. She checked and found a small hole in the hose that pumped the gas from the heater. She asked me to fix it right then and there, and I told her I had to get to Milwaukee before dinnertime, as I was invited. I suggested she fix the hose herself, as it would only need a shitty little piece of duct tape to hold it until I returned. Failing that, I said if it bothered her that much, we had a regular plumber who could be called at almost a moment's notice.

Then I got into my car and headed north.

It wasn't until I finished my speech the next evening the organization's treasurer handed me a check for ten thousand dollars and whispered there had been a phone call for me from the Chicago Police Department. I returned the call as soon as I could, thereby discovering my wife was dead.

When I arrived home in the middle of the night, the house was not much more than half a house because the gas exploded and blew the back half of it into a gazillion pieces. Dayna had been in the kitchen at the time, and apparently the falling ceiling over her head killed her. Yellow crime tape and a posse of Winnetka cops surrounded the place. I wasn't given the opportunity to grieve, because they questioned me for more than an hour sitting in one of the police cars. I was called to headquarters the next day, put in an uncomfortable room with a huge mirror on one wall I knew was two-way, as other cops were sitting behind it watching, listening, and taking notes.

I was grilled again by a heavy-set African American detective, this time for three hours. If I hadn't gotten someone in Tana Phillips' office to arrange a funeral and burial with the local corpse experts, I wouldn't have been able to do it myself. After about two weeks, with me living at the Palmer House in downtown Chicago, I was arrested, hands cuffed behind my back, and marched through the hotel lobby while at least fifty reporters shouted questions and comments at me. At the inquest, I was charged a hundred-thousand dollars bail, ten percent of which I had to pay in advance, and was released on my own recognizance until the trial, set for two months later.

At that time, I talked to Aubrey by phone and suggested we

not get together again until after the trial. She agreed.

That's the last time I saw or spoke to her until she appeared in the courtroom, as a prosecution witness. Where the Assistant District Attorney found out about us in the first place, I hadn't the foggiest notion. In any event, Aubrey was truthful as hell, and the fact we were engaged in a long and passionate affair didn't help my defense with anything.

The trial took ten days. Tana was no defense attorney, but she knew every other lawyer in town, and she hired one, Nathan Peara, to handle the courtroom work in downtown Chicago. His percentage of successes was somewhere in the higher eighty percentiles. I wasn't that shot in the ass with the percentage. Too damn many percentages of the defendants he took on as clients wound up in prison.

I won't weigh you down with a word-by-word report on what was said and done during the legal proceedings. It'd take you a month to read and interpret them. Besides, you can catch up with the same things on any lawyer TV show. But it was some surprise to me when the ADA pulled out his bag of tricks. They were magical.

His name was Ryland Chanock, a young, aggressive, snot-nosed little shit who had dreams of glory of the governorship or the United States Senator from Illinois. I didn't know anything about his background—maybe Harvard, Yale, or some other stuffy Ivy League factory that coddled and nuzzled the entitled kidlets of the very rich. When he first walked in the door, I recognized his suit as costing about fifteen hundred bucks. Now I had a few million tucked away, being a best-selling author, but I wouldn't spend that much money for a suit if my life depended on it.

When he got Aubrey on the stand, he approached her as a cobra would confront a rabbit paralyzed with terror. Here are a few highlights of Aubrey's appearance.

ASSISTANT DISTRICT ATTORNEY RYLAND CHANOCK: Good morning, Ms. Sinden. Am I correct in stating you are well-acquainted with the accused, Russell Reinert?

AUBREY SINDEN: Yes, sir.

RC: How long have you known him?

AS: At least a year and a half. I knew all about him from reading his books before that, but I got to know him personally after I met him.

RC: Personally? Interesting word. How 'personal' was it?

NATHAN PEARA: Objection, your honor.

JUDGE: Objection sustained. Counselor, please define the word for the witness.

RC: I apologize, Your Honor. Ms. Sinden, could you describe your relationship with Mr. Reinert as an intimate relationship?

AS: It was, yes.

RC: An intimate adultery relationship?

NP: Objection, Your Honor.

RC: (SMIRKING) I withdraw the question. Ms. Sinden—during this time together—this intimate time—did Mr. Reinert ever tell you he loved you?

AS: (Silence).

JUDGE: Please answer the question, Ms. Sinden.

AS: Yes. Yes, he did.

RC: How many times did he tell you he loved you?

AS: I didn't count them. How many times do you tell your wife you love her?

RC: I'm not on trial here. Did he tell you he wanted to marry you?

AS: Never.

RC: Did he mention he wanted to divorce his wife?

AS: He mentioned it a few times, but he said he wouldn't be protected financially, so a divorce was out of the question.

RC: Did he have a will?

AS: I have no idea.

RC: You never discussed a will with him?

AS: No.

RC: Without a will, and with no offspring and no living

relatives, if Mr. Reinert should pass away, whatever he owned would become the sole property of his wife? Is that true?

AS: I'm no lawyer, Mr. Chanock. I don't know the first thing about wills.

RC: All right, then. Did Mr. Reinert ever mention to you he wished his wife would die?

NP: Objection!

JUDGE: Sustained. Mr. Chanock, you're skating on very thin ice.

RC: Again, I apologize, Your Honor.

AS: Wait, I will answer that damn question. No, Mr. Reinert never wished the death of his wife.

RC: At least not to you.

JUDGE: (warningly) Mr. Chanock....

RC: Withdrawn. No more questions then.

JUDGE: Mr. Peara, your witness.

NP: Thank you, sir.

When Nathan Peara climbed out of his chair, he didn't look like the hotshot defense attorney who got all his clients acquitted. He looked like a rumpled and badly rattled bum. His suit was beige, wrinkled, and looked as though he'd bought it at Target.

NATHAN PEARA: Ms. Sinden—did you ever tell Mr. Reinert you loved him?

AS: I don't really remember. Probably I did. But there's a big difference between saying 'I love you' and "I'm in love with you.'

NP: Thank you, Ms. Sinden, for the etymology correction. What you must mean is you both loved each other, but this wasn't the end-all, be-all love affair of your life. Is that true?

AS: I—suppose it was.

NP: You knew all along Mr. Reinert was married?

AS: Yes, he told me on our first date.

NP: Did you ever tell him you had another lover besides him—at the same time?

AS: No. He never asked. He probably assumed, though.

NP: Why was that?

AS: There were many nights that one or the other of us had other things to do. We just left it at that.

NP: But you did have another lover?

AS: I did.

NP: Do you still have the same lover?

AS: I do.

NP: And this other lover—was he aware of your affair with Mr. Reinert?

AS: He probably guessed—

NP: He intuited?

AS: Yes, if that's what that word means. But I don't believe he knew it was Russell Reinert. He probably didn't care, either.

NP: Really?

AS: He was—is—married, too.

NP: Apparently all these cross-current relationships, these adulteries—and nobody gave a damn.

JUDGE: Watch your mouth, Counselor.

NP: Sorry, Your Honor. So, Ms. Sinden—-and forgive me if I'm repeating, or digging up whatever the prosecutor might have said—your marriage to Mr. Reinert was out of the question?

AS: More or less, yes.

NP: For both of you?

AS: Probably.

NP: And no mention from either of you the wish, or even the—fantasy—the death of Dayna Reinert was wanted or hoped for?

AS: Not at all.

NP: So this whole thing was not illegal, isn't that true? It was just immoral?

AS: Depending on your position toward immorality.

NP: Immorality alone doesn't usually send people to prison, does it?

AS: If you say so.

NP: I do say so. No more questions.

Aubrey looked at me with sorry, helpless eyes as she descended from the witness stand. Having to honor a subpoena, I thought she did pretty damn well. Oddly, though, the ADA never mentioned the fact her "other lover" was the richest and most powerful man in Chicago. Naturally my defense council didn't bring it up either, because at the time I had no idea who it was.

The jury was "out" for less than two hours, the time it took for everyone to pee and then elect a spokesperson. Seven women, five men—and they pronounced me guilty of involuntary manslaughter, a crime I didn't commit. The judge sentenced me to ten years.

In the Joliet Correctional Institution, I vegetated, rotting a bit more each day. Aubrey came to see me a few times, but finally told me it was too tough for her to wait for me in abstinence for an entire decade. She stopped coming. I didn't know she married until hubby Cole Cabot called me, told me she'd disappeared, and begged me to find her.

I also didn't know the other lover was Gaylord Ogilvy until Cabot told me that, too—and while that concurrent love relationship was brought up at the trial, the name of the man in question wasn't mentioned.

Did Ogilvy, with all his billions and his strength and influence in Chicago, maybe lean a bit too hard on Assistant District Attorney Ryland Chanock to avoid bringing his name up at all? Inquiring minds want to know.

So did this helpless and totally ignorant shithead.

CHAPTER SEVEN

"Mr. Ogilvy has you scheduled for a twenty-minute meeting," Irvin Greenfield reported when I returned from my Buckingham Fountain afternoon trip, at a few minutes before four o'clock. "No more."

"Brushing my teeth takes more time than that," I said. "What's the hurry?"

"He didn't want to see you at all." He held out his hand, flat, and tilted it back and forth. "The Aubrey Sinden romance thing. He's a busy man, as you might imagine."

"I don't have to imagine it. His name screams at me from the sides of buildings all over town." I corrected myself. "All over the country."

"All over the world," Greenfield said, his mouth sounding dry. He stood up. "Ready to go?"

We went out into his own personal waiting room. "I'll be in Mr. O's office," he told his receptionist, and we veered out into the hallway again. "Mr. O's" private office was very close by, but at the end of the hallway, and his personal receptionist was fiftyish, and physically incapable of smiling. She rang the boss's inside office, then hung up and pointed at the big oaken doorway without a word.

I entered Gaylord Ogilvy's throne room—and that's exactly what it looked like. My first thought was now I'd never visit the

Taj Mahal, because I've seen it all. Everything was painted either ivory or gold—and a closer examination would have discovered they were *not* painted ivory and gold—they *were* ivory and gold. On one wall were at least a dozen photographs of Ogilvy with various politicians like Trump, Lindsey Graham, Dick Cheney, and the infamous "running man" Josh Hawley, from the U.S. Senate. The rest of the pictures were Ogilvy shaking hands with movie and TV celebrities who are known to lean far to the right. Against another wall were about sixteen feet of filing cabinets made of the most elegant mahogany wood, all with locks on the drawers, perhaps because Ogilvy wouldn't allow his private files to be where he was not in complete control. Two visitor chairs, one of which I sat in. Against the wall with all the photos was a comfortable-looking white leather sofa and two more easy chairs, so pristine I imagined no one had ever put their asses in them before.

Ogilvy himself was in a white executive chair with a tall back that did indeed look like a throne. His desk, twice as huge as Greenfield's, had nothing on it but six—count 'em six—telephones, three of which were cellphones. One land line was red, which made me wonder if he were in constant contact with the White House. He wore a black suit and a long orange tie, and his glasses were thick, wide with tortoise-shell frames that probably went out of style in the seventies. He also wore a neat, graying Van Dyke beard that threw me off balance. Before I went to prison seven years ago, only a few young men wore whiskers, and never American billionaires. Now almost everybody does.

"Mr. O," Greenfield said a bit louder than usual, possibly because Ogilvy was hard of hearing, "this is Russell Reinert."

"Go away, Irvin," the old man mumbled, waving his hand in the air as though swatting at a lovebird who'd escaped from its cage. Greenfield left without another word. He was Ogilvy's Chief of Staff. *Go away, Irvin?* He must have some shitty job.

I said, "I appreciate your seeing me, Mr. Ogilvy."

"I do *not* appreciate it. You're here because Greenfield said something about Aubrey Sinden going missing. She's married, Reinert. Christ almighty, are you seeing her again?"

He looked magisterial when I walked in the door, but it didn't take him long to assure me he believed he really *was* a king. I answered, "I haven't seen or talked to her in almost seven years. I just got out of prison a few days ago."

"Am I supposed to congratulate you?"

"I don't expect congratulations. I'm here to find out what's happened to Aubrey."

"How long has she been gone?"

"More than a week."

"So why are you here?"

"Aubrey's husband contacted me," I told him. "For some reason, he figured I was a good detective and I could find her."

He scoffed. "You're no detective at all—just a washed-up writer."

"You're half right. I'm no detective, but I write about them."

"Not very well," he pointed out. "I started reading one of your books several years ago. I quit after about twenty pages—but then I never bother with fiction. It's a waste of time. I only tried reading it because Aubrey was fucking you on the nights she wasn't fucking me."

I didn't like hearing it. No surprise there—I just didn't like hearing it. I said, "I don't know why Cabot didn't call the cops in the first place, but I guess he has secrets. We all have secrets."

"I don't have secrets," Ogilvy said. "Whatever I want, I buy. I buy this office. I bought my four homes—two here, one in Arizona, and one on the French Riviera. I buy my cars. I buy art, especially French Impressionists from the beginning of the twentieth century. I buy pussy. I bought Aubrey's, and I even bought my wife's. Everything is for sale. The trick is to be able to afford it. I can afford it."

"You don't see Aubrey anymore?"

"Why should I see her? She's married now—and I don't fuck

around with married women. Too much trouble."

"Did you know back in the day she was seeing me at the same time?"

"I know everything, Reinert. That's something else I buy. Information."

"You actually hired private investigators to follow me around?"

He raised his eyebrows at me, as if I'd just asked a completely stupid question. "I hate private investigators. They went out of fashion with Sam Spade eighty years ago. There are people on this company's payroll, full-time, who do shit like that. Make inquiries. Do research." He closed his eyes for a few seconds. "Anyone connected with me in any way, I make sure I know what they're doing when I'm not looking."

"I see. Did Aubrey know about that?"

"I doubt it."

"You knew we were sleeping with the same woman. Weren't you jealous?"

"I have more money in my right-hand pants pocket right this moment than you've ever seen in your life, Reinert." He shook his head. "I wasn't jealous—because whenever I wanted her, she'd come. Nights or days I didn't want her, I didn't give a shit what she did. Or with whom. I just needed to know. Last thing I wanted was getting crabs—or the clap."

The clap? Aubrey Sinden was not a professional hooker who slept with ten men every day, and I resented the hell out of Ogilvy referring to her as someone who might have had an infectious sexual disease.

"Also," he went on, "by now she has to be close to forty years old—and I don't buy forty-year-old pussy." He allowed himself the smallest of frowns. "I'm married to one, for shit's sake."

This was a big learning day for me. Before this, the only ones I ever heard insulting their wives were stand-up comics. *Take my wife—please.* I ignored it. I said, "You don't know where

Aubrey is now?"

"If I knew where she was, Reinert, I'd never have let you into the office—or this building. I have people looking for her myself."

"Since she's forty," I said, trying to keep contempt in my voice from spilling all over his desk, "why do you care where she is?"

"Because." No more answer than that. Just *because*. "She wasn't only a piece of ass. She was smart, and I'm sure you know that. What you didn't know is she did some work around here for the organization. She'd advise us about projects. Signed some contracts instead of me that will enable us to borrow huge sums of money for new constructions. She was an executive in the organization—just to make everything nice and legal. I don't want to fuck her again, but I care about where she is. In case I need her."

"Need her?"

Ogilvy lifted his shoulders and then dropped them. "As I said earlier—she signed some contracts. I don't need her right this minute, but I want to know where I can reach her."

"Well, I'm looking for her because her husband asked me to."

He sighed. I feared this meeting dragged too slowly for him. "Her goddamn husband. Cole Cabot. Wimpy little jag-off faggot. Is he paying you?"

"No. I don't need his money," I said.

"Good, because he doesn't have bus fare."

"Maybe not. But I'm worried she's gone without a word. That's not her."

"I want to know what you're finding out.," he said in a tone that sounded more like a threat. "A phone report every day from you. I'll pay you for it—pay you very well."

"I don't need your money, either, Mr. Ogilvy. Just a little bit of help. A place to start. If not, I'll leave and never bother you again."

"Your sincerity breaks my heart. Did prison teach you to be sincere?"

I said calmly, "I'm certain there's a button under your desk to summon security to throw me out of here. But I assure you, I'll break your fucking nose and possibly rip off an ear before they get here. That's also what they taught in prison. You get tough in there—or you die."

Ogilvy nodded, frowned, studied the top of his desk for a while. Then he said, "Well, I need my nose and my ears more than arguing with you about it. What the hell do you want from me? Why are you here?"

"Just a point in the direction where I can begin searching for Aubrey."

"I haven't even seen or talked to her since her marriage. I'd think the husband would know more than I do. Didn't he give you a lead?"

"Just you," I said, "and it turned out, Irvin Greenfield, too."

"You really trust him? Cabot, I mean."

"Why would he come to me if he didn't know anything?"

"About his own wife?"

I admitted, "I haven't thought that out yet. I'm just a novelist."

He stroked his chin thoughtfully, like a bad actor pretending to think hard. Then he said, "I can give you a little shove in the right direction. Do you remember Ember Polland? Does that name ring a bell?"

"Vaguely," I said. "She was a friend of Aubrey's."

"She was Aubrey's best friend forever," Ogilvy said, and one corner of his mouth lifted slightly in what he probably thought was a smile. "I met her a few times, but I completely lost track of her. I don't know if she married, if she's still in Chicago, if she's even still alive."

"Amber Polland?"

"Not Amber. Ember, with an E." He put his hands on the desktop. "An ember is some little piece that's still burning hot after the fire goes out."

"I know what an ember is, Mr. Ogilvy. I use words to make a living."

"Not anymore, you don't. Let yourself out, Mr. Reinert," he said, and swung his throne-like chair around a hundred and eighty degrees to look out the window at the lake. I was afforded a view of the back of his head. I left without another word.

In his outer office, his receptionist had gone, but Irvin Greenfield was still there, looking concerned.

"All right," he said, his voice almost angry. "You get what you wanted?"

"I don't know yet."

"Well, you're through here, Mr. Reinert, one way or the other. You're no longer welcome at this company."

"Does that include all your tributaries, Mr. Greenfield?"

He took a few deep breaths, and I realized with some amusement he'd been breathing too hard. "Fuck off, Mr. Reinert," he said.

CHAPTER EIGHT

As I drove home from Gaylord Ogilvy's office empire—not much of a drive, only ten minutes once I ransomed the car from the parking garage—I realized I was one of the few who ever got into the Merchandise Mart if they didn't belong there in the first place, much less inside the sacred worshipping lair of the city's richest and most powerful man. The meeting was unsuccessful, but I felt myself extremely lucky. After seven years locked away and unable to go anywhere except when I was told to, I was free.

I was entitled.

Being an only child, adopted into a middle-class white family, I was cuddled, coddled, told every day how special I was and how handsome and how brilliant. Never mind I was overprotected and guarded like the prime minister of some banana country who hired someone to scratch his ass for him. God forbid he'd have to scratch it himself.

I was entitled.

I became entitled when my first novel found its way onto the New York Times Best-seller list, and six more after that. They all got made into major studio movies, for one of which I was nominated for Best Screenplay Oscar. I didn't win, but that didn't matter, I was entitled to whatever fame or stardom I could leach out of the New York Times Literati or the tight-knit Hollywood community. An only child gets whatever he or she wants.

By the time they sentenced me to a decade in prison for killing my wife, both my parents had died, so there would be no hysteria or tears or wringing of hands—but my entitlement went right out the window. There were a few truly terrifying days at the very beginning. I'd never even driven by a big prison, much less been in one, because I'd never learned how to fight as a kid—and in the Big House, fighting was a way of life, sometimes over a slice of bread or a glass of milk in the dining hall. Some were not so much fights as they were murders, as many lifers stole tablespoons from a meal and sharpened them to a killer point if they worked in the machine shop. I learned about that early in my incarceration.

I was no movie star stud, but fairly pleasant-looking, and on the third night in lock-up I learned several co-convicts had voted affirmatively I was going to become fish-bait. A candy-ass. A gunsel.

Few people know what gunsel really means and rarely have the reason or the instinct to use it. They all think it's what they called tough guys in old gangster movies, but look it up in one of those giant, heavy volumes like the Oxford English Dictionary, and you'll find a gunsel is also a male victim for any other male who fancied him sexually. Most long-time cons had lived on the outside as heterosexuals, but there were no women inside a prison to take care of their lustful yearnings, so young, attractive male prisoners—gunsels—filled the bill whether they wanted to or not.

On my third day in what many of my fellow cons refer to as the Crowbar Hotel, I was cornered inside the shower room—one of my two shower experiences allowed per week—by three men, long-timers. One, who I learned later was inside for life plus ninety-nine years because he serial-raped and murdered seven African American prostitutes who worked the south side of Chicago, and the other two were younger guys who fed some sort of Mickey Finn to women, often college girls who'd had too much to drink or smoke in the first place, rendered them unconscious and then raped them, frequently in alleys or someplace hidden, and leave them there, often naked, to be discovered by strangers the next morning.

These three guys were eager to get to know me personally—very personally. I learned later they considered me FMS—Fresh Meat Syndrome. I tried to convince them I just wasn't interested, but they wanted to make me a "keester bunny." I got pushed around as they worked themselves up to be really brutal, but I figured I was doomed—possibly for the next ten years.

That's when Denver Tolliver arrived on the scene—and I assure you, when he arrived anyplace, he *really arrived!*

Tolliver is a black man who was around forty years old at the time, and weighed upwards of three hundred twenty-five pounds, three hundred and ten of which were solid muscle. He was six foot, six inches tall, he had a voice deeper than Barry White's but nowhere near as sensuous, and was fast losing his hair, as the front of his head was bald, shiny and gleaming like a gold brick from Fort Knox.

None of my would-be attackers stood any taller than five foot ten. Just the sight of angry Denver Tolliver was enough to scare them off, even as he warned them any further encroachment on the slim body of the new kid—me—would be one of their all-time major mistakes. But he didn't let them go that easily. He beat the crap out of all three of them at the same time, saving his most fiendish castigation for the serial killer. He left them all bloody and naked under the showers, which he switched to ice-cold to run on them before we left, giving two of them severe head colds and the third with pneumonia. All three went to the doctor's office the following morning, and the serial killer wound up spending three weeks in the prison hospital with a concussion, a broken jaw, a broken nose, and about seven fewer teeth than he had when he walked into the shower room.

None of these victims blamed Denver Tolliver. They didn't dare.

Tolliver hardly spoke to me until we got clear away from the showers and on our way to our cells, though I kept trying to thank him. Finally, he said, "Damn, boy. You so fricken pretty, you might as well have a big sign on your forehead screaming *Fuck me!* You stick close to me an' I'll try takin' care of your ass, or else you ain't gonna survive six months in this joint."

"I appreciate it," I said, trembling like a dried-up leaf on the harsh, windy last day of autumn. "But why watch out for me? Why me out of all the men that are in and out of here all the time?"

His smile was not something to write home about, but his eyes twinkled. "I don't read much, an' my daddy, he couldn't read at all. But he worked thirty-three years on a trash truck for the Sanitation Department—and him an' me an' my little brother, we saw all those movies they made outta books you wrote, three, four times each, mostly on television. But them— whatchacallem?—them private eyes you wrote about—they did good shit and always made the cops look like dumb assholes." His eyes took on that far-away look of an airborne peregrine falcon spotting an unsuspecting rabbit getting a nibble of greenery. "Us cons got no use for cops."

I said, "I've only been in a few days. How come you know I wrote books that turned into movies?"

"Anybody come into The Bastille—or anybody walk out—I know about it, my broh. I know all about it."

On this day, seven-plus years later, as I was driving home from a short, awkward meeting, what Gaylord Ogilvy said a few minutes earlier and what Tolliver said seven years ago sounded very much the same.

Denver Tolliver had an excellent sense of humor when he felt like it. He often mentioned he'd been born in Denver, Colorado—thus the first name—and said he was lucky he wasn't born in Charlotte, North Carolina.

I learned several weeks into residence in Cell 6-22B why he was in prison, though as I have mentioned, one doesn't ask. Tolliver, however, laid the story out for me. He and his younger brother, both unarmed, were hanging around on a South Side street corner. Four white police officers, two each in squad cars, rolled up, got out, started harassing them for loitering. They argued, naturally, winding up face down on the sidewalk. Tolliver's brother, Tyree, was the smart-ass bigmouth of the two, and he enraged one of the cops so badly the officer actually stood on his head with both feet, trying hard to grind his face into the dirty sidewalk. His police weapon was in his hand.

Big as Tolliver was, he was on his feet in a mini second, wrenched the weapon away from the cop, and shot him between the eyes. Killing a police officer in Chicago means wherever you go, even hiding in an ice-fishing hut in the middle of Greenland, the Chicago constabulary will find you—even if you stay hidden for fifty years.

Denver Tolliver did not run, did not hide. He was arrested on the spot by one of the other cops, thrown into jail, tried for murder within six weeks of the killing. It was no surprise he was found guilty by the jury after less than four hours of deliberation. Only his squeaky-clean background kept him from a death sentence, but life-plus-ninety-nine years without possibility of parole wasn't much better.

I was damn glad he picked me to watch out for. He made me feel safe, as safe as one could be residing in the Illinois Bastille—and there were eight thousand tenants who quickly learned if you fuck with me, you're fucking with Denver Tolliver, too.

In his own special way, Denver Tolliver was also entitled.

It wasn't until two years later, when most everyone on both sides of the law in that joint learned who I was and gave me the opportunity to teach lit classes to any inmate who wanted it. I couldn't discuss my own books, which are all about murders, and it's hard to pick out books to read that never made crime pay and did not offend either white prisoners or black ones, but I managed. *Rebecca* by Daphne du Maurier was a favorite, even though several African American cons wondered why every character in the novel was white.

To make a long story short, I was released relatively unharmed after seven years instead of ten, which Tolliver called a Get-Out-of-Hell Free Card. I truly miss his friendship. I grew up and flourished amongst many good friends of color, hard to even admit they were a different hue than I was. But there has never been anyone like Denver Tolliver, and never will be again. I so wished I could return his friendship, but there was no way. He was twice my size, and all our fellow inmates were terrified of him. He was a non-elected Emperor of The Homeboy Hotel and will probably remain so for the rest of his life. I hugged him goodbye and promised to keep in touch with him—but I knew he was going to age and die in that prison.

I landed in a pretty neat situation the day I walked away, thanks to Tana Phillips. Because of her, the book money I'd earned before going inside well was taken care of and invested beautifully, though I couldn't touch a nickel of it while still a prisoner. Now out, I found myself in the soft middle of new clothes, a new car, a new apartment, and even a new MacBook Air laptop on which to take up writing again. It was gold-colored, too—surprising because most laptops these days are always black or gray.

One thing Tana forgot, though, was pajamas. I haven't owned a pair of real pajamas since I was ten years old, but I'd spent my adulthood sleeping in soft pajama-like pants and a T-shirt—or in underwear while incarcerated.

No one in their right mind would ever sleep naked in prison. *No one.*

In the past few days, I was shocked and dismayed my agent

and my publisher wanted nothing to do with me, so I hoped someone else in the publishing business would remember who I used to be and take a chance. I know I was damn good at what I did and hated the idea of building up my career again by using a *nom de plume*. My ego was healthy enough I wished to be known for my own work, good or bad. There have been famous novelists who have published under an assumed name, but took great pains to let their readers know who they were anyway, i.e. *'Erle Stanley Gardner'* writing under the name of *'A.A. Fair'*, right on the front cover and on the title page. What was the point? I wish the noted creator of Perry Mason was still alive so I could ask him.

But there's that damn Cole Cabot demanding I find his missing wife, once my mistress as I unknowingly shared her sexually with an infamous gazillionaire. Cabot's spinning a bothersome story shook me up badly. Now free, I was searching for peace, not nightmares.

It was past five o'clock when I returned home, and I didn't imagine any more activity that day would require a suit and tie. I changed into jeans and a polo shirt, made my dinner—a turkey sandwich on pumpernickel—poured myself a Mountain Dew, and opened up my laptop.

Tana, or one of the technological geniuses in her office, had set me up on the Internet, along with Facebook and Twitter. I knew I'd never use Twitter. It seemed so ridiculous unless you were a President of the United States who used it to rant every day—but I checked Facebook. The profile photo of me Tana selected was the author photo on the back cover of my most recent book (most recent being seven years ago). The profile was filled out completely—Home Town (Chicago), Now Living In (Chicago), Job (published novelist), Relationship (single), minus the fact I am a convicted felon. I argued with Tana a lot of famous people are known convicted felons and came out all right, whether on the Internet or anyplace else— boxer Mike Tyson, actors Robert Mitchum and Bobby Blake, and housekeeping angel Martha Stewart for examples—but she talked me out of including it on my main page.

Finally, I looked up Aubrey's best friend from the old days. Ember Pollard. I'd heard her name from Aubrey several times, but I had no idea what she was like. I'd seen her very few times for only brief moments, like when I was meeting Aubrey in a bar and her best friend was sitting with her, though she left almost immediately—-and all that time I thought her name was Amber, with an *A*. I knew few of Aubrey's friends. Maybe it was because I was married, and she didn't want her other gal pals to know much about me—but I didn't introduce her to my friends, either. Adultery is best left a secret.

I didn't think there were many people named Ember in the world, and was surprised there were quite a few of them on Facebook. Many women used their maiden name and their married name on this particular social correspondence, so eventually I came across Ember Pollard d'Anjou who lived in the Hermosa area in Northwest Chicago. Pretty decent neighborhood, though I barely remembered it other than it was the birthplace of Walt Disney. Her profile photo was of a smiling African American standing with her arms around a white male looking to be in his mid-forties, their heads leaning toward one another as if they might really be in love. She had studied psychology at the University of Chicago, and after graduation, became a social worker. Her FB profile told me she was married to one Joseph d'Anjou. She had 246 Facebook friends, but I was not one of them. This was my first FB use in seven years, and Tana had given me the profile name RussAuthorReinert, possibly because there might be few other Russell Reinerts in the world who never wrote mystery fiction for money.

I worried what I should correspond to Ember, who might not even remember me. I'd have to be careful what I put online, but at the moment she was my only lead to find out what happened to Aubrey. I desperately wanted to meet with her.

I spent several minutes trying to find her phone number on

the Internet, or one that might be her husband's, but it was to no avail. An operator informed me their number was unlisted. Whatever happened, I wondered, to the big fat phone directory book, which was delivered free every year? I used to page through them in the old days, looking for interesting names to use in my novels.

Now all I could remember were the first and last names of guys I met and socialized with in the Stony Lonesome, and most wouldn't want their names on Facebook.

I sent Ember a private email. I composed it more slowly than my novels, weighing every word. Close to being a Luddite terrified even to use the Internet, I still understood whatever you put online will exist somewhere out in the ether for eternity, even though you've put it in the Delete department and hoped it would go away forever. I didn't want people to know, three days after I walked free, I was desperate to locate anyone.

Hi, Ember. I typed slowly, checking each word for mis-spelling or mis-typing. *I don't know if you remember me. We only met a few times, briefly, but I've heard a lot about you. I'm Russ Reinert. I used to go around with Aubrey Sinden several years ago. I know you and she were best friends. I haven't been in Chicago for quite some time, but I'm back now and I'd really like to see her again, even for old times' sake, but have no way of getting in touch with her. I was hoping you might know. If so, can you message me here on Facebook? I'd appreciate muchly. After such a long time away, I have no friends in town anymore. Anyway, nice getting in touch with you. Oh, congratulations on your marriage. Hope you're well and safe. Best, Russ.*

I sent my profile picture to her, too. Again, the old one. I need to get some new photos taken. My most recent pictures, which I never share with anyone, were left profile, right profile, face front, with a number across my chest.

I fumed for a while, went out, found a department store where I could purchase some sleeping clothes, and paid for them via Mastercard—but it wasn't a credit card, at least not yet. It was a debit card, meaning the minute I made a purchase with it, "they," whoever they may be, immediately deducted it from my bank account. I might not even bother with a credit card anymore, as they charge interest for everything, but no charges for a debit card. I had enough cash in the bank, so I'd never have to worry about it. Besides, Tana takes care I have spending money to spare.

Do I want to buy a new home? A new car? A trip around the world? I wouldn't want to brag that "I'm very rich," as some rich people do, even though it makes them look like drooling idiots. I *am* rich, I suppose, meaning I could chug through the rest of my life without writing one more word. I'm not even in the same galaxy as Gaylord Ogilvy, because I don't own half the city and don't put my attention-getting name on every building one can see. But unless I turn into a raving maniac and decide to buy all the North California coastal islands and build mansions on them no one in their right mind could afford, I'd be financially comfortable for the rest of my days.

Despite my many notebooks full of ideas I scribbled in my cell, I wasn't ready to begin another book. I was finding out how much Chicago changed. Restaurants I used to patronize are gone. Jazz bars have mostly given way to blues bars or hip-hop joints, not really my favorite music. New buildings now stand where old ones used to in my youth, but the "L" trains are *still* running overhead through downtown and out into the suburbs. I didn't care. All that drove me for the moment was to find Aubrey, ASAP.

I got to thinking, though—remembering. Tana Phillips. Aubrey Cabot. Cole Cabot. Ember d'Anjou. Even Gaylord Ogilvy. Everybody I'm connecting with in the last three days is married. Denver Tolliver was married, too, and had a young son in his late teens. Though Tolliver could not write legibly, he phoned his family every two weeks from the public phone in the hallway at the prison. His wife, Kalinda, swore on a regular basis she'd been celibate from the day he walked into prison, and he happily chose to believe her.

And me? Since I was arrested and convicted for manslaughter of my wife Dayna, I haven't had any sort of sexual experience for more than seven years. Masturbating, especially in a barred cell, with a cellmate watching and guards gliding by every two minutes and peering in, didn't happen that often for me, either. Even in a state prison, one needs to have *some* privacy.

Professionals, working girls—in the old days they were called courtesans—had never appealed to me. I know some of them are stunningly beautiful, if you have enough money to pay for one. For many years I'd been able to afford the best, but high-level prostitution never got my attention. Oh sure, I've taken women out to dinner and then to the theater before lovemaking, or even taken a few on Hawaiian or Cancun mini-vacations, and I guess that was kind of paying for their physical company, but it didn't feel like that. They all seemed like real honest-to-goodness dates.

Besides, the women I chose could have easily said NO. A few of them did.

Funny, though—when you're single, not committed, even though you might have a steady lover about whom you're very fond, sex can be wild. Crazy. Overwhelming. An astonishing learning experience. After you get married, though, things change—sometimes slowly but often almost immediately. Too many other things demanded your involvement. Money. Career. Making married couples your friends rather than single ones. Families, yours against theirs. Children, the raising thereof. Overeager lovemaking often takes a back seat after marriage and never moves up to riding shotgun again.

Dayna and I had a hot and heavy relationship at the beginning, but it wasn't too long into the marriage I realized Dayna wasn't in love with me at all. She was in love with being the wife of a best-selling author who always got the best tables in Chicago restaurants without having a reservation. I made tons of money from publishing and movie rights, and she tried getting all of it into her grubby fingers. Otherwise, we had little in common.

I was a baseball fan, loved the Chicago Cubs and going to games at old, tottering Wrigley Field. Dayna never went with me—not once. She never really knew what a shortstop did for a living, nor cared. She was an avid tennis player, and even joined a country club so she could volley any day she wanted to with women just like her—trophy wives, entitled wives, religious users of Botox, skin creams that made their wrinkled arms look smoother, and the removal of facial hair. Tennis lacked any interest for me, golf with a bunch of paunchy old white men even less so. I adored theater plays and musicals, but Dayna always preferred waiting until they made a film version—and then we had to watch them on Netflix or Turner Classic Movies, because those who actually attended theaters were, according to my wife, low class. Worse than anything was I preferred having sex at night, and she wanted to do it in the morning.

Our conjugal bond wasn't ghastly, horrible, traumatic. It was just—dull.

A few occasions were given over to discuss the possibility of divorce, but she wouldn't hear of it, and threatened to take me for every cent I had, even money I hadn't even earned yet because I had lots of novels yet to write. So together we drifted into an existence rather than a marriage, only going out together to some tight-assed benefit event where she was more fussed over than I was.

We had extramarital affairs with others—I did, and I'd bet the farm she did, too. She flirted shamelessly with other men while I sat there watching. Would her flirting turn into something more serious? I'm sure it did, but I never knew. The adulteries quickly lost their ability to hurt and enrage. They were simply something to keep one from getting bored out of their skull.

That's when I met Aubrey Sinden. The chemistry was instantaneous in that first moment. We both knew it, felt it, actually showed it somewhere south of kissing and groping in public. We didn't care whether we got to know one another, although eventually we did. Even on the first night, there was no discussion of *If*. It was only about *Where* and *When*.

We had our own lives. There were times when one or the other of us was not available. Aubrey knew about Dayna, as I'd been honest about my marital status from the beginning. She worked for a huge international company, but would say no more about it. She told me she was single, but never revealed anything else about her life, and I guess I was pleased not knowing about it. I never considered divorcing Dayna to marry Aubrey, because I had no urge to marry anyone again, ever.

Some of my friends—*my* friends—knew my marriage was not a happy one. The old places I went, I went alone. I'm sure these longtime Chicago acquaintances thought, in one of their weaker moments, I'd be happy if Dayna died. That wasn't true. I'd never wish that on anyone. We no longer liked each other much, but there were many moments of bliss, passion, lust, and even laughing out loud we recalled and cared about. If she decided on a divorce to take a large chomp of my hard-earned money and then disappear from my life, that was not a consummation devoutly to be wished.

We moved into an elegant home I'd just bought in Winnetka, a north-of-Chicago suburb. Probably built around 1965, the ranch-style house at the top of a sweeping hill still presented a beautiful picture to visitors, but fifty years had taken its toll with things like the roof, the worn-out driveway, and leaky plumbing and heating.

Dayna didn't give a damn about all that. Optics bothered her, which meant beautiful and expensive clothes, dinners out at high-end restaurants where she sipped the most expensive wines in the joint, traveled around the world, and obscenely worshipped opulent cars, though I did give an unbridled *No!* to a

Rolls Royce. After all, enough was enough. I had plenty of money already, but if I spent at all of it on her, she'd be out of the house day and night, and I'd find time to write another book and make more money for her to spend.

If Ember didn't answer my email, where could I go next? I gave it a lot of thought—and then I phoned Cole Cabot.

CHAPTER NINE

I was back at the damn Viking ship again, this time at twilight, so there were few passers-by. But what kind of meeting spot was this, looking at what remained neglected, an ancient copy of an older ship? Get down on one knee and ask your girlfriend to marry you with an ugly, rotting, covered-with-pigeon-shit old boat peering over one shoulder? What am I doing here? Four days from prison—-stuck in another meeting with Cole Cabot.

And it was my idea to call for this get-together! Sheesh!!

Cabot was there already, wearing a very heavy sweater, probably knitted from llama wool dripping with lanolin and never to be washed—just brushed out on occasion. I had on an autumn-weight jacket. He was smoking a cigarette as I approached him. I'd never smoked before, but got into the temporary habit imbibed in prison, maybe because most fellow inmates were smokers. I stopped a few weeks before I was freed, but on this cool evening, I wished I could smoke, but I'd die before I asked him for one.

He glanced up at me but made no effort to rise. Did the centuries-old polite habit of shaking hands become illegal while I was in stir? Or was Cabot still living in the fifteenth century?

"Have you found anything?" he asked, again without a hello.

"I have little to go on," I replied. "I'm doing this strictly for you, and I could use a little more help."

"What help? Aubrey is my wife. She's gone. If I knew where, I wouldn't have asked you to find her."

He was at one end of the park bench. I sat down at the other end. "How about I ask the questions and you answer them?"

He looked sullen. "You sound like a cop."

"That brings up question number one. Why didn't you call the police in the first place?"

"Because," Cole Cabot said, "she never told me much about her relationship to the Ogilvy Corp, or her relationship with Ogilvy himself. She mentioned her part-time work there in passing a few times, but she wasn't open to share with me a lot of stuff I don't know about. It might be legal, or it might not be. I got no idea. I didn't want to take the chance of getting her in trouble. I don't want her to be in trouble now."

"Getting her in trouble? She's gone without a trace! She could be floating in Lake Michigan for all you know."

"I *don't* know!" His eyes grew teary, and his shrug reached his entire body. "Christ knows what else she was into."

I sucked in lungs full of air. "I don't want to ask—but was she having an affair with someone?"

"Not with you, Reinert. You were in jail before I even met her."

"What about during your marriage? Was she cheating on you with anybody then?"

"I don't know!" He thought that over. "Probably not."

"And she wasn't still sleeping with Gaylord Ogilvy?"

"She quit that when we got engaged."

"Are you sure?"

"Ogilvy said no, and so did Aubrey. He's so goddamn rich he wouldn't have to lie." He was sitting slumped over, his forearms on his thighs, studying the sidewalk under his feet. "That's all I can tell you."

"Not necessarily. Tell me about your relationship."

"Huh?"

"Your marriage."

"That's none of your goddamn business."

"You made it my goddamn business when you contacted me in the first place—-so talk! Was it a good marriage?"

"What does that mean?"

I gritted my teeth. My stomach burned, as if I'd just eaten a large meal full of spices and hot peppers in an Indian restaurant and the waiter forgot to bring out the rice. Asking Cabot questions was like talking to a brick wall with no windows. "What do you think it means? Were you happy together? Did you argue a lot?"

"It's a marriage!" he protested. "Married people argue. All married people. It comes with the territory."

"Argue? Do you ever hit her? Or does she ever hit you?"

"It's not that kind of argument."

"What kind was it?"

He looked away, though from his expression I don't think his mind caught on what his eyes captured. "Money—or not enough of it. Or my business, I guess, because I spent too much time working and not being with her more."

"Did you have fights?"

He shook his head slowly. "Not that often. Mostly on Sundays. All married couples fight on Sundays. They ought to make it a law, y' know? Every Sunday, you take a day off from your marriage. Don't cheat—just go away somewhere and do whatever it is you wanna do without having to explain it.."

He unknowingly opened a wound somewhere inside my stomach. During my marriage to Dayna, Sundays were frequently bitch days—and I worked at home, too, damn it! I had one bedroom remodeled into my office—two laptops, a large TV screen on the wall across from my desk if I wanted to write and watch sports at the same time, and a door that was kept closed while I worked.

Back to the job at hand, I asked Cabot, "Did you have a fight that day—or the day before she disappeared?"

He shook his head. "To tell you the truth, we had pretty great sex the night before."

"Good for you," I said. "She left the next morning?"

"I left," he said. "For work, like I always do. She wasn't working then, not full time. When I got home that night, she was gone."

"No phone message? No note?"

"Nuh-uh."

"She didn't take anything with her? Clothes? Make-up? Jewelry?"

"She just took her purse—her car was still there when I got home."

My instant thought was she was removed from her home against her will. No woman alive would simply run off and disappear without taking her make-up with her. I said, "Did you get in touch with Ember Pollard? She was Aubrey's best friend—back when we were together."

"I didn't think about it. I never knew her very well. I didn't like her much. I was glad Aubrey stopped seeing her."

"Why?"

He twisted his mouth up, unwilling to answer. I said again, "Why, Cabot?"

Eventually he said, "Let's just say black is not my favorite color."

"You're a racist prick."

"I'm no racist, dammit! Black people are okay as long as they keep to themselves."

I made tight fists, my fingernails digging into my palms. "I'm just itching to lay you out in lavender, right here on the sidewalk."

He gave me his big tough guy look, which was more like that of a peeved Jerry Seinfeld. "You think you could?"

"After I spent seven years in a state prison? Take your first swing, Cabot. It'll be your last, so make it good."

"Forget it, Reinert. I'm sorry I ever called you. You're fired."

"Fired? You already fired me—from a job that didn't pay a salary. I got news for you, pal. I'm going to find Aubrey on my own. She's an old friend, so I'll forgive her for marrying a dumbshit like you who's too stupid to dial 911 when his wife disappears." I stood up, moved closer, looming over him and making him nervous. I put my face close to his. "And stay out of my way. If you get me mad enough, I'll put you in my next book as a psychopathic transgender serial killer who ends up being kidnapped and eaten by a herd of Australian dingoes."

"I'll sue you."

"You'll get laughed out of town. But if you want to sue, I have the name of a great lawyer." I began walking away, then turned back. "Stay right where you are, Mr. Cabot. If you follow me, I'm going to break your nose."

It was almost dark by the time I found my way out of Lincoln Park.

I wasn't hungry when I got home, even though I walked all the way. Funny, but since resuming my more-or-less normal lifestyle, I preferred walking to driving my new car. Maybe because for the past seven years, I had not been in any sort of motorized vehicle. Joliet is a huge prison, and it's a long walk to get anywhere besides the shower room. My legs had grown stronger.

As for the bad words between me and Aubrey's husband, I knew more tough ones than he did, and for good reason. I had a few fistfights in prison during which I came out okay, and I worked those out on my own, without extra help. Denver Tolliver was not my babysitter. But when the really bad guys tried their bully intimidation tactics on me, Tolliver was always there to step in between us.

I don't know why he seemed to care about what happened to me. Different ages, different races, different backgrounds. He knew little about me at the beginning, but somehow caught on I was intelligent—and people who knew how to use brains needed protection from the locked-up despots who would form into gangs to terrorize those not big enough or mean enough to hurt them back.

I consider Tolliver the best friend I ever had, and I promised myself I'd write him every month or so to let him know I still think of him. He won't write back, mostly because he always misspelled damn near every word. I doubt I'd be able to visit him. Prisons don't look kindly on former inmates dropping by to say hi to their malfeasant buddies not lucky enough to have gotten outside. Denver Tolliver will never get through that iron gate to breathe freely. His life sentence is a death watch that lasts forever.

I kicked off my shoes, poured a drink, and sat quietly. Television doesn't make it for me, only filling up the boring spaces during which I have nothing much to do. In my old days, I had few times that weren't active. I was either writing a book, which enveloped my life, or romancing someone exciting—like Aubrey Sinden. I read, too, at least two books a week unless I took on something mammoth like Stephen King's *It*. The last time I tried reading something that long, it was James Joyce's *Ulysses*—and I barely got through half of that before bailing out. Now, after seeing only the vintage books the librarian pushed past my cell door every week on a broken-down cart, I had no clue who was writing good stuff these days.

It wasn't until I fixed a second drink when I thought to check my laptop for emails or Facebook messages. There was no real reason to do so, but Tana Phillips had set Facebook up for me in hopes of selling a few of my older books before I could squeeze out a new one.

The urge, the commitment, the *addiction* to writing had not yet returned. That troubled me. I had enough money to live well until I'm in my nineties, but for me, life *is* writing, and always has been. But It was impossible to think about it just then when my full time was looking for Aubrey—a woman I hadn't even seen in seven years.

There were several entries on my news page, many old Facebook friends I never met personally, telling me they'd missed me, were glad to see me back, and asked when my next book would come out. Some, I believe, had no clue I'd been locked up in a state prison.

But there was one private message, and I opened it with a combination of eagerness and fright—an answer message from Ember Pollard d'Anjou.

Hi, Russ. Naturally I remember you, Hell, you were famous already, but I didn't want to make a fuss over you because you were Aubrey's fella.

Since she and I both got married, we don't see each other much afterward. We talk maybe once every ten days, and sometimes grab a lunch together, or even a dinner-and-drinks night. I think she still works part-time at Ogilvy Corp, but I never knew what it is she did there.

I have no idea where she is now. I haven't heard from her. I called Ogilvy's, and I called her husband, but he was pretty cold to me, and either couldn't or wouldn't tell me a goddamn thing.

She was pretty crazy about you back then, but there must've been some reason she rarely let you and me get together. Like I say, I don't know much, but if you want to meet for coffee or a meal or a drink sometime, I'll be glad to. Give me a call in the evening.

She left her home phone number, and then she added something, a P.S. that made me smile.

BTW, after I met you through Aubrey, I loved reading your books. Thought you should know.

Ember xoxoxo

CHAPTER TEN

The nearest Cook County Adult Probation Office to where I lived was in a not-too-tall building on downtown Washington Street, a few steps west of State Street. This was my first trip there, and not knowing anything about probation or parole officers, I was scared silly. I didn't think when I got out I might be forbidden to use alcohol, or even enter a restaurant in which alcohol was served—and I'd already broken that rule. Would I get slammed back into prison to complete my ten-year sentence for having a fucking drink?

The parole officer's name was Roman Bellini. How Italian could one get?

The office was tacky, as was the building itself. The receptionist, if that's one would call him, was a guy in his middle twenties, wearing a cheap suit and a tie too bright and playful for his job or location. I guessed he goes to school at night and majors in law enforcement, as no one in their right mind would want a receptionist job at a place like this. The waiting room was stuffy, probably not cleaned every night, and the smells that hung in the air were ghastly familiar. Unless you've either been in military combat or in prison, you wouldn't realize how badly terror stinks.

The student pointed at one of four uncomfortable-looking folding chairs against the wall and told me to wait. I'd arrived five minutes early for my appointment, but I wound up waiting for half an hour before someone came out of the inner office.

A man of color, close to sixty but looking older, wearing a blue suit he probably bought used at a Salvation Army store, medium-to-dark skin, and grayish hair disappearing at an alarming rate, waved a timid goodbye to the receptionist, but got no reply. The fear stink in the room grew that much stronger.

After he left, the phone on the desk tinkled and was answered. The kid listened for mere seconds, hung up and said, "Reinert," and jerked his head toward the inner door. I figured if he ever got his law license, he'd forever be one of those junior guys who spends his life looking up things in dusty old law books.

Inside, the room looked even more shabby than the one in which I'd just waited. Roman Bellini sat at a desk that probably came to fruition somewhere during the Lyndon B. Johnson Administration, scratched, marred with dried-up liquid rings from generations of coffee in cardboard containers, and cigarette burns on the surface that arrived before smoking became illegal in government offices. Behind it was Bellini, whose last smile was probably at a Road Runner cartoon when he was eight years old.

In his late fifties, I guessed, and like his last visitor, losing his hair. Short, chunky, a man who never saw or knew about Buster Keaton, Laurel and Hardy, the Marx Brothers or Abbott and Costello, and thus unable to smile, laugh, or even look pleasant. Hated his job but was too old to work as a Starbucks barista or as an assistant-assistant manager at Burger King. He apparently bit his fingernails during odd hours.

What the hell—it's his job. Maybe at home he is kind, loving, cheerful, and puts on a Santa Claus suit every Christmas.

Yeah, right.

He looked up as I entered, and frowned as if a Tyrannosaurus rex just walked into his office. Without speaking, he jerked his chin toward one of the two visitor chairs. He seemed to study my folder for at least a minute. Then he said my name aloud: "Russell Reinert." HIs tone was as if he'd just announced Benito Mussolini had entered the room.

He put down my file and leaned back in his chair. It squeaked. It hadn't been oiled since the LBJ years, either. "It says you were a perfect prisoner. No mistakes, no trouble. Taught classes to fellow inmates. Good boy. Evidently, you have a damn good lawyer."

"I do?"

"Why you think you're walking around when you were sentenced to ten years and you're out after seven?"

"I don't know why, Mr. Bellini. I didn't ask."

"Just accept whatever comes along, eh?"

"I did while I was in prison. And I'm here—with you."

"Why is that?"

"Am I not on parole?"

"No, Reinert, you're not. Because you're a big shot. Big best seller. That's what they call you, right?"

"I couldn't write while I was inside. Took lots of notes, but I haven't had a book published for the past seven years." I realized I was sweating. My hands were clammy and the underarms of my shirt were damp. "Am I supposed to be looking for a job?"

"Handing out shopping carts to old ladies at Walmart?"

"I don't think Walmart pays people to do that anymore." I shrugged. "I'm just guessing, I haven't been inside a Walmart in a while."

"You won't need going to Walmart. A whole lot of your money was put into trust when you got convicted. Now you can get it whenever you want."

I didn't answer, didn't even nod.

"You're a lucky guy then, huh?"

"Everybody's lucky—and unlucky, too."

"You're unlucky because you murdered your wife."

My sweat turned ice cold within seconds. I said, "I didn't murder my wife. They called it involuntary manslaughter—and I didn't do that, either."

"Twelve jurors say you did, so you did."

"That's where the unlucky part comes in, Mr. Bellini. But I'm out now."

"That's right, you're out now. You can drink, you can fuck, you can write another goddamn book, you can do whatever you want. And you don't have to come see me every two weeks, either. We're done."

"Wow," I said softly, meaning it. "How did that happen?"

"Ask your lawyer," Bellini said. "In the meantime—if you litter on the street, if you drive one mile faster than the speed limit, if you grope some strange female, if you talk bad to anybody at all—I'll see you're back in prison to finish out your sentence and add ten more years. Now get out of my office before I lose my temper and shoot you dead."

I couldn't believe it—or maybe I should. I'd thought I had to present myself to Parole Officer Roman Bellini every month for the next three years at least, hat in hand, head down and mumbling "Yes sir" whenever I was forced to, and not much more. Now, though, I could take my millions out of wherever Tana put them, move to somewhere like Fiji, and live the rest of my days on the always-sunny white sand shore with exceptionally gorgeous, topless, dusky-skinned women all over the place.

Nice thoughts—but do they have Wi-Fi in Fiji so I can write my next book? Besides, I had to stick around Chicago until I found what had become of Aubrey Sinden.

Bellini, though, said something that stuck in my craw, and before I did anything else, I wanted it cleared up. That's why I went up to the law office of Tana Phillips, in the elegant and unique Wrigley Building at the banks of the river on Chicago's Miracle Mile.

Arly Singleton was not only the receptionist in the main lobby on the seventeenth floor, she was also the office manager, and had been for as long as Tana had been my lawyer. When I stepped off the elevator, her face lit up, and she stood and came around her desk to greet me with a hug.

"Russ," she said, finally backing up to take a good look at me, "you can't imagine how happy we are you're here. It's been too damn long."

I hugged her back. "How come you're prettier and sexier since the last time I saw you?"

"Tea instead of coffee, soy and veggies instead of meat, water instead of Pepsi, and waiting around for hunks like you to hug me again." She was married, by the way, so hugging was truly friendship, nothing more. "Does Tana know you were coming?"

I shook my head. "Life is full of surprises. Is she in—or down in court getting a serial killer a fifty-dollar fine and a slap on the wrist?"

"She's right here in the office, Russ, getting ready for a big trial in about two weeks. I'm not supposed to bother her—but for you, we'll both make an exception. Come with me."

Arly took my hand and marched me down a long hallway to the double doors on the big office, knocked and opened the door without asking.

"Tana," she announced, "a surprise delivery for you." She stepped aside, pushed me through the doorway, said, "Ta-dah!" and disappeared back down the corridor.

I'd been in the office many times before, but it had slightly changed since my former days. The desk was larger, more beautiful, and the visitor chairs were also new. There were different elegant drapes on the windows, and on the wall was mounted a very large dramatic painting by early twentieth century Chicago art genius, William S. Schwartz.

"Russ!" Tana stood, too, and gave me another hug. The day was turning sunny and beautiful, all right. Tana was especially beautiful, too—her black hair long and entwined with colorful threads, her mascara an interesting purple, her lipstick strikingly crimson. "What brings you here? You want your millions to go play craps at the nearest Indian casino?"

"Not all of it. I'd want to keep about thirty bucks." I glanced at her desk, so full of papers I couldn't see even a sliver of wood. "I'm sorry, hon—I see you're busy."

"I'm always busy," she said, "but this is your first visit in a long time, so I'll stop being busy for five minutes. What up?"

"I just came from the office of Roman Bellini."

"The parole guy? Why'd you go there? You don't need to."

"Nobody said I shouldn't," I said. "I thought I was out on some sort of parole. But he didn't know why I was there, either. When I asked him, he told me to talk to my lawyer. That's you."

"You want to hear about my magic wand?"

"If you were a guy," I said, "that would sound dirty."

"Have a seat," she said, "and I'll talk dirty some more. You want a drink?"

"Not now," I said, sitting down. "Tana—I'm so happy I don't *have* to know. But I want to. It'll let me sleep at night."

She sat on the edge of her desk—on some of the thick piles of paper. "Russ, you know I love you. Jack loves you, too."

"I know that."

She cleared her throat. "From the day you went inside, I've tried to get you released or re-tried, or something else. Nobody wanted to listen to me. The DA was so delighted to imprison a celebrity and get major press attention, he could hardly stand it. The mayor back then kind of flipped me off—saying there was nothing he could do. The governor, who figured you didn't vote for him, just wasn't interested."

I nodded. "Sounds right. I didn't vote for him."

"I tried every six months or so. My nose got flattened from having doors slam in my face. I was frustrated."

"You and me both, Tana."

"But then—guess what? Election Day! New DA. New

mayor. New governor. They're all big football fans, especially the Chicago Bears."

"Nobody gives a damn about the Bears since Mike Ditka won a Super Bowl more than thirty years ago—and I never played football," I said.

"No—but guess who did?"

"Big ugly defensive end who goes around marrying gorgeous lawyers? Nope, never heard of him."

Tara laughed. "Jack put it together on his own. He made calls to the governor and the new DA" She lowered her voice to a near whisper—for what reason I'll never know. "The new mayor is a woman, and I don't think she's into football, so Jack ignored her. And—here you are."

I slapped my hand against my head. "Oh, my god! Jack did that?"

She grinned. "He hates it when my clients get locked up."

"How many of those get locked up?"

"Just you. He didn't want me to tell you he got into this, Russ. He likes you, and that was it."

I put my face in my hands for a moment, mostly to keep from crying. Then I said, "I'm going to build a statue of him and put it right smack in the middle of the Miracle Mile."

"He doesn't want a statue. He just wants them to retire his football jersey and hang it up in Soldier Field where everyone can see it. And that ain't gonna happen." She reached down and squeezed my hand with hers. "We love you, Russ—and in seven years we never stopped trying." She let go. "And just so you know—we never, even once, thought you were guilty."

I threw my head backwards in the chair and closed my eyes. "Now maybe you can convince my thousands of fans to agree with you."

"You've got to do that yourself, babe, by writing a new book."

I hesitated for too long a moment. Then I said, "Tana, there's something else I want to talk to you about."

"Should I sit behind the desk again and be your attorney?" She squirmed into her chair and took up a ballpoint pen. "I'm ready."

"Don't bother writing this down. Remember Aubrey Sinden?"

Her expression didn't change, but her eyes got less friendly. Cold. "I remember her. She's what sent you to prison."

"As I recall, she said nothing but nice things about me."

"That's the point," Tana said. "You were married, but Aubrey Sinden was your girl-on-the-side. Your—mistress, if you want to use a 1920s word. Prosecutor Ryland Chanock just ate up her testimony like bacon and eggs for breakfast, because he made the jury think you killed your wife to permanently be with Aubrey. They took that juicy scandal into the jury room with them, and bingo-bango—guilty of manslaughter." Her look softened. "Why are you mentioning Aubrey? Are you seeing her again? Seriously?"

I shook my head. "No, she's married now."

"Phew!" Tana exclaimed, wiping non-existing sweat from her forehead.

"But her new husband—his name is Cole Cabot, by the way, and he's an asshole—he got my phone number from Owen Fullmer and called me. She's missing—been missing for more than a week."

"And?"

"Since I write about detectives, he wants me to find her."

And then I told her the whole story.

CHAPTER ELEVEN

"I had no idea," Tana said when I was through with my tale, "that Aubrey was sleeping with Gaylord Ogilvy at the same time she was seeing you."

"Neither did I," I replied. "Her husband told me that. It shocks the crap out of me. It wasn't the romance of the century, but we were good friends who enjoyed having sex together."

"I'm surprised he told you."

"I don't know how much help I can be when my hair still smells like prison, but I suppose he knows Aubrey and I were pretty damn close, so for whatever reason, I got the chance to interview Ogilvy in person—along with his second-in-command, Irvin Greenfield."

Tana got up and walked to the window. Whenever she's in her office and she's thinking, she loves staring out the window at sprawling Lake Michigan—cool and blue in the autumn, waves dancing among the daytime stars in the sunny summertime. In winter, it's rough and mean, violent water crashing high in the air whatever it happens to touch. "Irvin Greenfield," she murmured. Then she put her hands on her hips. "I've never heard of him. What does he do for Gaylord, anyway?"

"I don't know what you'd call it. Chief of Staff? Executive Vice President? Guardian of the Galaxy? His office is right next door to Ogilvy's, but smaller. I had to go through an interview with him first before I could get into the actual presence of royalty."

"Did Ogilvy know about you all that time?"

"He said he always knew, but I doubt if he gave a damn. He probably had other friends with benefits."

Tana grew flustered. "This Cabot guy knew about you, too?"

"Only after they got married. Normal, I guess. Did you tell Jack your previous lovers when you two decided to make it serious?"

"Only when he asked me. I was afraid he'd hunt them all down and kill them—because one of them is a cabinet secretary for the current administration." She leaned against the floor-to-ceiling window. "The husband hired you to play private eye, Russ?"

"There was no mention of money. I don't need money. He—asked me. Then he got pissed off at me and I told him to pound sand."

"But you're still looking for her."

"I cared for her. I wasn't *in* love with her. That's a different thing altogether. But I loved her."

"Okay, fine," she said, pushing herself away from the window and sitting down again. "Why didn't he call the police?"

"He was vague about that."

"Vague?" She thrust her head forward as if she was going to bite off the head of a live chicken. When Tana Phillips gets angry, you're better off trying to teach sit, stay, and roll over to a sex-starved wolverine. "His wife vanishes without a trace, he doesn't call the cops, you're busting your ass to find her when you've only been out of prison for ninety-six hours—and *he's* vague? Holy shit, Russ! I think I'll have Jack make another phone call and put you back in the stir. At least inside there you'll be safe!"

"No one calls prison *safe.*"

"You haven't heard a peep out of Aubrey Sinden for years.

She's married, it's her husband's problem. And face it—you don't love her anymore."

"There are different kinds of love, Tana. You're married, you have a husband, but I still love you, and I'd put my life on the line to help you." I tried to sound pleasant about it. "And not only were you and I never lovers, we haven't even tongue-kissed—and it's been almost twenty years."

"We should do that—somewhere around never." She laughed in spite of herself, then got serious. "Russ, we haven't talked about—well, do you plan to start dating again?"

"Oh, sure," I said. "Whenever I meet a drop-dead beautiful woman who's desperately lonely and wants a man in her life, I've got a pickup line, and for seven years I perfected it. *Hi there, I'm famous, I'm rich, I'm dazzlingly good-looking, I'm self-employed so I can see you any time you want, it's your decision. And oh yeah, I was convicted of murdering my wife. What time shall I pick you up?*" I lifted one eyebrow. "You think that'll work, Tana?"

"Only if the woman is looking for an asshole to hang out with," Tana replied. "And it wasn't for murder."

"I know what it was for." I turned my head away. "I don't even remember how to fuck, Tana. I think I'm better off forgetting about it."

"Don't be a jerk. Nobody forgets how to ride a bicycle once they've learned it."

Driving home, what Tana had just said to me hurt me more than anything ever said to me before. I wouldn't forget how to ride a bicycle because I've never in my life done so. I believe I mentioned that earlier, as I was an only child, revered and overprotected by my father so I would never do anything that might somehow produce an injury, and terrifying my mother, who was too frightened to hold me as a baby.

It dawned on me in all my fictional work, I'd never dealt with any parent-child relationship, not wanting to unearth my own home situation.

Too much love? Something I've thought about all my adult years. Every so often, I stop and wonder why I was given up by my biological parents. Was my mother a fifteen-year-old girl whose boyfriend was too dumb or too broke to buy condoms? Were my bio-parents unmarried adults who made a mistake, were too young, and couldn't allow a baby to throw a saboteur's shoe into their career machinery? Were they married with three older children and couldn't handle the pressure of Number Four? Or was I the result of a rape?

Some so-called pro-life religious fanatics hysterically swear babies as a result of a rape were "God's plan," one of a gazillion reasons I've chosen to be an atheist, though I am relatively healthy and not some half-finished creature who arrived two months early, didn't make the healthy cut, and got thrown out with the rest of the garbage.

My adopting parents were not young, so it never occurred to them to adopt another one, a sibling for me with whom I could fight and argue and support and love. They aimed every thought and impulse at their magnificent prince, who could not simply fall and skin his knee, bloody his nose, or God forbid, break a finger.

There was no whipping boy around to punish for my transgressions, either.

Nobody is my family. I'm alone.

I've only been out of prison for hours, and I miss Denver Tolliver more than everyone else.

Changing clothes at home to jeans and a T-shirt, I found plenty of deli meat in the fridge, thanks to Tana, but the fact is I loathe packaged salami, bologna or even that yucky blood sausage wrapped tightly in cellophane. If not in a deli where they cut and slice the meat as I ordered, I wasn't interested.

On my laptop, I looked up the phone number of the late and much missed Lou Malnati and his pizza restaurant. There was no pizza in the world like it, and no pizza in Chicago like Malnati's. I ordered delivery of a large pizza with everything except pineapple and anchovies. Neither belong on a pizza, and anchovies don't belong on *anything*. I look askance at those who eat pizza that way.

I quickly checked my Facebook. There was a private message from Ember Pollack d'Anjou.

Yes, I know Aubrey has been gone for about two weeks. I keep calling her, emailing her, messaging her, even talked to her husband once, but never a response from her. I'm sure she's not mad at me for anything—we've been friends since high school. Glad you're trying to find her.

Can we get together tomorrow at six o'clock? Here's my phone #. Ciao.

When did people start saying 'Ciao' instead of just 'goodbye?' Random thought. I dialed her up.

CHAPTER TWELVE

I'd always lived as a night person, going to bed at three in the morning and sleeping until ten o'clock, but in The Joint, we were awakened early whether we liked it or not, shuttled down to the dining hall, and then put to work. One of my jobs was feeding the Canada geese who showed up every morning during three of the four seasons—I had no idea where they went in the wintertime. The rest of my job was in the prison library, and every few days I had to wheel my cart up and down the cells in case anyone wanted to read a book. They didn't have any of my books available, as they're all about murder and violence, and cons aren't allowed to read things like that and get any bad ideas.

Bedtime all over the prison was at ten o'clock, but from what I could hear, few people went to sleep when the lights were off.

Now no one was around to tell me when to sleep, when to wake, when to eat, when to take a dump. It felt good. I'd made a phone connection with Ember Pollard d'Anjou the night before, and we'd set a meeting at six o'clock at a nearby Chicago saloon. This was the day, basically. Nothing to do, except sift through the three hundred plus pages of notes I'd scribbled down while in the slammer and re-typed by one of Tana's assistants. Plots, characters, random ideas—that's how writers live. Where and how they live makes no difference. The writer's brain churns out ideas every waking moment.

I suppose if I only wrote books based on all these jottings, and never made another note, I'd finish one novel every year until I quietly pass away at the age of ninety-eight.

I didn't get through fifty pages before there was a sharp rap on the door that startled me. Few people knew where I lived— and the Near North was not the most welcoming neighborhood for little girls selling Girl Scout cookies.

I opened the door to two of the largest men I have ever seen, including Denver Tolliver. One black and one white. Weightlifters? I doubted it. They wore well-pressed suits, white dress shirts and moderate ties. It was hard not to notice bulges in suit jackets covering their under-the-armpit artillery.

"Mr. Reinert?" The black one said, putting out his huge paw for a shake, "my name is Walter Yellen. This is my associate, Hayden Fantus."

Hayden Fantus didn't offer a handshake or even a smile. These two guys were not Jehovah's Witnesses.

"Would you like to come in?"

"We're working," Yellen said. "For the Ogilvy Corporation."

"Oh?"

"We were sent to bring you to an important meeting."

"I see. And when does this meeting take place?"

"Now," he said.

"I'm not dressed for a business meeting," I said. "As you can see, I'm in jeans and a T-shirt."

"That makes no difference. Just throw on a jacket and come along. They're waiting for you."

I thought to be as tough as I could be. I said, "Suppose I don't want to come right now?"

"Ah, well—that would probably cause some trouble, Mr. Reinert."

Hayden Fantus spoke up for the first time. His voice, low and gruff, could have come from a villainous movie alien invading the earth. "You don't want us to lose our jobs, do you?"

Was I living in an episode of *The Sopranos?* I weighed the moment. Denver Tolliver taught me how to fight mean and dirty. Eye gouging, choking, ripping off an ear was possible—not probable but possible. I could take one of them, probably Walter Yellen. Both of them? Unless I had Denver Tolliver standing behind me, I was doomed.

"Hang on," I said, "I'll get my jacket."

Their new-smelling black Cadillac Escalade had too many technical gewgaw improvements to count. Back-up video. TV set in the rear seat, along with a well-stocked liquor bar and crystal glasses of three different sizes. The TV set wasn't on, and no one offered me a martini. Two telephones, one in the front seat and one in back. Wi-Fi Connection. More buttons on the dashboard I didn't know what to do with. Many top-level wealthy men drove Audis, BMWs and Mercedes-Benzes, but if one wanted to be considered obscenely rich, they owned USA-made Lincoln Continentals or Cadillacs, especially the Escalade. Walter Yellen drove, and Hayden Fantus sat in the back seat with me. Nobody talked—until I did.

"I was in Chairman Ogilvy's office just yesterday," I said, trying not to sound nervous, "but we're not heading for the Merchandise Mart, are we?"

Fantus didn't bother looking at me. "We have meetings at other places besides the Merchandise Mart," he mumbled.

"So, where is the meeting today?"

"You'll find out."

I looked at the buttons on the back door. I was certain they were locked and unlocked only by the driver, meaning I wouldn't be able to leap out and escape at a stop sign.

I shut up for the next twenty minutes—neither of them wanted to talk to me anyway—until we got out in the no-man's-land where houses were huge and far between. Yellen stopped at an iron gate, leaned out the window, and pressed a button. The gates creaked open, and he turned down a long driveway, tall trees on each side touching each other's top branches and making a leafy overhead canopy—heading toward a majestic residence that could only be called a mansion.

Not what anyone might refer to as just a big house, or an elegant country retreat. Other than the Palace of Versailles, it was like nothing I'd ever seen before. It's a goddamn royal estate on the outskirts of Chicago, the house and grounds filling up at least fifteen acres. A guest house was off to one side of the main building—just in case they had a party and wound up with twelve party-goers in a person sleepover houseguest party. At the other end of the mansion, a swimming pool shimmered in the sunshine.

The size of the house itself, sprawling, with turrets and towers, approximately four stories high in spots, was big enough for eight bedrooms and twelve bathrooms. Summer visiting grounds for the entire Illinois National Guard? There was no crocodile-filled moat surrounding it, but otherwise it was very, *very* royal. I guessed the resident had paid for at least ten houses that once stood there to be destroyed.

It wasn't hard to guess who the resident was. What puzzled me is why we were meeting at his home and not his office again.

I expected a tuxedoed butler with a British accent no one could understand to answer the door, but an African American housekeeper in a black-and-white maid's outfit appeared instead and said good morning to me. She seemed pleased with her job in such a once-in-a-lifetime house. I figured there were other domestic employees on board but out of sight—cooks, chauffeurs and a whole cadre of gardeners who did all the cleaning and panting and fixing. She smiled at Yellen and Fantus, and they smiled back. A happy crew.

She said, "Will you step into the parlor, sir?" and led the way. The two big galoots stepped back. I called over my shoulder, "Don't go anywhere, kiddos, I don't want to have to walk home." The face of Fantus grew red and angry. I guess he resented being called "kiddo."

Tough shitsky, Fantus.

The parlor was bigger than my whole apartment, damn near as big as my old house, and certainly a sixty-person guest crowd could sit and watch a musical concerto without crowding each other. The furnishings seemed a throwback to the 1930s, but they looked brand new, meaning someone designed them for this room. The curtains on the windows could have hung in Buckingham Palace. In a place like this, one can actually *smell* the money.

In the far corner of the room was a fireplace big enough to roast an entire ox, horns and all. Hanging directly over it, shining and glowing from the four lights set into the ceiling from different angles, was a double oil portrait of Gaylord Ogilvy and what I assumed to be "the little woman."

She was no little woman, though. She was gorgeous. Traffic-stopping gorgeous. If you're old enough—and I'm not, but I love watching old black and white films from the 1940s on Turner Classic Movies—you might remember Hedy Lamarr. She was generally thought then to be the most beautiful woman in the world. Ogilvy's wife fit into that very narrow category. Olive-skinned and midnight blue-black hair in the painting, and cornflower blue eyes that followed one's moves across the room. Not surprising, she was definitely a trophy wife. The wealthier one was, the more startling—and expensive—the trophies they buy.

I stared at the painting until I heard a soft, melodic voice behind me. The tone was like one might use when proposing marriage.

"Mr. Reinert, I'm so pleased you could come. I'm Lilith Ogilvy. Something to drink? Coffee? Tea? Something alcoholic?"

She was taller than I'd imagined from the painting, probably due to the three-inch heels on her white shoes. Her hair was combed back tight into a bun. Her off-white jumpsuit was silk, flowing over her body like gentle rain. The diamond on her right hand was almost the size of a golf ball. The smaller diamonds encircling her wedding band sparkled as she talked and moved.

Her necklace—gold and sapphires—fell around her neck and into her cleavage. She was not busty. She was not flat. She was—hmm, I think I'm momentarily out of words. Even big celebrities who walked on the Oscar ceremony red carpet didn't dress as elegantly as she did—and it was only eleven o'clock in the morning.

I was humiliated being in Levis, a white T-shirt, a lightweight fall jacket, and sneakers—no socks. I felt as silly as if I'd worn my orange prison drag.

I could barely open my mouth—it took about ten seconds, which is a long time—but I fought through the shock and croaked out, "I'm… delighted to meet you, Ms. Ogilvy."

"Lilith," she said. The name sounded intimate, sensual, even erotic when she said it.

"Lilith." It didn't sound that way when it came out of my mouth. "I think I'm supposed to have a meeting with your husband."

She shook her head. "He's not here in the mornings. He's hardly here at all. No, Mr. Reinert, your meeting is with me—and we're about to have it." She pointed to two matching easy chairs. I eased myself into one, and she occupied the other. From the fresh, smooth look of her outfit, this might have been the first time all morning that she sat down.

"I wonder why you didn't call me first, Ms. Ogilvy," I said, "instead of sending your muscle guys after me."

That seemed to amuse her. "Muscle guys? Is that what you call them? Hardly. They're my personal security."

"If your personal security were five-foot-six and a hundred fifty pounds, I wouldn't have busted my ass to get here. You could have just phoned."

"If I called, you might have said no, so I sent the men. I dislike wasting time, don't you?"

"I wasted seven years of time without stopping," I said. "Now I want to use every minute."

"I won't keep you long. You had a meeting with my husband yesterday."

"I did."

"Asking about Aubrey Sinden."

I nodded. "Nice your husband discusses his appointments with you. I'd think you were both too busy."

She ignored that. "How do you know Aubrey Sinden?"

"I knew her from—before I went away."

That didn't shock her. The Ogilvys knew everything. "You haven't seen her since?"

"No."

"Spoken to her, or written letters?"

"She saw me in prison a few times, but eventually we agreed to call it off."

"She's been married since."

"That's what I hear," I said.

"Then why did you contact Gaylord?"

"Aubrey's husband called me the day I got out of prison and told me she was missing. I'm no private eye, but I used to write about them, so that's why he contacted me."

"How did he know you were out of prison that very same day?"

"I guess he read it in a newspaper. Aren't you a *Chicago Tribune* subscriber, Mrs. Ogilvy?"

She ignored that. "You're famous."

"*Was* famous," I corrected her. "I've been out of circulation for a while."

"Her husband knew about you and Aubrey."

"I guess she told him."

"Did she also tell him about her affair with Gaylord Ogilvy?"

"That's what he said."

She shifted around in her chair and looked up at her likeness hanging on the wall. She was far more beautiful in person. I wasn't too sure about her husband in the portrait because I hardly looked at him. She turned back to me. "I assume she was seeing both of you at the same time?"

"I didn't know that until Cabot told me."

She took a deep breath. "We have what you'd call an open marriage."

"Mine was, too—or I guess it was."

"Is that why you killed your wife?"

"Try not to be so damn insulting, Mrs. Ogilvy. I didn't kill my wife."

"Lilith," she corrected me.

"Lilith," I repeated.

"You were both cheating?"

"I don't know," I said. "I was."

"With Aubrey Sinden?"

I nodded.

Lilith said, "I knew about her and Gaylord from the beginning. It didn't bother me."

"Don't you love your husband?"

She laughed. She actually laughed. Then she said, "I'm very lucky, Mr. Reinert, to be born attractive and intelligent. I could have been anything I wanted to be—but rich was Number One. I live an amazing life. I have every single thing I want, and yes, I have lovers. No, I don't love my husband, never did—and I can't remember the last time we made love to each other. He's more than twenty years my senior, but he's really too involved with money to care about me. I guess we're both happy enough. I'm his trophy, I spend a lot of his money on things I care about, I'm treated like a queen in Chicago, and usually when I travel, I go by myself or with—other people."

"Lucky you. Why do you care about Aubrey Sinden?"

She cocked her head, thinking about it. Then: "I know for a fact she signed several business agreements for my husband's company—and that means money. My money as much as his.

When you approached him, I wanted to know if she was missing or if you were just on her side and playing a game."

"I don't play games, Lilith. Not at my age."

"You're young."

"Not so much."

"I've read one or two of your books."

"Glad to hear that."

"A long time ago. Now that you're free, are you going to write again?"

"What else can I do?"

"Live on your money for the rest of your life."

Now it was my turn to laugh. "You know about my finances?"

"I know about everything I want to know about." With her left hand, she began stroking the diamond on her right hand. "I'll pay you, Mr. Reinert. Can I call you Russ? Russell? I'll pay you to stop looking for Aubrey—triple whatever Cole Cabot is paying you."

Triple zero, I thought, but didn't point that out. I also didn't tell her I was continuing my search without Cabot's approval. I said, "I'm not for sale."

"That disappoints me."

"I don't imagine you're disappointedtoo often."

"True. Can I up my offer?" She did some math in her pretty head. "How about thirty thousand dollars to back off?"

"I'm not in the same universe of wealth as you are, but I don't need the money."

Now her eyes became slits and the corners of her mouth turned down. "I'm not used to being refused, Mr. Reinert. I don't like it."

"Sorry about that."

She lifted her head so her chin was pointing right at me. "I can call in Hayden and Walter, you know. Maybe they can persuade you."

"They'll try. But I've had lots of fights in prison, and I'll probably rip Hayden's ear right off his fucking head and make him eat it before they beat me unconscious."

She shriveled up her face. "What a terrible thing to say!"

I said, "I can do prison slang you never even dreamed of."

She rose quickly and walked toward the fireplace, which probably hadn't been used for about six months, and though the temperature outside was in the mid-sixties, it was still far too balmy to turn on a roaring fire. She leaned against the bricks for a moment, positioning herself right below The Ogilvy Double Portrait. Then she focused her attention on me again.

"I can suggest a bonus, too," she said.

"What's the bonus?"

Long pause. Lowered chin. Lowered voice. Eyes sparkling. Breath heavier than usual. Then she simply said, "Me."

That knocked me completely out of my comfort zone.

She continued, "You're quite handsome in addition to being talented. We'll have a lovely long-standing affair. Gaylord doesn't care where I am or what I'm doing. And if he did find out—my guess is he won't give a damn."

"I'd give a damn," I said. "I'm an old-fashioned guy. I do my own propositions."

She moved closer. "We can do it right now, right here on the sofa—and everyone who works here is loyal to me, not to my husband or his goddamn company. Nobody will mention it to Gaylord." She smiled, almost chuckled. "You know you want me, Russ Reinert. You've wanted me since I walked through the door. I could tell—right away."

"You're right on the button, Lilith. I wanted you the minute I saw you. Even before you came in, I wanted you from your portrait. You're exceptionally beautiful—but I'm sure you know that."

She came over and perched on the arm of my chair, leaning down to purr in my ear. "We can be beautiful together," she whispered.

I nodded. "But guess what."

"What?"

"My desire for you has decreased ninety-eight percent in the past forty-five seconds."

She stiffened as if she'd just touched a high-voltage fence. I stood up so quickly I nearly knocked her off the chair and onto the floor. "I haven't had sex in seven years, Lilith. I guess I can wait a few days more. So why don't you call Beavis and Butthead to drive me back home? Otherwise, it's too damn long a walk." She opened her mouth to say something, but I moved right along. "Having them beat the shit out of me won't get me to do what you want—it'll just made me angrier. And kill me? I survived prison—I guess I'll survive your leg-breaking tag team." I started toward the door. "It's been fascinating meeting you, Lilith. It's something I can tell my grandchildren—or better still, write it all down in my next novel."

CHAPTER THIRTEEN

Ember Pollard d'Anjou and I decided to meet at an Irish pub and restaurant on the north side in the neighborhood forever known as Wrigleyville, because the legendary baseball park, Wrigley Field, was right in the middle of it. They've jazzed up the inside of the playing field a bit, because for decades they only played games during the day. But the outside of Wrigley looks just as it did 90 years ago—and they still have green vines growing on the outfield wall.

There've been many Irish joints in Chicago for the better part of two centuries, because it was an Irish city. In earlier days, every mayor, cop, fireman and politician was Irish, and most of the female teachers in elementary schools were Irish, too—and mostly single. To this day, all Chicagoans, Irish or not, celebrate St. Patrick's Day by having a parade and dyeing the Chicago River a bright Irish green.

The town's comeback from the great fire turned it into a beautiful, powerful city, which makes me proud to be a native. However, I doubted I'd eat anything at the Irish pub when meeting with Ember, as the Irish menu was a turnoff. Most of the imported food recipes from the Emerald Isle, like colcannon, cuddle, boxty, and champ are slightly different versions of mashed potatoes. In prison, I had to eat potatoes every single night, as they are cheaper for the wardens to buy than most other edible meals. I'm not much for potatoes these days.

As I waited for Ember at the bar, I sipped on a Jameson's whiskey, now brewed in County Cork. It's the best-selling Irish whiskey in the world. I'm not much of a Gaelic imbiber, but when in an Irish pub, what the hell? It left me with a warm, safe rumble in my stomach. I was probably ten years older than everyone else present, and I couldn't help feeling I was in the wrong joint.

At length, Ember Pollard d'Anjou came through the door—one of the few people of color in attendance, and virtually none at the bar, so she was noticed by almost everyone. The sound of loud conversation lessened by half, at least for the moment. Chicago is a city entranced by female beauty. And it's still racially divided.

Striking-looking, she recognized me, smiled, waved, and came over. We halfway hugged and pressed our cheeks together for the briefest of moments. Considering we'd never been real friends and had only met a few times, the hug seemed to fit.

"Good to see you again, Russ.," she said. "It's been a long time." She stepped back to get a better look at me. "You've hardly changed at all. A little gray in the sideburns area, but otherwise, you've aged well."

"I'm too pale. I never got out in the sunshine. I mean *never*. You look great yourself. Marriage agrees with you. Congratulations."

"Thanks. He's a good guy," she said, "and with a very French last name, he gives me all the class I need."

"I'm glad you're happy, Ember. You've always been Aubrey Sinden's best friend." I looked around. "Shall we get a table?"

We found one clear in the back. This eatery always has Irish folk singers on Friday and Saturday evenings, but this was not a weekend, so there was no music. It was relatively quiet—for a gin joint. I ordered her a red wine and another Jameson's for myself.

Small talk for a few minutes, mostly from her. A little bit

more about this good guy she married, and where they lived, right here in Wrigleyville. I had nothing to say about my incarceration, and I had little in the past to discuss.

Ember finally said, "You're looking for Aubrey, too? It's scary. I usually talk with her every other day or so, but I haven't been able to reach her for almost two weeks."

"Her husband doesn't know where she is, either. He asked me to find her, but then he backed out for some reason. I'm still looking for her."

"Cole Cabot?" She shook her head. "He's a wuss, I'm afraid, but that was her choice." She looked around, then leaned forward and spoke softly. "Russ, did you know she was seeing someone else the same time she was with you?"

"I didn't know that at the time. I heard about it from Cabot."

"You know who it was?"

"Yes. Her other lover was the first one I talked to—Gaylord Ogilvy."

Ember gasped. "You've gotta be kidding."

"I wish I were." I licked my lips as my mouth was going dry. "I had to talk to Irvin Greenfield first. He's Ogilvy's front-line protector."

"I never knew it was Ogilvy. She never told me. Why didn't she? He's the most powerful guy in the Midwest." She shook her head angrily. "Well, whoever she was seeing, she made money out of it."

"That sounds shitty, Ember."

"She's a great person—and no goddamn hooker. Whatever she was doing had more to do with money-making than just opening her legs."

It sounded a lot like fucking for money, at least to me—but I chose to let it go. Aubrey had been a high point of my pre-prison world, and I was going to find her now, no matter what.

The waitress arrived with our drinks, then went away. We clinked glasses and then Ember said, "I hope life is easy for you now. Have you contacted all your old friends?"

A moment standing at the edge of the abyss. I bit the inside of my cheek and said, "I'm afraid I don't have friends anymore. Most of them—" I paused. I didn't want to say it—but I had to. "Most of them think I'm a murderer."

My words were painful. Ember said, "Well, I don't. Please keep me out of that other column."

I tried a smile, but I could tell it wasn't working. I brushed it aside and said, "I also talked with Lilith Ogilvy this morning."

She took a deep breath and leaned back in her chair. "His wife? Oh my god, why?"

"It was her idea, not mine," I said. "She offered me a lot of money to stop looking for Aubrey."

"Did you accept it?"

"I have plenty of cash. I don't need hers. Or his." I took another sip. "Do you have any idea how Aubrey was making so much money with Ogilvy?"

She shrugged. "She just told me it was big business, and she was in on it."

I ran my hands through my hair. I felt like pulling it out by the fistful. Big business? Aubrey? That sounded to me like an adult fairy tale. "Ogilvy is part of the one percent big rich in this country," I managed to say. "I can't imagine what she was doing for him."

"She cared a lot about you, Russ. She wouldn't tell you she was sleeping with somebody else, too. That would have been mean—and tacky. You weren't the love of her life, but she'd never do anything to hurt you."

"Cole Cabot is the love of her life?"

"Doubtful." She lowered her voice even more. "I hope you'll understand, but after you went inside, she had to make a decision. She couldn't just wait around for ten years."

"It was only seven years," I reminded her, "but who's counting?"

"She hooked up with Cabot, and finally married him. She

told him about you before the wedding. Unless they're a complete shit, when someone gets married, they tell the truth. That's when she quit having sex with Ogilvy, and she told Cabot everything, including about you."

"She actually told him all that? Even that I was married?"

Ember chuckled. "She was in her thirties, Russ, just like you were. She wasn't exactly a virgin. She had plenty of money of her own, or so she told him, and Cabot was happy to use it as if it were his."

Deep in thought, I rubbed my chin—a habit. Bristly, even though I'd shaved that morning. Five o'clock shadow. It felt normal, but until three days ago, I was only allowed to shave twice a week. Rules. I think prisons make up half those rules because they love exerting power over the inmates. "That's why Cabot wanted me to find her."

"I think she was still involved with Ogilvy and Company money, even if she wasn't having sex for it anymore."

That troubled me. When Aubrey and I were together, I knew she had money. She lived well, dressed well, drove a newish Mercedes—but I doubted she was rich enough to empty out her bank accounts and disappear into the mists of memory only to show up in Uzbekistan or the Canary Islands to live luxuriously with a hunky beach boy or two hanging around when called for.

"Ember," I said, "what was her marriage like? To Cole Cabot?"

"It was kind of like you and her. She never brought you around much, and I only met him four times, just hello and goodbye. She talked about your books all the time. Cole? She doesn't discuss him at all."

"Is he good to her?"

"As far as I know. She never has any bruises showing."

"It'd be Aubrey shelling out bruises. Does Cabot have money of his own?"

"He drives a five-year-old Chevy Malibu, and he buys his clothes right off the rack. He's far from a poverty case, but nowhere near rich." Ember raised, then lowered her eyebrows. "I'm just guessing."

"I'm guessing too," I said. "He came to me and not the police because he knows something about Aubrey's financial relationship with Ogilvy, and he wouldn't want that to go public."

"Ogilvy's wife tried to buy you *out* of this search, Russ. Maybe for the same reason? Maybe Aubrey owns a bigger hunk of his companies than anyone realizes."

"You're smart, Ember," I said, meaning it. "You knew Aubrey a lot better than me."

"Well, I knew her longer." She spoke more softly. "Did you love her, Russ? I hardly ever saw you together. Did you really *love* her?"

I rubbed my forehead with both hands. The essence of a headache was forcing its way behind my eyes. "I loved her—as much as I could. I didn't know there was anybody else, but I knew something was keeping her from me more than half the time."

"That," Ember said, "and your wife."

That was a harpoon through the gut, so I chose not to answer. My wife. My late, great wife. I was in love with her once, which was why I married her. It didn't take long until I realized love was like a cold sore, disappearing quickly. She didn't want me—just my money. Dayna and I hardly saw each other anymore. I moved into the guest room at night, shut myself in my office every day. I even got a second coffee-maker to keep beside my desk, so I didn't have to see her when I had to head for the kitchen. When I met Aubrey, she became important to me.

I said, "My marriage was headed for the rocks. If we got divorced, Dayna would have gotten most of my money and possessions. But even before I went to trial, my lawyer put everything I owned into a trust so the state of Illinois couldn't take it. Now that I'm pardoned—I guess I'm pardoned—I'm halfway rich again." I had to shudder. "All that money and nobody to spend it on."

Ember put her hand over mine and gently squeezed. "I knew you were innocent, Russ—and Aubrey knew it, too. She should have waited for you."

"Ten years? A quarter of her life? That's insane. I told her not to wait that long, and eventually she believed me."

"Now you're wasting your freedom trying to find her."

"Not a waste," I said.

"You should be writing again."

I looked troubled. "I haven't figured out how to use my new laptop. They change them every year so one can't keep up. New rules, new apps, new technology—and I'm a Luddite."

"You'll catch up." She looked down at her drink and her tone changed. "Is there a woman in your life now, Russ? You and I should know each other better—have dinner sometime. Bring a date if you want. You'll meet my old man. Everybody likes him."

"He's French?"

"His grandparents were French. He was born in New York City. Brooklyn, actually. I'll call you. We'll set something up for next week."

"That would be—nice," I said. It was true, it would be nice.

She stood up. "Be good to yourself, Russ," she said. "These new days are precious for you. Live every minute of them."

She hugged me again, tighter than the last time, and I watched her make her way through the crowd of too-loud drinkers, out the door and onto the sidewalk.

Aubrey's best friend.

I learned a little bit about Aubrey from her, but I've learned a little bit about myself, too. A little bit.

Put them all together, jumble them around some, and discover what a startling discovery I'd made?

Bupkiss!

CHAPTER FOURTEEN

I had to replay the whole conversation in my mind as I drove home. What dug its toes into consciousness is what I said to Ember about my friends. I didn't have any—not anymore. Even the great comrades of yore tend not to hang around when their BFF has been convicted of killing his wife. What questions will they ask?

"How did you do it?"

"Was it spur-of-the-moment or was it planned?"

"I've seen the movies—but what's prison really like?"

Jesus Christ! If an old friend bothered calling me now, I wouldn't even answer the phone.

So—no friends to speak of. What's more painful than that? No siblings.

Sure, I loved being the only kid in the household, the one who got all the love, all the attention, all the gifts, and the wishbone every single Thanksgiving. But now, as a convicted felon with dead adoptive parents, biological parents unknown, and a literary career formerly on its climb to the pinnacle now stopped cold for the better part of a decade, it would've been nice to have a brother show up to go out with for a drink or two and remember the old days when we played together or fought each other or busted our asses trying to make our parents like us best, or a pretty, loving sister who hugged and really meant it.

When my first novel was released, I was cordially invited to the biggest Mystery Writers and Fans convention anywhere, named the Bouchercon after the late brilliant reviewer of crime fiction, Anthony Boucher. The organizers have it in a different city every year. My first was in San Diego.

When I arrived there and looked around at all the famous crime authors, I realized I was the only one at the convention I never heard of.

The mystery writers were friendly, supportive, fun to be with, great drinking buddies, male and female—unlike authors of more serious, classy novels who are solitary, self-aggrandizing and cranky. Some of the Boucherconians became longtime friends, especially those who also lived in and wrote about Chicago. From that day until I wound up in the slammer, I never missed going to a Bouchercon.

I used to see locals once a month at the meetings of the Mystery Writers of America. Some of us went out to dinner or lunch in between meetings, just to chat. Before my marriage I dated one of them for a short time. Wherever I went in the country, when some big deal book festivity was going on, I always ran into many Bouchercon friends.

Three or four of them wrote letters to me after I was put in Joliet. The letters were sent kindly, but were almost all awkward. Eventually they stopped because if I wanted to answer them, I had to write by hand. The warden not only wouldn't let me work on a laptop, he wouldn't even loan me a typewriter.

Typewriters? Dial telephones? Movies with a cartoon and a newsreel? Youngsters should look them up in the dictionary. Dictionary that's actually printed and not on the Internet? Forget it.

I considered calling a few of my so-called friends after I got out, but thought better of it. Some have moved away, some died, one or two had gone to live on some unknown tropical island and closed the door on the world. My Chicago agent dumped me, my publisher cut me off at the knees, and even the Chicago bartenders who knew me well might have moved elsewhere, passed away, or sold the screenplay they hammered out in the middle of the night to Universal Studios and are now living in Beverly Hills with an Olympic-sized pool, and wondering what kind of world this has become since all the movie studio heads have not reached thirty years of age.

I dozed off in my recliner that evening while watching a Western movie on television, directed by the great Budd Boetticher. Randolph Scott was the star—always the good guy. I didn't care whether he was good, bad or indifferent, as I was half-tanked and fell asleep before the final shoot-out.

In the morning I ate a relatively good breakfast, showered first hot and then cold to wake myself up, shaved with my new electric—I shaved closer with an old-fashioned blade razor, but where the hell was I going for the rest of the day to look good? Then, dressed in a sweat suit and sneakers, I turned on political news on MSNBC.

When I got bored, I phoned Cole Cabot again. When he answered, there was a hubbub in the background, so I assumed he was at work.

"What the hell do you want, Reinert?" he demanded. "I fired you."

"You never hired me, jag-off. Remember? I'm on my own time now."

"Why?"

"Because," I said, "Aubrey was once part of my life."

"Yeah—but I'm her husband."

"I know—but unfortunately, you have no experience investigating."

"Neither do you."

"True. I'm rusty, but maybe if you helped me a little—-" I left the rest of the sentence hanging.

He was quiet, too, thinking about it. Then: "What do you want?"

"We should meet."

He sighed. "By the Viking ship again?"

"Fuck the Viking ship," I almost barked, irritated. "Come to my place tonight, eight o'clock. I'll pour you a drink, and we can talk openly—no mommies pushing past us with baby strollers."

He took a good fifteen seconds to answer, making me think he really wanted nothing to do with me. He was still enormously disturbed by his image of me in bed with his wife before he and Aubrey ever met.

I still had half a pot of coffee, so I filled my large mug, settled down in front of my laptop, and got onto Google to find out every single thing I could about Mr. Ogilvy—his life, his businesses, his history.

I've never been an efficient searcher of internet secrets, but I kept at it for three hours, making notes, most leading me in some sort of direction rather than just walking around town knocking on doors. I stayed with it until I got bored.

Gaylord Ogilvy came from the Hyde Park neighborhood on the south side of Chicago, the only child of Cedric Ogilvy and Beatrice Worthington. Both families were born to the purple, as they say. Daddy Ogilvy's fortune came when they closed the legendary Chicago Stockyards and he bought up most of the land for cheap, razed it, and built and sold middle-class homes, mostly for the lace curtain Irish.

Gaylord's education was in expensive private schools, including legendary Phoenix Military School, during which time he grew even more wealthy—as he had more money than everyone and set his classmates up with good-looking college prostitutes, pocketing twenty percent of the fee. Upon graduation, he enrolled in the University of Chicago, suddenly began studying hard for a top degree in business, and wound up the salutatorian in his graduating class, which left him loathing the valedictorian who had two points more than he did on their university efforts. Then he spent five more years at Harvard, earning both a Master's degree and a Doctorate. Afterwards, dripping with money, he married Lilith Shadburn, also from an extremely wealthy family in Evanston.

Borrowing some thirty million dollars from his father, knowing he would inherit it anyway, he built office buildings and housing developments all over the city. In five years, he changed the skyline of Chicago—and in those five years he not only made back his thirty million (which he never repaid to Daddy), but one hundred seventy-eight million more.

Both personally and professionally, his reputation was far from squeaky clean. Since opening his own corporation, he kept a series of mistresses in elegant apartments all over town. Building houses and hotels as if playing Monopoly and owning Boardwalk and Park Place, he hired contractors and builders and conveniently forgot paying them the full amount for which they had agreed, though he spent almost as much on attorneys who dug him out of his endless holes. He wielded tremendous power over City Hall and almost every Chicago department head or director. He got legendary Chicago awards no one else ever dreamed of. The magnificent house in which I'd visited Lilith Shadburn Ogilvy cost the company nine million bucks plus change. But its real cost, according to the New York Times, was closer to seventeen million. Anything about that in the local *Chicago Tribune* or the *Sun-Times*? No. I wonder why he bought the most exquisite mansion in the state at a ridiculous bargain, do you? Need I explain?

By the time Ogilvy was in his mid-fifties, he'd extended his real estate power to other cities, i.e. Philadelphia, Tucson, Kansas City, Omaha, Seattle, Toronto, Montreal, Liverpool and Marseilles, frustrated to the point of hysteria he hadn't yet raised up buildings in Eastern Europe, Africa or the Middle East. Four elegant private country clubs in Georgia, South Carolina, Virginia and Basalt, Colorado. Three towering new skyscrapers in New York City's Long Island, and a vast housing development for the upper-middle-class executives, just outside

Newark, New Jersey.

He bought a controlling interest in a distillery that produced bourbon in Kentucky, and actually changed the name of the bourbon to Ogilvy's Best—but it wasn't a very good bourbon to begin with, and it went out of business within two years of his control. I guess great bourbon drinkers know an asshole when they see one.

He bragged openly he gave millions of dollars each year to needy charities like the Cancer Society, the Diabetic Society, Multiple Sclerosis, Saint Jude Children's Hospitals, and several other charities, but the fact is in the past twenty years he'd written and delivered to philanthropies benefit checks less than twenty thousand bucks.

Total.

According to the info I gleaned from the Internet, Ogilvy's companies were worth approximately twenty-three billion dollars.

Billion. With a *B*.

By 3:30 in the afternoon, I'd learned as much about Gaylord Ogilvy as I could unearth on the Internet. There is not much more to uncover about Chicago's Money Lord to know he was an out-and-out criminal, being sued by more than twenty-five different companies and individuals. However, the city and state's most powerful tricky-dick lawyers will make sure none of this info is released to the Great Unwashed who don't read newspapers or watch the local news shows. Ogilvy had more money and more overpaid attorneys than almost anyone else in the country, and he could wait his angry citizens out, buy them out, or just ignore them and hope they'd go away.

I shut down my laptop, pushed myself away from the desk, and stretched, hearing bones pop. My body was in fairly good shape, as I had spent lots of prison time doing push-ups, pull-ups, jumping jacks and stretches, especially when I got the chance to watch exercise TV shows, always hosted by beautiful women, which had attracted my interest in the first place.

In my younger days, I'd been a runner. Most days, when the weather was decent, I'd trot for a few miles outside. It caused my thighs to feel like solid rock, helped my lungs breathe deeply, and I suppose made my heart healthier. There was an exercise room in Joliet, but it was impossible to do any running during the one hour per day we were let outside in the yard. It was more important to meet and keep on the good side of so-called friends—and real ones like Denver Tolliver. In seven years, my running skills had practically disappeared.

I didn't expect Cole Cabot's visit for another four and a half hours, and the weather outside was sunny and warm-looking, so I thought I'd give running the old college try once again.

Dressed for it, I walked the half-block on Oak Street down to Michigan Avenue, where the beach curved. I'd run on the beach years before, though the sand made exercise more difficult, so I figured I wouldn't get far on this first day before the legs and knees began excruciating.

I loped slowly, heading north, hoping to make it to the North Avenue Beach without collapsing—a ten-blocks' distance from where I lived. My new Tana-bought running shoes churned up the sand as I trotted rather than ran, but it was damn difficult. There were few people actually on the beach—it wasn't warm enough for sunbathing or swimming, but the wind wasn't doing much, and the lake waves were more clement than usual, so it was a good day for me to get back in the groove. Slowly, of course.

A few people wearing zip-up jackets sat on benches just off sand to watch the waves, which only splashed rather than threatened. The sun was toasty, the lake-lookers noticed me trotting by, and most smiled, nodded or waved, not knowing who I was.

North Street Beach loomed. No one could miss the huge Beach House planted right in the middle of the sand, looking like the top deck of a cruise ship. It had been there since long before my own parents were born—another Chicago landmark.

I had too much confidence in myself, as the last hundred and fifty yards were murder. I could barely breathe. My feet were hurting as though hammered with a crowbar. I aimed for a bench and plopped down on it, my head thrown back, gasping for air, trying to rub some good feeling into my legs. The thought of running back home was an oncoming nightmare. I checked to make sure I had my cell phone and wallet with me, as I planned to call a taxi to take me home.

After about five minutes, my legs still throbbed and my running togs were sopping wet, but my breathing was almost normal, so I could sit up and see what was going on, wiping at my eyes to clear away the sweat. Several other joggers pounded by me, looking as if they were in pain, too. Most of them just stared ahead, focusing on not dropping dead from exhaustion after running in the sand.

Damn! I thought, *I should be home writing a book. But what would I write about this time? A novel all about sand runners?*

That's when *she* came along.

She looked right at me and slowed down to a trot. She smiled and breathlessly said, "Hi," as she passed.

More than polite, I said hi back to her, but that would be the end of it. That's what I thought, anyway.

She covered another twenty yards or so, then turned and came back to me. "Are you okay?"

"Fine," I gasped, lying. "This was my first run in a long time, and I came too far and too fast."

"Do you want some water?" She wore a fanny pack, which definitely got in the way of displaying her amazing once-in-a-lifetime great ass. She probably had enough stuff in that pack to take her through most of Europe.

"No," I said. "Thanks, but I'm really okay."

I wasn't okay yet—but just looking at her was making me

happier than I'd been in—seven years? More?

Probably five-feet-eight-or-nine. Long beautiful legs with a tan that had faded from the past summer, shining with clean sweat. Medium-sized breasts beneath her T-shirt—but I've never been a breast freak, so they looked perfect to me. Hair caught up in a ponytail—light brown or dark blond, I couldn't tell.

Eyes. Oh my god, *eyes!* I first thought they were blue, but a second—and third—glance convinced me they were gray. Her oval face reminded me of paintings by Modigliani, except his models were all brunettes. She wore no make-up—most women don't if they're serious about running—but her lips looked kissable.

And don 't forget what I said about her butt.

Lilith Ogilvy was beautiful—and she knew it. The problem is, even touching her might give one a serious case of frostbite. The woman standing in front of me was different.

Very different.

"How far did you run?" she inquired.

"From Oak Street, which is too far—but I didn't realize until I got here."

She cocked her head to one side as though studying me. Then she said, "You're Russell Reinert."

I nodded. "Have we met before?"

"You've never met me—but I've met you. Every time I read one of your books, or see you on a television interview, I feel as if I'm meeting you all over again. I was at one of your signings, too—I think for the last book—at the bookstore in the Water Tower."

"Did I sign your book? I'd remember."

"No, I didn't buy one. Back then, I didn't have the money to spare. I got your books out of the library every time. Anyway, I can afford the next one."

"What do you do for a living—besides being terminally adorable?"

"Terminally? Wowzer!" She took a deep breath. "I teach Fashion Design at Northwestern. I got my degree there in the same subject."

"When do I get to see your creations?"

"I don't really create anymore. Instead, I teach other people to create." She indicated the space next to me on the bench. "Mind if I sit down?"

"Sure," I said, shifting my ass to the left. "It's a bench made for two."

She turned to study the lake. She had an amazing profile. Beautiful forehead, almost-stubborn chin, and a nose that was aristocratic but not in the least bit perky. "I hate to take up time you should be writing."

"I'm not writing now," I said. "I had to take a time-out for a while."

She smiled with a kind and generous understanding that told me she knew where and why I'd taken that time-out. "Better get back to it, Mr. Reinert. There are thousands and thousands of people waiting."

"Not thousands and thousands," I said. "More like fourteen or fifteen ardent readers. But I never saw one before that looks like you." I managed to sit up straight, even though my legs screamed at me not to move at all. "Since you've met me so many times, you should probably call me Russ."

"Oh, my."

"Why an oh my?"

"Because—well, because you're famous."

I couldn't help chuckling. "Not anymore. But I bet I can guess your name."

"You've known me for ninety seconds and you can guess my name?"

"Of course," I said. "I'm psychic." I closed my eyes, hand over my forehead, pretending to concentrate. Then: "Got it. It's Hortense."

"Oh my god," she laughed, "that's a horrible name."

"Why? It's a beautiful name, from the Latin. It means 'gardener.'"

"I live in a high rise. No garden, just a relatively small balcony on the fourteenth floor. But Hortense sounds like a prostitute having a nervous breakdown. Whore-tense." She pushed the hair back from her forehead. "You can lead a whore to water, but you can't make her tense."

Now it was my turn, realizing for the first time since I was convicted of manslaughter, I laughed. Heartily.

She scolded, "I'm not giving you a second chance, buddy. Who knows what you'll invent next? Griselda? Fatatatita? This time, try Cassidy. Cassidy Hammond."

I shook my head sadly. "You're making it up. It's really Hortense. But just so I don't piss you off, I'll call you Cassidy from now on."

She raised her eyebrows, wiped the sweat from her eyes, and licked her lips. "From now on?"

I took a deep breath of the fresh Lake Michigan air and realized I was no longer frightened to jump into the water. "I think so," I said.

CHAPTER FIFTEEN

My second shower of the day was almost too hot to stand, but I needed it after my run, although I didn't have the strength or the energy. I walked back—strolled, actually, and on Lake Shore Drive sidewalk and not the sand—and tried not to get too close to anyone because, overheated as I was, I was sure to offend them. Antiperspirants are fine on ordinary people—but after a long strenuous romp through sand, it would be like using a water pistol to take down an elephant. I can't recall any other time I was sweating gallons, even on a hot day in a prison that never heard of air conditioning.

It was only a few days past saying goodbye to the hoosegow in which I lived that had an infallible rule for convicts—two showers per week. Period. No matter if I were filthy, stinky, had crapped in my pants, spilled hot soup in my lap or sweated through my clothes, if it weren't my scheduled shower day, that was tough shit. Therefore, I made a point of being thankful for that late afternoon shower in my own personal bathroom.

I wasn't hungry for dinner, because my body ached in places I never knew I had. It would be hell getting out of bed the next morning, and I hoped I'd heal up by tomorrow evening, because I had a date.

An honest-to-god date.

Cassidy.

Not a "Hi, can I buy you a drink?" kind of date. Not a "Let's meet in some bar—but feel free to leave if I don't show up" kind of date. It was a "Let's get together at 7:30 and we'll go out to dinner" date. A "Let's get to know each other" date.

But for a convicted felon who's never even touched another woman in almost a decade, it was a "Holy-crap, I'm-terrified!" date.

I poured myself a single-malt Scotch—straight up with one single ice cube to smooth it out while I drank it. I found classical music on TV to relax me—mostly Mahler—and tried not to think of Cassidy Hammond. Not to envision her as the leading lady in the next book I was going to write—assuming I'd ever get around to writing another book. Not to think about her in a sensual or erotic way. When you're in prison for a lengthy stretch, you try not to think about women and beds and sex at all. It wrenched my guts trying to become the normal good old American guy.

I wasn't sure I'll ever be that again. It wouldn't be easy.

The classical music switched from Mahler to Edvard Grieg. I'd never been to Norway, never even thought about their music, and it always surprised me someone as famous as Grieg had lived and worked there. I had no idea where he died. Maybe slumped over the keys of his grand concert piano—but I doubted it.

I expected Cole Cabot at my door, and even though I yearned for a second drink, I wanted my head clear when we talked. My personal job was to find Aubrey Sinden or discover what's happened to her. Cole probably knew a lot he hadn't told me to begin with, so I had to stay on my toes and not miss anything.

He was only five minutes late. I switched off the music before I opened the door. Cabot slouched in like he'd rather be almost anywhere else.

I sat him down opposite me in the living room. I didn't offer him a drink.

"I'm trying to fill some empty spaces," I said.

"Give it up. You don't work for me, you're not making any money, and you haven't even seen or heard from Aubrey for years."

"No, I haven't," I told him, "but she and I were important to each other back in the day, and it's still important to me."

"Sit back and enjoy, Reinert. You're rich, for crysakes."

"There's rich," I pointed out to him, "and then there's *rich*. Did you ever meet Gaylord Ogilvy personally?"

He shook his head. "He's been on TV—mostly local news—and that's about it. Don't forget—when we got married, Aubrey stopped seeing him. I mean, I never thought I was getting a virgin or anything, but I insisted—no more her fucking anyone else but me."

"But she continued working for him?"

"Not for him. It was for the company—Ogilvy Corporation. She only worked part-time—mostly from home or on the Internet. Sometimes one of his people showed up at our place so she could read some stuff and sign it, but that was it."

"What stuff?"

"I got no idea. It was her thing, not mine."

"How about these people who came to your place for her signature? Did you meet them?"

"It was always the same guy, so sure I met him." He screwed up his eyes and mouth, trying to remember a name. Then he said, "Irving Greenfield."

"Irvin," I reminded him. "No G at the end."

"Whatever."

"Irvin Greenfield is the number two guy at Ogilvy Corporation. I don't know what his title is, but his office is right next to Gaylord's. Whatever he brought over for Aubrey must've been pretty damn important."

Cabot looked away. "I paid no attention. I guess she was still on the payroll."

"Did her money and yours go into the same account?"

He said, "We have a common account—rent, car payments, groceries—like everyone, and she contributed. But she had an account of her own someplace else."

"Not at your bank?"

He shook his head. "I don't even know which bank."

"You never asked her?"

"Not my business."

I found that strange. From the very beginning, Dayna and I had an abrading marriage—arguments galore and infidelities too myriad to count—but we always had a common checking account and savings account. When she perished, Tana Phillips made sure that money was mine free and clear, as Dayna was an only child as well.

I said, "You have the freedom to use the common checking account and the savings account in both your names. Right?"

"Right."

"But not her personal account."

"I told you, I don't know what bank. Maybe she's got a secret account in Switzerland, where our federal government can't touch it."

"Since she's been gone, did you ever look through her drawers and papers, her desk, any files she might have? Any phone numbers?"

He looked humiliated, as if we'd been at an elite black-tie benefit ball and someone told him loudly his fly was open. "Jesus," he almost whispered. "That never even occurred to me."

"Well, do it the minute you get home tonight. Who's your accountant?"

"We go to H & R Block every year to do our taxes. They have an office on Lincoln Avenue for people who make big deductions."

"She has offshore accounts too?" I demanded. "Numbered accounts no one can touch unless they know the number? Money the federal government hasn't a clue about? And you don't have a top-drawer CPA to help you."

"Aubrey has one of her own, I think," Cabot said, "for whatever she makes from Ogilvy—but I don't know a damn thing about it." His face paled, and he wiped his hand across his mouth.

"Which one of you made the most money? You or Aubrey?"

He raised his voice. He didn't shout, but he let me know he was damn annoyed. "None of your fucking business."

"Sorry," I said—but I wasn't sorry in the least. His snotty-nosed answer told me Aubrey brought home the larger share of the bacon—by a lot.

Cabot said she no longer had sexual relations with Gaylord Ogilvy. Maybe she was lying to him—or maybe he was lying to me. The problem was Aubrey Cabot always worked from her home, and no one, not even the richest man in Illinois, would drop by her home for a quick screw. I made love to Aubrey many times—and she was never one for "hurry-up-I'm-busy."

I changed my focus. "Personal question. Are you in love with Aubrey?"

His eyes bugged out, and his chin hit his chest. "Wh—what? What kind of question is that?"

"You don't have to answer it—which tells me a hell of a lot about you."

Furious, he sputtered and stuttered for a bit. I let him flail around until he calmed down some, and I asked the question again.

"Of course I love her, you asshole," he snarled. "I married her, didn't I?"

I said, "I understand love. I love pepperoni and sausage pizza, I love the Cubs. I love springtime. I didn't ask you if you loved her—I'm sure you do. I asked if you were *in love* with her. A different meaning altogether."

Cole Cabot closed his eyes, his fingers gripping his thighs as though they were about to fall off. I think he might also have been biting his tongue. Finally, he slumped back in the chair, opened his eyes and said, "Look, she's beautiful, right? When we go places together, men just stare—and that makes me feel like a million bucks. She's smart as a whip. Fun to be with. Supportive. She cares about me, cares about my life. And the sex is—fantastic." Then he glared at me. "I suppose you already knew that." He looked away again, at a wall that was so far denuded of any art or decoration. I'll have to get busy on that, buying paintings and other hangings.

"In love?" He continued more quietly. "Hell, I don't know. I'm—happy when I'm with her. Isn't that enough?"

"She's got her own money tied up somewhere," I asked, trying to get back on track. If I had to find her money, I wouldn't know where to begin looking for it.

He leaned forward and doubled his fists. "Why are you looking for her money?"

"Because so far, I've not run into any of her personal enemies, unless you forgot to mention them." I didn't try changing my tone, but it still came out dangerous. "You dragged me into this disappearance in the first place. Never calling law enforcement puts you at the top of my suspect list."

"I avoided cops," Cabot whined, "because I didn't know what she might be into." He shook his head almost violently. "I don't know, man. She was in some sort of shit with the Ogilvy people. Whether or not it's legal."

"Define shit."

He said, "I can't. It just worries me."

"Okay," I said, "but why not hire a private investigator?"

I'm unsure whether the question it enraged him , or he had started to cry. In any case, his emotions exploded, "Because I can't afford any goddamn private investigator!"

"Calm down," I warned him. "You're getting on my nerves."

His head was down, and he was sniffling. There are two things that happen to people when they lose their tempers. The first guy does what Cabot did—get furious, scream and rage, and then cry about it afterwards. The second guy—well, the second guy kills somebody.

"Get your act together, Cabot. Stop blubbering and talk to me." I pushed a box of tissues over to him and waited until he stopped weeping piteously. It took about two minutes, and seven tissues.

I took out my little pocket recorder and switched it on, pointing the microphone toward him. "Who's her CPA?"

"He won't talk to you. He doesn't even talk to me."

"What's his name?"

"Bryce DeBower is his name. I think his office is on Wabash Avenue."

"I'll find him," I said, clicking off my recorder and putting it on the table at the side of my chair.

He sniffed, took another tissue, and wiped his nose. "I want to be kept informed, Mr. Reinert."

"Kept informed? You pulled me in on this hunt, hating me because I slept with your wife before you even met her. You refused to pay me, and now you want to be kept informed?"

"I'm entitled," he insisted. "I'm Aubrey's husband."

"Well, Aubrey's husband," I said, "go fuck yourself." And I snatched the box of tissues away from him before he used them all up.

CHAPTER SIXTEEN

I hired a Certified Public Accountant after my first book hit the *New York Times* Best Seller List. We only met twice as he was Jack and Tana Phillips' CPA as well, and she set me up with him to do my taxes and things. I generally talked to him on the phone at least twice a year, after I'd turned in my tax information to him, pleased his main job was saving me money. Even behind bars, I still got great royalties from the books I wrote—and he worked it out for me to keep most of it. After all, for seven incarcerated years, royalties were my only source of income. That's one more good reason I was pleasantly wealthy when they finally unlocked my cell door for the last time.

Before that, my parents—mostly my mom after my dad died—took care of everything for me. It wasn't until I got into college and became a full-fledged Illini I understood how to write a check and to keep track of my money. I had little use for ninety percent of college, other than writing classes and acting onstage—I had a supporting role in Moliere's *Tartuffe* when I was still a freshman. I was a whiz on my electric typewriter, a fresh-faced Junior Terror with the coeds, and I had a remarkable consumption of anything alcoholic.

I had two doctors back then—one when I lived at home and one when I stayed in Champaign, both chosen by my mother.

During that time, I had a roommate—a red-headed kid named Larry from Centralia, downstate, who was studying to become an electrical engineer. We were friends because I got drunk at least once a week and he helped me through my hangovers more than once. We had little to talk about. He'd never read fiction in his life, and I barely knew electricity beyond changing a light bulb. I had no clue about those living in small towns and going to church every week. Larry confessed he had never even seen a Jew until he arrived in Champaign. He asked me seriously, and with no menace, how come Jewish people were called *shikes,* and after I laughed my ass off, I had to explain to him the proper word was *kikes,* and not a nice word at all.

I dropped out of college after two years and missed Larry. I moved back to Chicago and stayed with my mom for a while. There, I never had to wash a single dish. My cooking skills began and ended with peanut butter and jelly sandwiches. I learned to drive a car when I was twenty-two—back then the city's public transportation was amazing and many people never owned cars in their lives. I didn't live by myself in my own place until I was twenty-five, and for a few years after that I took my dirty laundry back to Mom so she could launder and *fold.* To this day, I am impatient and inept when it comes to folding a clean T-shirt.

It's the same with only children like me. Parents devote their whole lives to make sure we are safe, secure, and don't have to lift a finger. They don't realize they won't always be here to wrap their special kiddies in soft cotton and tuck them away somewhere safe—and that's when a person with no siblings damn well learns how to actually live as a grown-up.

The only things I've ever really succeeded without help or assistance are writing and fucking—and for seven years in Joliet, I did neither.

When I found myself acting out Cole Cabot's weird fantasy as an unarmed private eye, I was ready to rack one more peculiar search, along with everything else I had to re-learn by myself. Still less than one week of freedom, and I went downtown to flush Bryce De Bower, CPA, from where he'd gone to ground.

I discovered him so close I didn't have to drive. It was only a brisk ten-in-the-morning walk. His office was actually inside the beautiful white Wrigley Building on Michigan Boulevard on the eleventh floor, right next to the river. Like so many of the truly lucky Chicagoans, his windows looked out upon the lake, too.

It took me fifteen minutes to fight my way through three receptionists and/or secretaries before I was reluctantly allowed to enter the hallowed halls of Aubrey Sinden's CPA.

"I see people only by appointment," Bryce De Bower said to me by way of greeting. "I only gave in because you used to be a pretty famous guy here in Chicago—and all over the world, too. Not to be rude, but whatever you have to say had better take ten minutes or less. I don't want to get backed up here." He pointed to a visitor's chair opposite his desk.

De Bower was somewhere in his early sixties. Five foot eight or so, maybe fifteen pounds too heavy, balding, peering through too-thick glasses and wearing a three-piece suit with a dull necktie no one could describe five minutes after leaving his office. On his desk was a large framed photo of what must have been his wife and children at least twenty years earlier. They didn't look like movie stars, either.

I was able to tell him about my visit in far more quickly than ten minutes.

"I didn't even know Aubrey was missing. Holy crap!" De Bower's tone was that of a man who spent the morning searching for his reading glasses. "I don't hear from her all the time—maybe once a month."

"Are you aware of anyone who might be her enemy?"

"Everyone in the world has enemies," he said, "or at least people who just don't like them." He sat up straighter, a smirk on his lips. "Even me." Apparently, people who disliked him gave him a scintilla of pride. "I can't think of anyone so angry at Aubrey to spirit her away and keep her hidden."

"I'm thinking not so much of anger," I said, "but of money. You're her CPA, you know all about her money."

"I do—but I can't discuss it with you."

"Why not?"

"Because I wouldn't stay in business for the next half hour, spilling my guts about the moneys earned by all my clients."

"You get a percentage?"

"No comment."

"What about the money she earns from Ogilvy Company?"

"Again, sir—no comment. But Aubrey Sinden found her way to my office to deal with her connection to Ogilvy. My brother Richard—he's two years older than I am—happens to be the CFO of Ogilvy Corporation." He looked at me with contempt. "That means Chief Financial Officer."

I hated being talked to as if I were a blooming idiot. "Thanks for reminding me," I almost snarled, hoping I scared him.

It didn't work. I'll have to work harder at my snarl.

"Be that as it may," De Bower intoned, "Richard De Bower's biggest job at Ogilvy's is keeping his mouth shut about Ogilvy money."

"I see. Can we just talk about Aubrey's own money?"

"That's immoral and illegal, Mr. Reinert. It's much like being a lawyer. Communications between lawyer and client are deemed private. Same with clients and CPAs."

"A general question, then. Is Aubrey really rich?"

De Bower considered that for a time. Then he said, "Pro athletes are rich. Movie stars. Arab oil sheiks. Guys who invented Microsoft and Apple. Gaylord Ogilvy. They're rich. Goddamn rich. Aubrey is not all that rich." He made finger quotation marks around the word *rich*. "She's financially—comfortable."

"And Cole Cabot?" I queried. "Is her husband comfortable, too?"

"I have no knowledge of that. Cabot isn't my client. Just Aubrey. But I'm guessing—this is a guess, mind you—Aubrey has most of the money."

"What happens if she passes away first? As her husband, doesn't he automatically get at least half of her money?"

"It depends," he said, "if they made a pre-nuptial arrangement—and that could mean damn near anything."

"Like what?"

"Like Cabot only gets ten percent or twenty percent, or every goddamn nickel of it. Or the entire estate can go to some weird charity for elderly ladies who tend to a rose garden and harbor twenty cats. I have no idea. If there is a pre-nup, it was all handled by Aubrey's own attorney."

"And who is her attorney?"

"Hang on," he said, and removed an iPad from his top drawer. He poked and prodded at it for about thirty seconds. Then he said, "Dean Bosley."

"Where can I get in touch with him?"

Bryce De Bower said, "He's an associate with a pretty powerful outfit—the Tana Phillips Law Firm. You want their phone number?"

The last time I felt that terrifying feeling was the moment the jury foreman stood and announced I'd been found guilty.

Tana Phillips.

I finally took a deep breath, though my mouth had suddenly gone as dry as the Mojave Desert in the midst of summer, and I managed to choke out, "Thanks—but I have the number."

Until I wound up in Tana Phillips' elegant law office, taking up an entire floor in one of the newer buildings that lined Lincoln Avenue on Chicago's North Side, I didn't realize it was my first visit in more than seven years.

Tana was surprised seeing me across the desk from her, unbidden. I think she wished I hadn't showed up. We were best friends forever—but she's a powerhouse owner of a huge law firm, and I was an unemployed ex-con with time on my hands.

"I've got about fifteen minutes," she said, standing behind her desk checking a stack of files, putting some in her briefcase and setting others aside. "You're lucky I can squeeze you in. Much as I love you, Russ, you need to make an appointment." She shrugged. "In the evening, you can knock on my door at home any time. But office-wise, I'm pretty busy."

"You're my attorney, Tana."

"When you got out of the pen less than a week ago, you walked into a lovely and sophisticated lifestyle—and I set up all of it. I wanted you to feel halfway decent. I wanted you to feel free."

"I do," I said, "and for the thousandth time this week, thank you. But you're also Aubrey Sinden's attorney."

Her pause before answering was deliberate. "Not her personal attorney, Russ. I have forty-three associates and three other partners in this firm."

"And Dean Bosley is her personal lawyer."

"Not all that personal. Besides, Dean Bosley is a three-year associate, and he probably has more clients than he can even remember." She rolled her eyes heavenward. "I imagine he has to make fresh coffee for the people in his wing at least two days a week."

"How did you wind up being Aubrey's attorney?"

Her eyes sparkled. "When you were inside, she decided she needed a lawyer and came to me. I couldn't represent both of you—conflict of interest—so I passed her on to one of my associates, and now I haven't the slightest idea where she is, personally or financially." She tucked the last file into her bulging briefcase. "By the way, she's very pretty."

"Why," I pressed on, "did she need a lawyer?"

Her pleasant demeanor mortified into a heavy frown. "No lawyer openly discusses their clients with a third party."

"Sorry."

"Okay then—my turn to ask questions. Why are you here, Russ? Why is one of this firm's clients your business?"

"Because she's been missing for more than two weeks."

Tana's face changed again, this time with surprise. "I didn't know that. It wasn't in the news. How do you know she's missing?"

"Because," I said, and I heard the outraged defense creeping into my tone, "her husband—Cole Cabot—approached me and asked me to look for her."

We stared at each other for several long seconds. Then she quietly sat back down in her chair and pushed her briefcase away from her. "Jesus H. Christ," she whispered.

"He didn't offer me money," I said. "I would have turned it down if he had. Besides, the next day, he changed his mind. He asked me to stop."

Tana just looked daggers at me. "Then why didn't you? You're not a cop. You're not a private eye. You're no fucking *priest!* You're a convicted felon! You must be nuts even to hang around the edges of what might be a crime."

"I've had a few meetings—one with Gaylord Ogilvy himself."

"Ogilvy? You actually got in to talk to him personally about Sinden?" She leaned her head against the back of the chair, closed her eyes and put her hands up on either side of her temples, rubbing away what was beginning to be a migraine. "What did they teach you in Joliet prison? How to hammer in large nails with your forehead?"

She took her hands down and looked at me as though my x-rays had just come back positive. "Russell, it took me seven years of hard luck getting you out from behind bars. I made deals with the warden. I made deals with the district attorney. I made deals with the governor! I spent weeks looking for a place for you to live—a classy, elegant place. I bought your car. I bought your clothes. I bought the TV and the kitchen applianc-es and even the toilet plunger. I haven't spent one dime of your money for myself. You're a writer, damn you, so write! Quit running around thinking you're Sam Spade."

"At least," I said, "I won't get blamed this time because when Aubrey dropped out of sight, I was still in prison."

"Blamed?" She stood up quickly and charged around the desk toward me. "As far as you know, no crime has been committed. She bugged out, left her husband without a word, and you're blaming me—or my associate, Dean Bosley—for being her lawyer? And while we're at it, I have no idea what she's cooking up with Dean. Personally, I only handle rich clients who can't find their butt with either hand in the dark."

She picked up her briefcase and headed for the door. "Like you," she said over her shoulder, "I love you, but don't ever mention Aubrey Sinden's name to me again—unless you're being held by the Chicago police for killing her."

I doubt anyone alive would understand how cruelly that last sentence left me standing alone in her executive office, looking out at the lake and feeling I was once again a convicted felon.

CHAPTER SEVENTEEN

All alone once more. What's new and different about that?

Lawyer Tana Phillips and her husband Jack were the only two living people I could trust when I walked through the iron gate of that prison to freedom—not counting Denver Tolliver, who will be locked up in there until they truck him out in a body bag.

Not Aubrey Sinden, my so-called mistress for a year and a half before my wife died of an accident I was blamed for, who is now using Tana's high-end law firm that keeps her secrets, even though she'd vanished for a reason none of us could figure out.

One of the strongest arrows in the prosecutor's quiver after Dayna died was I killed her off so I could marry Aubrey—which was not true. One miserable marital mudslide was enough.

Now I feel incredibly stupid for setting out to look for her—but it didn't stop me. Why? Hell if I know.

So—here I am. No family at all. No parents. No siblings or cousins or aunts and uncles or kindly white-haired grandmas to whom I can turn. No more literary agent, no more publisher, no real friends. No wife, no lover, and a longtime, loyal attorney, I suddenly find it difficult to trust anymore.

Nobody.

It tickled my mind over the years—my good years—to search for my biological progenitors, but according to the rules of the day, the adoptive parents found me through a private agency, so my true background was a closed one. Even mom and dad had no clue who my real antecedents might be. When I thought about it carefully, parents who loved and raised me were a hell of a lot better than those who brought me into the world and then dumped me, whoever they were, so I never considered going on a real search.

What if I tried finding them now, at the same time I was searching for Aubrey? Ask around, write letters, close in on the adoption agency, if it still exists. Find who my real parents were, ring them up on the phone and tell them cheerily, *"Hi there, mom and dad. Surprise! This is your real true son. Remember me vaguely? Yeah, those other people call me Russell. What would you have named me if you'd kept me around? Percy? Elmo? Chauncey? And what's my real last name, anyway? Schmidt? Shanahan? Bacciagalupe? Jacobowski? Anyway, I'm a multi-millionaire, and I just got out of prison for a killing I never committed. Want to get coffee together, or maybe even a quick dinner at Applebee's where I can tell you about the books I wrote more than seven years ago?"*

Bad idea.

So here I am, crawling toward middle-age, adrift and forsaken as I've been all my life—not counting the years I was married to Dayna, who cuckolded me as often as most guys read the sports pages with their coffee and cereal.

I suppose I should discuss what happened that got me locked away.

Dayna, my wife, spent my money as if FedEx delivered thousands of it each morning. When we moved into the big house, she spent a fortune having the entire kitchen re-designed: hidden overhead lights, a new tile floor, new cabinets, a worktable in the middle of everything, expensive tile backings behind the sink, stove-top heaters, and around the one window she paid to have knocked out and enlarged to twice its normal size so the kitchen would be filled with glorious light. Of course, if one liked Chicago year-round, there wasn't much glorious kitchen light from November to May—but that didn't stop Dayna.

And let's not forget every flat surface in the kitchen and all three of the bathrooms were replaced with granite, the cost of which would supply a lower-middle-class family with rent and food for an entire year.

However, it was not a new house, but forty-six years old—and even in the best constructions, some things go wrong after four decades, like a leaking roof, stuck windows, worn-out plumbing, etc. After a few years of calling that house a home—most difficult for a number of reasons—Dayna somehow found herself in the basement, and noticed that in a hose through which gas was pumped to keep the water hot was a rip about an inch long.

She came pounding up the stairs, screaming like a banshee that I tore the damn thing myself trying to kill her, and I should fix it immediately. I was damned if I'd stop, make myself late for driving to Milwaukee for dinner to do shit little home repairs at the last minute. I' d just finished packing a suitcase!

There was another truth Dayna missed: I'm not at all what you'd call a "fix-it" guy, especially when I'm running late. I snapped at her to call a plumber or a heating-and-cooling guy to come out and fix it the next day, and left the house.

I'm sure she'd phone the most expensive person on the internet to come and fix the damn leak in a hose, and possibly give him a blow-job too, if the idea struck her.

It was the next evening the Winnetka police tracked me down by phone in a Milwaukee hotel and informed me my house had caught fire in the middle of the night, and my wife was dead.

I had stopped loving Dayna more than two years earlier. I stopped liking her shortly after that. But I never hoped, even on my most bitter and tormented days, she would die—or I would kill her. I showed her no physical violence. I never hit her or kicked her or even pushed her, and the only times I raised my voice to her was when she started screaming first. But the district attorney, hot for a big-time election to come, loved the *glory* of humiliating and convicting someone relatively famous—not in Chicago, but all over the country. All over the world.

Tana Phillips was in court almost every day, but she functioned best as a corporate attorney. My defense lawyer came from her office, as she was not the type of lawyer who personally tried to convince the jury I was a step and a half short of sainthood.

The DA assured those twelve stoned-faced jurors I wanted my wife Dayna gone so I could legalize my relationship with Aubrey, so I deliberately made a cut in the gas pipe just as I was leaving for an out-of-town appearance, knowing the house would catch fire and she'd die—horribly burned.

He even subpoenaed Aubrey to testify we'd been lovers for eighteen months or so. She tried her best to paint a positive picture of me, but he was the kind of snake that could twist testimony around for his own benefit.

The sequestered jury—the prosecutor made goddamn sure none of them had ever read my books—took only a few hours to return with a verdict of guilty, and all watched as I was handcuffed and led from the courtroom. I spent six weeks in county jail before returning to hear my sentencing.

Then I was loaded onto a well-guarded bus and motored downstate to my new "home" in the city of Joliet. The outside of that prison looked exactly how I figured it would. Inside, it was ten times worse.

But at length I got out. Pardoned. Excused. Not forgiven, exactly—not by anyone I've run into, except maybe the guy who parked my car in the garage a block from my new apartment. But free.

And lonely as hell.

And rich.

* * *

Now I had a date.

A real date, with a woman I met once and talked to for ten minutes when we were both dripping wet from exertion. We exchanged phone numbers. I called her. And now we actually had a date.

I'm not sure anyone uses the word "date" anymore. "Hanging out" is probably what teenagers say these days, though that also meant a bunch of people of both sexes going someplace all together. It didn't sound sexy or romantic. "Hooking up" meant fucking, or that's what I was led to believe.

If I didn't "hook up" with my new date, it's because I was terrified. I hadn't had sex in more than seven years, hadn't spent more than half an hour in the company of any woman in what the prison called the "Visitor's Room." Those women, naturally, were Tana Phillips and Aubrey Sinden—and Aubrey stopped coming.

And now I had a whatever-it-is, because calling it a "date" somehow went out of style in about 1995. I was going to meet up with Cassidy Hammond.

I phoned and asked if she'd have dinner with me.

"I've kind of lost track of restaurants around here," I explained, "but I'll be happy to drive to Evanston if there's a favorite place of yours."

"I don't live in Evanston," Cassidy explained. Her phone voice was low, confident, and subtly sexy. "I work at Northwestern, but I live in a high-rise on Sheridan Road, close to Devon."

I had to smile as I always did to Chicagoans' pronunciation of Devon. The British and the rest of the world pronounce it *DEV-un*, but in Chicago they call it *De-VAHN*. I hadn't heard either pronunciation for the past seven years. Then again, Devon Avenue is now very much known as "Little India," as almost every business on the street is owned and operated by East Indians. If you enjoy Indian food, just driving Devon Avenue, breathing heavily with the car windows open would blow you away.

"Why don't I come your way?" Cassidy continued. "I love the Near North, but I don't much get there anymore."

At our first meeting on the beach, I mentioned I'd just moved into a brownstone apartment on Oak Street. Nice that she remembered.

We met at an upscale eatery on Walton Street at eight o'clock, just around the corner from my new apartment. I was wearing casual pants, a white dress shirt, under a colorful Australian pullover sweater that was now out of style. But I didn't know that.

Cassidy had on a pretty dress—yes, a *dress*. Before I was imprisoned, it was rare to see a woman in any dress unless she was a celebrity wearing a ten-thousand dollar evening gown, trotting the Red Carpet on the way to a big-time entertainment award.

Or if she were a nun.

Cassidy Hammond's hair was down past her shoulders instead of in a ponytail, and it looked amazing. More than that, her dress was dramatic and attention-grabbing. Soft gray in shade, broad collar turned up at the back of her neck, just the tiniest glimpse of cleavage, medium sleeves, and medium-short skirt, and set off the color of her gray eyes. As soon as I sat down with her, I told her she looked terrific.

"Thanks very much," she said. "I designed the dress myself."

"Amazing. You should be a fashion superstar, not just teaching fashion design at a university."

She brought her shoulders up around her ears. "I gave that a shot. Went to New York—got a job with a big fashion house. I only lasted a year."

"You're kidding! They fired you?"

"No," Cassidy said, "I quit, cold. I couldn't stand the bullshit of the super-rich and the obscenely giant egos of the designers. And the men? Well, every man I came into contact with in the business was either gay or insisted on going to bed with me within the first twenty minutes." She shook her head hard and her long hair bounced. "You can have New York—with instructions."

"Then you came back to Chicago," I said.

"It's a big city, too—but there's decency here. A feeling of—America. And most Chicago men have a slight touch of class."

I cocked my head. "I'm not sure I should thank you for the compliment."

"Considering I've only spent twenty minutes with you in my lifetime," Cassidy pondered, "I'd have to say you're on the bubble."

"Because of my books?"

"Hmm. Partly."

"Since you've followed my career so closely, you might think, as do some people, I'm a murderer."

"Wow," she said with a little gasp. "You're in the shock business now?"

"It's no shock to me, Cassidy. You know I've been in prison."

"I did know. I just didn't expect you to throw it on the table before we've even ordered drinks." Her gray eyes narrowed. "And nowhere during your trial did anyone use the word *murderer*."

"Manslaughter, which means the same thing. Involuntary manslaughter. My God, you followed that trial so completely?"

"It was that or walk the streets and pick up sleaze-bags."

"I've only been out a few days," I said. "Give me some breathing room to learn how to be a human again." I looked away from her and lowered my voice to a near-whisper. "I'm sorry. We shouldn't be here together. It's too soon. I got sucked into serving time for a crime I didn't commit, and I'm sticking my neck out all over town about it. I shouldn't have done that, either."

We didn't say anything for almost a minute. Then she murmured, "I understand. I really do," and she took my hand in hers. "Let's order drinks, Russ. Take a few minutes so we can enjoy ourselves. I don't want anything from you except companionship, a pleasant evening." She squeezed my hand, then let go. "Or we can leave, if that's what you want. I just think you need to be peaceful."

"You give me peace, Cassidy. Odd, because we're on the edge of being total strangers. I'm sorry I got off track so fast. I'm like an immigrant, just off the boat and into a civilization which makes me sad because nobody in my new country speaks the same language I do, and they eat sheep eyeballs for lunch. Don't leave me. Please. I promise I'll behave."

Her smile was soft and giving. "I won't leave, Russ. I'm kind of an immigrant myself, because I never talked to a celebrity before—not counting saying thank you to Mike Ditka years ago for holding a door open for me—and he never answered, either. Let's take it slowly—walk on tiptoes until we both know where we are. Okay?"

"Okay," I said.

We had drinks—two apiece, and we talked. My so-called crime and imprisonment was not mentioned again. Cassidy expanded about her life up to that moment, including the fact she ran at least four days per week, often on the sand, until Chicago weather turns wintry and impossible to deal with. I told her I was adopted and never bothered to look for my biological parents. She told me she was an older sister of a boy who took R.O.T.C. in college and then became an officer in the United States Army—at the moment a major, stationed in Germany. She'd never married, and was now past the clock-ticking baby period and figured she'd never have one.

We mostly talked about my writing—what made me start, what made me work like a maniac, writing almost every day of my life from high school on, to become the huge success I unfortunately had to put on hold.

Neither of us mentioned past lovers. On the first date, that alone would put a kibosh on bringing up old romances.

She had a few questions about what was it like to be a literary luminary. She wanted to know what led me to writing about murder all the time.

"Read the bible," I said. "After fifteen minutes, you lose count of how many people were murdered, starting with Cain killing Abel. That goes for almost all fiction—certainly my favorite works, whether it's *The Great Gatsby* or *The Grapes of Wrath,* or even *Huckleberry Finn.* Death is a big part of life, Cassidy. Death by design enhances what people read. It sure fascinates me."

"Do you own a gun?"

"I know how to shoot one, or used to—but I've never owned one. I have a set of new steak knives in the kitchen in case I want to kill somebody."

"I'll remember that," Cassidy said, "in case you ever invite me for a home-cooked meal. I'll stick with matzo ball soup and cheesecake."

After our drinks were gone, neither of us was hungry enough for dinner. We walked outside into a sixty-five-degree autumn evening, the breeze off the lake catching everyone's attention.

"Where did you park your car?" I asked.

"A few blocks from here in a garage."

"I'll walk you there," I said.

"Don't you live right around here?"

"A walk of five minutes. Three minutes if you're in a hurry."

"I'm in no hurry. Show me," Cassidy said. "I've imagined you in your new place, writing."

Fear returned, almost choking me. I finally got out, "Are you sure?"

"I'm sure right now. Tomorrow—or next week—or next year at Christmastime, I might not be sure. Come on, Russ—or I might never get to look at your apartment."

I had trouble swallowing. "Then—I promise I'll be—a perfect gentleman."

Her eyebrows went up and her gray eyes almost twinkled.

"Did you ever see that old movie, *Some Like It Hot?* Marilyn Monroe and Jack Lemmon?"

"Sure," I said. "A long time ago."

"Remember the last line in the film?"

"I don't think I do."

"If I tell you," Cassidy said, "do you promise to follow it and act accordingly?"

"I promise."

"Okay. Well, this rich old guy is in love with Jack Lemmon, who'd been dressing as a woman for the whole film to avoid getting killed by gangsters. At the very end, when Jack tears off his wig and confesses, 'I'm a man,' you know what the old guy says?" She hooked her arm into my arm and started down the street toward Michigan Boulevard. "'Nobody's perfect.' Remember that, Russ."

CHAPTER EIGHTEEN.

I wasn't very good in bed. In fact, I was astonishingly lousy.

It's not that I'd forgotten what two people do with each other between the sheets. I'd learned that when I was seventeen, from a somewhat older woman, Mary Jane Grant, who bragged all over the Near North neighborhood she'd boffed a teenager. That did wonders for my reputation, by the way.

But after more than seven years without even a female handshake, it just seemed—awkward. Strange. I was more turned on by Cassidy Hammond than any other woman I'd ever known, but a severe case of overpowering nerves made it quite a while before working up a half-ass erection—and premature ejaculation after about two minutes was humiliating to the nth degree.

She put her head on my shoulder. "This was a first. I never went to bed with anyone on a first date before. Usually on a first date, I don't even kiss."

Which made me feel more shitty, more maladroit.

I seriously—*seriously*—considered taking my own life, right there and then. But that would be awful for Cassidy. She'd remember it for the rest of her days, and that would screw up *her* future sexual dalliances as my inept failure would keep coming back to remind her.

"Don't be upset, Russ," she said to me soothingly. "Really. I figured this might happen."

"I forgot how to do it," I said, turning my head away from her as we lay in my bed. "For the last seven years, I tried hard to not even think about it."

She was silent for a moment. "When you're totally out of practice for a long, long time, it doesn't come back right away."

I chewed on my lower lip before saying, "I wanted it to be good for you."

"It's been a year and a half for me, too. Look—I loved you when I read your books, fell *in love* with you at your book signing, but I was too scared to approach you. After all, you're a famous guy."

"I was famous." Vinegar taste was on my tongue. "Not anymore."

"To me, you still are." She lay on her back under the covers, looking up at the ceiling. I was on my right side, listening to her, studying her profile.

"I felt awful about your conviction," she went on, "and sympathetic, too, but there wasn't a damn thing I could do about it. I thought about writing you a letter, making us pen pals until you came back to Chicago—but lots of weird women do that with prisoners, so I never tried.

"When we met on the beach, it was totally by accident," she continued. "Was it fate? I don't know. I was thrilled to see you, gasping for air on a bench by the lake. I thought you were on your last breath, but I had to stop and talk with you—and dammit, the feelings came back with a rush."

"I had feelings, too," I said. "A few minutes on a bench didn't change my life, but I thought you were beautiful, and funny, and I asked for your number." Now I flipped over onto my back so she couldn't really see my face if she made the effort. "I had no idea we'd be—here—tonight. I was scared, and it turned out I was right. I'm sorry, I'm a lousy lay."

"It's possible I'm a lousy lay, too."

"Cassidy, that's a kind and generous lie."

"Well, it's sort of my fault," she said. "I didn't think you'd invite me to bed tonight. I was the one who asked to see your new apartment, and I made damn sure we wound up right where we are."

"Big mistake."

"Not at all. Years ago, I read your books and loved them. I loved the way you use exactly the correct words you wanted, and sometimes those exact words get someone to hunker down even more and read your work to find some words no one ever heard of—like *arcane,* or *jacaranda.* Where in hell do you find words like that? I'm a Midwesterner, born and bred, and I never heard of a jacaranda tree before. I loved your plots with twists in them every few pages, and I thought your author photos on the back cover were cute. That's why I showed up when you did your book signing at the Chicago Fire Tower. Remember, I couldn't afford a book then, but I wanted to see you in person, hear what you had to say."

"It was a talk I gave at a hundred different book signings and speech-making. Even now, I could do it in my sleep."

"It was a first for me," she said. "And yes, I seriously fell in love with you."

"But you didn't approach me. You didn't even say hello."

She took a deep breath. "You were married then, Russ. I don't do married men. I never have." Her chuckle was without mirth. "I'm no slut—but I'm no virgin, either."

"There are hardly any virgins over the age of fourteen," I said.

She ignored a comment I'd hoped she'd laugh at. She didn't. "You don't know me," she continued, "and I'm sure you're nowhere near in love with me, so if tonight upset you so badly, I'll quietly go away. But I'd rather hang around a little and see if it gets better."

I didn't answer for a few moments until she added, "You'll remember how to fuck all over again."

I rolled back over toward her, and she put a cool hand against my chest. "Slow down, commando," she said. "Another try tonight isn't a good idea. Take a few days, think about it. If it's too much pressure, I'll understand—but I'd hate like hell to lose you."

"I'd hate that too," I said. "But now, just walking free again is only half the problem. I got drawn into a ridiculous mission I can't seem to get out of."

"A mission?"

"That's what I'm calling it," I said.

Then I told her the story about my search for the missing Aubrey Sinden.

It was probably the most uncomfortable moment of my life, worse than hearing of Dayna's death, worse than the trial, the verdict, worse than my first day behind bars. But telling a beautiful woman with whom I'd just had inept and boring sex all about my former mistress I hadn't seen in seven years, about Aubrey Sinden's current disappearance, about my impossible wife. It probably took a half hour to tell—especially lying naked with her in a bed I had not yet grown accustomed to. To me, though, it seemed longer than Salome's tales of a thousand-and-one nights.

We were quiet for a while after I finished. Then Cassidy said, "Were you in love with her, Russ? And are you still?"

I pondered that. Then I said, "No, not really. It was fun and exciting, but nowhere close to *in love*. I was never in love with my own wife, either, though for a short time I thought I was. But I went to prison for her accidental death. Aubrey's married now, and her husband is an ignoramus. He came to me for help."

"Why didn't he contact the police?"

"You'll have to ask him that. But when he backed off, I figured to spend a few days looking for her before I got serious about writing again. She's in my past, a short but shining moment in my life, and I can't just sit on my hands when she's gone missing, and no one is looking for her."

"Gone missing?" she asked. "That could be dangerous. For you, too."

"Because of my record? I suppose. But I committed no crime and don't intend to start now, not even trying to walk and chew gum at the same time."

"Please," she said with a soft little chuckle. "Please tell me you don't chew gum anymore."

I laughed out loud. "Is that the red line you won't cross?"

"Damn right."

"I crossed a few red lines myself," I said. "Mostly with Gaylord Ogilvy. You know who he is?"

"I know who Warren Buffett is, too. It's hard to live in Chicago and not to know about Gaylord Ogilvy. You actually met him? In person?"

"Just a few days ago. Aubrey was his mistress at the same time she was mine, though I only found out about it the second day I was free. Her husband said she was financially involved with him, so I had to get through his Number Two guy, Irvin Greenfield, and I finally got to Gaylord—probably because they both know who I am." I swallowed hard. "Or who I was."

"What did you learn?" Cassidy wanted to know.

"Not a damn thing. The next day, though, two muscle guys walked in here and took me out to the Ogilvy estate to talk with Gaylord's wife."

"And?"

"She offered me a lot of money to drop my search."

"Did you accept it?"

"Hell, no," I said. "I don't have as much money in the bank as Lilith Ogilvy has in her pocket—but I'm not poor. Even if I were, I'd turn her down."

Cassidy covered her eyes with one hand. "And then I came along to mess up your life even more."

"Mess up my life? I'm *so* glad you came along." I took her hand and held it in mine. "Don't desert me, Cassidy. I need you."

"There are lots of women in the world who think you're a literary lion."

"At the moment, I'm a literary prairie dog. But I don't care about them. I care about you—even more because I screwed up so bad, and you didn't hold it against me."

She sat up in bed, pulling the blanket over her breasts. "Circumstantially, you're kind of a born-again virgin."

"Oh, shit!"

"You're out of practice and you weren't expecting it. Take a few days. Focus on looking for this Aubrey person. Don't even think about me or sex. A week ago, you were behind bars. Now it'll take time to feel free again. When you do, call me. I'll be there for you." She got out of bed and walked naked across the room to where she'd tossed her clothes. She had the most beautiful ass I'd ever seen in my life. "Even if you change your mind, call me anyway." She slipped on her bikini panties. "Don't worry. I've waited for you for many years, so I guess I can wait a few more days." She put on her bra. "Or longer."

I got up, too, and shrugged myself into a robe. "I'll walk you back to where you parked your car."

"Don't be silly. I'm a big girl. Besides, it's eleven thirty, and this is Near North. You could walk Rush Street alone at three o'clock in the morning and no one would bother you."

She finished dressing, then stepped into the bathroom for a few seconds to fluff out her hair. I guided her to the door. "I'll miss the hell out of you," I said. "But you're way too kind about it. We have to start all over again."

She twisted her mouth to keep from laughing. "I guess your memory doesn't last for more than twenty minutes. We already started—and I can hardly wait for Step Two."

Then we kissed goodnight—a medium-long kiss, but there was little passion involved. Just caring. Then she waved a small goodbye and moved quietly out the door.

The gentle kiss of those soft lips and the teasing tip of her tongue left me with knees that could barely hold me upright.

* * *

There are times to meet people, spend a certain amount of time with them, even know them for thirty years, and they never really become a friend, just someone who just fills up the gaps in one's life. There are other times when a first meeting lasting ten or fifteen minutes makes them family.

Forever.

When Cassidy Hammond first ran past me at North Avenue Beach, I hardly paid any mind to her, as I was totally wiped out after a long run on the sand. "Pretty girl" popped in and out of my mind within seconds—a flash of movement against the background of a choppy lake and a fairly deserted beach. It was not until she stopped, came back, and told me she'd read all my books that she got my undivided attention.

I find myself most attracted to women who are beautiful in a way most women are not. The ones that make my heart flutter simply don't look like other women. The face comfortably oval. The hair? Like many men, I prefer hair that spills across the pillow, but I love the much shorter look, too. The mouth soft and inviting. The eyes—I couldn't tear myself away from her eyes, which are windows for what hides behind them.

That was Cassidy, in one explosive moment at the beach. Not that she outshines every movie star or high-fashion runway model who ever was. But what beauty there is about her just struck me, hard. I can't explain it—but then few men can when they fall in love at first sight.

How could I fail so miserably? I didn't plan having sex with her just twenty-four hours after I met her. I knew how long it had been and how I needed time to focus, think about it, and wonder whether everything worked properly. It was Cassidy who invited herself to my apartment, but she was no wham-bam-thank-you-ma'am. I figured another drink or two, kiss a lot, and then say goodnight and we'll get together soon, even set a date.

Then, to both our chagrins, we somehow got to the bed-room, my sexual performance closely related to that of a sixteen-year-old boy screwing for the first time. Though she was kind and tender, even saying she looked forward to the next try, I was terrified our kiss goodnight was the last kiss ever.

My late wife had never been family, nor Aubrey, and my adoptive parents were really not blood relations either, because I was biologically conceived and birthed somewhere else.

But Cassidy Hammond, after a brief meeting on the beach, one evening, after one disappointing sexual try, both of us out of breath and dripping perspiration, to me she was family.

It will surprise no one I didn't get one minute of sleep that night, tossing and turning and taking a cold shower and even imbibing two more drinks of single-malt Scotch, neat. Nothing would help, and I was in the worst turmoil of my life, even during those first months in prison.

Still an only child. Still an only adult. The only ones sustaining me were the characters I created out of my imagination and put down on paper to share with the rest of the world—and they always did exactly what I asked them to do.

I hadn't even done *that* in more than seven years.

In the morning, I made an entire pot of coffee and drank it down. My breakfast consisted of two pieces of buttered toast, though I only ate only one. Then, dressed casually, I went outside and strolled down to Michigan Boulevard, the Drake Hotel on one corner and Lake Shore Drive and the Oak Avenue Beach on the others. During the wintertime, the city actually hangs ropes on the side of the Drake Hotel to grab onto so the wind off the lake doesn't blow you clear off your feet. It wasn't wintertime yet, so the familiar intersection perked me up and made me glad Tana Phillips had found me a place to live within a heartbeat of this familiar Chicago spot.

Too much coffee already. I didn't want to get sand in my shoes again, and it was way too early for bar-hopping. Those who drink in saloons at eight o'clock in the morning have a real problem. I began walking south, toward the Chicago River, breathing deep and thinking hard about Aubrey Sinden.

There were four possibilities, considering the tricks and

twists I gave my own work so one had to read to the very last page. First, Aubrey probably did not skip out, leaving all possessions behind her, and not even a simple goodbye to her idiotic husband. Second, she could have been kidnapped, but if so, why, and by whom, as after more than two weeks, there was no demand for ransom. Third, I doubted she took her own life. Suicides don't go somewhere far away from everything and anybody, to a place no one would dream of looking, and check themselves out, not even leaving a note. Most unpleasantly last was Aubrey had been murdered.

Cassidy Hammond warned me continuing my search might be dangerous, but I didn't think so. When Aubrey first went missing, I was still behind iron bars, so I'd have nothing to apologize for.

And that gave me another idea.

Nobody has paper telephone books anymore—right up there with the long-ago candlestick telephone or actual dials to twirl, or the party lines—so I powered up the computer and got myself onto Google so I could write down the number I wanted. I stared at the piece of paper, and my hand was trembling. I had to convince myself I had the balls to make such a call.

It took me ten minutes, during which I broke out in a sweat. I'm a free man. Not on parole, I guess I've been pardoned. I can do any damn thing I want to if it isn't illegal. But my lower back still ached, and probably would forever from sleeping on a prison cot for a good chunk of my adulthood, and I was frozen in my shoes staring at that number and my cell-phone.

Finally, taking such a deep breath most of the air in the room wound up in my lungs, I tapped out the number.

A man with a gruff voice answered. It was a new voice to me, but for the past seven years, gruff voices were the only ones I heard. This sounded like a police desk sergeant with a slight Irish tilt to it.

I forced myself to say: "This is Russell Reinert calling. May I please speak to Detective Easton Dorn?"

CHAPTER NINETEEN

In 1871, according to frivolous myth, Mrs. O'Leary's cow kicked over a lantern in the barn and started the Chicago Fire that burned down most of the city. No one blames Mrs. O'Leary or the cow anymore because they quickly rebuilt Chicago to be one of the most beautiful urban cities in the country. But let's face it, that was a hundred and fifty years ago, and those then-new buildings grew old and tired, and now sag with age and disappointment.

The police precinct I entered that afternoon was not built right after the big fire—but close enough so once inside you can smell, taste and feel the sweat, farts, body odors and the fear of criminals who walked inside—and some never came out again, either.

The first time, I went in with my hands cuffed behind me, under arrest for killing my wife. Everybody knew I was in Milwaukee when my house burned down, so I didn't strike the match—apparently Dayna *did* turn on the gas—-but celebrities are thin-skinned, and more vulnerable than everyone else. The Winnetka house was not in Chicago proper, but the District Attorney of Cook County, who planned to lock me away forever, believed my prosecution would be more fitting if it happened in downtown Chicago.

Now, just one week out of prison, I found myself walking

into this particular precinct again—of my own free will—to meet up with the cop who arrested me in the first place.

Police Detective First Grade Easton Dorn was a tall, dark African American who looked tougher than the worst steak you ever bought from a guy who stored them in his automobile trunk. I hadn't seen him since they shipped me away, but sitting across from him now in his semi-private office, I couldn't help notice the changes.

He was close to my own age but towered over me for two or three inches. Maybe about fifteen added pounds since last I saw him, which didn't make him look fat but even tougher to walk around if you foolishly decided to ignore him. His hairline had climbed a few inches, and what remained had turned salt-and-pepper, and he'd grown a beard and mustache, also semi-gray. When he'd arrested me, I'd noticed him wearing a wedding ring, and figured he was one of the nice-guy policemen who didn't get snockered every night after work and then go home and smack the crap out of his wife because she folded his clean T-shirts the wrong way. But now his left hand was bare. I felt for him. It's hard to be married to a cop.

I'd never seen him interact with other people besides his then-partner whose name I'd forgotten, but I think he'd smiled only once in 1986 and had forgotten how since then. He sure wasn't smiling when I entered his office, but of course no police officer in his right mind is glad to see someone they've arrested for murder and spent time in prison for it.

He was wearing a light blue dress shirt with small red lines in it. Open at the neck, tie pulled down past the second button. Just like cops in movies.

Neither of us offered to shake hands.

"I couldn't believe you wanted to see me, Reinert," Dorn said. "I figure you're not here today to kill me out of revenge. Idiotic thing to try in a police station in the middle of the morning—and whatever else you are, you're not dumb." He stroked his Van Dyke beard with his fingers, making me believe he hadn't been wearing it that long. "I even read a few of your books after you went to prison. They weren't bad, except your private eyes are heroes and you make cops look like fucking morons."

"Mostly they aren't morons—but that's in real life. I make up fiction." Then I added with intensity, "And I never killed anyone. I suppose you don't buy it, though."

"I don't buy or not buy. I investigate, and I arrest. In your case, I was ordered to do so. I don't judge, that's not my job. Other people judge—and convict."

"Well, you did your job with me, Detective Dorn—so I didn't come to kill you. I have no revenge in mind."

"Then why are you here?" Dorn demanded.

"I have—a problem."

"You want the name of a good psychiatrist?"

I ignored that. "Do you remember a woman who testified for the prosecution at my trial? Aubrey Sinden?"

"The name doesn't ring a bell," he said, "but I recall the only woman who testified for the defense. She was your mistress while you were married, right? Everyone thought you killed your wife to be with this broad full time."

"Not broad," I corrected him, my tone abrasive. "Her name is Aubrey Sinden. Aubrey with a B."

"I don't care how you spell it—but that relationship got you convicted."

"I realize that."

"So, what have I got to do with it?"

"Nothing—except Aubrey disappeared a week before I was scheduled to get out of prison."

Easton Dorn frowned, turned halfway away from me, and thoughtfully chewed on his thumb for a while. Then he said, "You weren't around when this woman went missing. Did you plan on taking up with her again?"

"After seven years? Hardly. She's married now. That's how I found out she's gone. Her husband asked if I'd try to find her."

"Her husband?"

"His name is Cole Cabot."

"Sounds like a real douche bag," Dorn mused, "running to a mystery writer for help who got out of the can hours earlier, not to the police."

"You'd have to ask him that. But I found out a few other things from him."

"Like?"

I breathed deeply. "You know who Gaylord Ogilvy is."

His whole face changed, and he swung the chair around to face me, sitting as straight and regally as a king, and fixed me with one of his don't-fuck-with-a-cop glares. "Gaylord Ogilvy? This Aubrey person was somehow mixed up with Gaylord Ogilvy?" He placed both palms on the desk in front of him. I'd never realized before how large his hands were. "Tell me all about it, Reinert."

Easton Dorn was quiet after I finished. I watched his frowning face as he tried putting all the pieces together I'd laid out for him. He wasn't a cop who shot first and asked questions later. He'd rung the bell politely at the door of my half-burnt house and informed me I was under arrest for the murder of Dayna Reinert. He didn't physically hurt me, except when he cuffed my hands behind me too tightly, and deposited me in the back of his car. Businesslike rather than rude, Dorn never swore at me, or called me names, never warned what might happen to me in prison, and even put his hand on the top of my head when I got in the car to make sure I didn't bump it too hard.

Few cops would allow a convicted felon he'd arrested for murder to come sit in his office with a strange tale to spin. Therefore, I don't think he ever believed I was guilty of killing my wife.

Eventually his face relaxed. I said, "Any thoughts, Detective?"

He nodded slowly. "Gaylord Ogilvy is a shitheel."

"Everyone in Chicago knows that already."

"When this Aubrey was your mistress, you had no idea she was also in a relationship with Ogilvy?"

"No."

"Does that bother you now? Sexually, I mean?"

I lifted and lowered my shoulders. "It was more than seven years ago. Since then, she got married, and her husband says her business with Ogilvy now is just that—business. They aren't sleeping together anymore."

Dorn said, "This husband of hers is a dumb jag-off."

"That may be, detective—but he came to me for help."

"And not the police."

"Not the police," I said.

"Well, he wouldn't come to me, anyway. I'm in homicide. Look, Reinert—I have no contact with Ogilvy or his crowd. But a couple of his so-called marginal people have disappeared without a trace. My guess is they ripped off the company, deposited their ill-gotten gains in a numbered-only account in a Cayman Island bank, and are living someplace like Costa Rica where they can't be legally extradited by the United States of America."

"I can't see myself living alone in Costa Rica," I said.

"I can't see you getting involved in something like this, fresh out of prison after less than a week, with the richest and most powerful guy between New York and San Francisco. You're already in trouble, and every Chicago cop itches to arrest you for littering—including me." Dorn pushed himself away from his desk. "Quit trying to be a private eye, Reinert. You're busting your balls for nothing. Write another book, okay? That's what you do best."

My eyebrows arched skyward. "I can't believe you actually read my books?"

"A few, after they took you away from your typewriter."

"Typewriter? Seriously?"

"Seriously—I'm just an old-fashioned cop." He reached up, and with one thumb softly wiped the very corner of his mouth. I never saw anyone do that besides Humphrey Bogart.

"Tell you what," he went on. "Write another book and I guarantee I'll buy it—assuming you won't write cops up to be morons." He suppressed a grin. "But I only make a police department salary, so I'll wait for the paperback." He stood. "Now pound salt, will you? I've got murderers to catch."

Still no handshake. Oh, well.

It wasn't until I was home, stripping out of my suit-and-tie outfit and into denims and a sweatshirt I remembered telling Dorn the story of my own "investigation," I 'd mentioned my meeting with Lilith Ogilvy at the mansion, but forgot to tell him she had sent two clones of the Incredible Hulk to pick me up and deliver me.

Strange. A phone call would have done the same thing.

CHAPTER TWENTY

I had one more person to question, so I made the phone call. I didn't give my name to the secretary, or whoever she was—-if I had, I would never have been connected. We argued for more than a minute, but I guess I wore her down because she finally gave in and connected me.

The gentleman I was calling sounded pleased to be talking to me and invited me to his office, but I insisted on going someplace for lunch where we wouldn't be noticed. I still was not familiar with most of the restaurants, so he suggested one close to me in Near North, far enough away from downtown so nobody would catch on. Lunch time: one o'clock.

Dean Bosley was a few years younger than I, and a few inches taller. So light-skinned, I guessed he might be the child of an interracial marriage. After making the appointment, I Googled him and learned he went to the University of Michigan for his bachelor's and master's degree, and University of Chicago for his law doctorate.

He somehow got noticed by Tana Phillips, hired, and within five years' time handling his own roster of clients.

"I wouldn't want Tana to know about this meeting," he said after we ordered lunch. Neither of us took advantage of the bar; I ordered coffee, and he got a ginger ale. "You're one of her biggest clients as well as a very good friend—but she wouldn't want me talking to you about another client. I heard from her Aubrey Cabot was missing, and I'll do anything to help her. To help you, Mr. Reinert."

"I appreciate it—and it's just Russ."

"Russ, then." He grinned, slightly embarrassed. "I don't much read fiction—but I'll catch up with your books one of these days. It was Aubrey's husband who first contacted you about finding her? Cole Cabot, I mean."

"If not for him, I'd never know she's missing," I said. "The last time I saw or talked to her was shortly after I went to prison. She visited me a few times, but we both decided it was time to move on—emotionally."

"I can't imagine why Cabot contacted you."

"Maybe because I write about private detectives, I act it, too. But that lasted for one day before he changed his mind." I relaxed against the back of our booth and said, "Are you Cabot's attorney, too?"

"No. I hardly know him." Dean frowned. "Why don't you let it go, Russ? You've got a new place to live, a new laptop, you should be writing a new book. Tana is the best lawyer in Chicago—and that includes me. You have adjustments to make. Forget Aubrey Sinden and live your own life again."

"We were lovers—a long time ago. That doesn't ever really go away."

"Tana explained that to me—but I can't discuss Aubrey with you, either. Lawyer-client privilege."

"Then tell me this. Did Aubrey work at Ogilvy Corporation full-time? Or Part-time?"

"Neither," Dean Bosley said. "I don't know how often she went into their office, or whether she worked at home, but every so often they'd issue her a pretty substantial check for doing whatever it was she was doing."

"Were you aware Aubrey was Gaylord Ogilvy's mistress?"

He nodded. "Tana told me she used to be—before her marriage. After that, from what I hear, Aubrey and the corporation were strictly business."

"Then why in hell would they kidnap her?" I asked.

"Are you saying they did?"

I just shrugged. "I can't figure out anyone else doing it."

Dean Bosley nervously straightened some of the silverware on the table, took out an expensive ballpoint pen, and fiddled with it into several different positions, clicking it open and closed. "You're an ex-con. You have no clue what Aubrey was doing while you were gone."

"You might be right," I said. "Does she have a safe deposit box somewhere?"

He nodded. "A bank here in Chicago."

I wanted to know, "What if something's happened to her and someone will need to empty that box? Who has the key and the number? Her husband?"

"No. This law firm has it. Tana knows where it is—and so does one other partner in this company. Not me."

"Is she cashing those big checks Ogilvy is giving her and keeping the money in that box?"

"I don't know," Bosley said. "Maybe she's got a numbered account in Switzerland or someplace. I doubt she sticks it all under her mattress."

"That might piss off Cole Cabot."

"Maybe. But if she dies before he does, he won't inherit much money." He winked. "I wrote her will, but I can't tell you what's in it. That's the law."

I attempted to cross my legs, but there wasn't enough room in the booth. "I'd give my right nut to know what she does for all that money."

"As I understand it, she owns several big companies under the Ogilvy umbrella."

It took me a while to close my mouth after his comment jarred it open. "Why would she do that?"

"I doubt she actually owns any of those companies. They're mostly Ogilvy-owned outlets for constructing gigantic buildings—

some of them in foreign countries like Argentina or Belgium. I'm just guessing, here."

"Buying those companies would have cost millions," I said. "Billions."

Bosley's eyebrows lifted skyward. "I don't think Aubrey had billions. Millions, maybe. If I had a million or two, I wouldn't build a luxury condo complex in Buenos Aires. I'd buy a nice house overlooking the lake and live in it. Cabot wouldn't gain much by doing away with her."

I already had the money to live in a house by the sea in Buenos Aires if I chose to, but all I remembered from taking Spanish in high school was *'El burro es un animal.'* That wouldn't fly very well in Buenos Aires. I said, "If Cole Cabot did anything to her, why would he ask me to find her in the first place?"

Bosley explained, "He'd be a desperate man. He lives well because she does. A hell of a lot of men marry rich women because it serves their purposes. If Aubrey Sinden Cabot dies, Cole is out on the street."

I took a few bites of lunch, quietly running all this through my mind. I was reaching a dead end, and it was driving me nuts. I said, "So Ogilvy put up the money but let her sign the ownership contracts. Why?"

"Tax purposes, I imagine. Or maybe he bought them up so no one else in the world can."

"That's fucking crazy," I said.

"Gaylord Ogilvie is no Dalai Lama. He's a monster with the deepest pockets in the world. He owns everything. For all I know, he even owns this fucking restaurant—or the building it's in. Everything he does makes him more money. I cautioned Aubrey, but those deals made her rich. If Ogilvy paid me as much as he pays her, I'd sign those contracts in a New York minute."

I scratched my head in frustration. Aubrey goes from part-time mistress to part-time *partner?* Has she vanished because of money? I put down my fork. "Dean, if this is all true, why would Ogilvy kidnap her? Or kill her?"

"Easy there, big guy," Dean Bosley said in the tone parents used to scold their children. "He's a miserable asshole, and everyone knows it, but there's no record of him killing any-one—or having them killed."

"I've heard rumors. People in his aura disappearing without a trace."

"That's because he threatened them with ruination in the courts unless they got out of town, fast. I know of one guy in particular Tana represents. He was a real estate guy with a great record of collecting clients and buying and selling upper-price homes. He was no millionaire, but he had money. Five years ago, in the middle of a real-estate deal, he suddenly left town. The last I heard, he lives in Ottumwa, Iowa—running two or three dry cleaning stores."

"Leave or get killed? Is that what you're saying?"

Bosley shook his head. "Leave or get humiliated in court and maybe go to prison—that's more like it." He filled his lungs with air and expelled it slowly. "I wonder what it's like in Ottumwa, Iowa."

"This real estate cat left everything behind?"

"No—he packed some up, but he left an expensive apart-ment he owned, right on the lake. Tana hired a real estate lady to sell the apartment, but the on-site manager has no clue where he is."

"How do you know that, and his manager doesn't?"

"Because I'm a damn good lawyer," Dean Bosley said severe-ly, "but Tana's is ten times the lawyer I am." He stood up. "Let it go, Russ. You've been out of prison less than a week. Stop being such a goddamn sucker!"

CHAPTER TWENTY-ONE

One nice thing about having a family—I've heard about it—is basically they tell you the truth. Sure—little white lies, maybe, like "I didn't take the last Pepsi in the fridge," or "Don't look at me, I didn't wear your favorite sweater."

Little white lies from close family members really don't hurt anyone, and maybe thirty years later, someone will bring one up from the past and everyone chuckles about it.

I didn't find myself in that situation. The only person who told me the pure unadulterated truth was Ember Pollard.

But Cole Cabot, Irvin Greenfield, Gaylord Ogilvy, his wife Lilith and her two muscle boys Hayden Fantos and Walter Yellen, my ex-agent Owen Fullmer, CPA Bryce DeBower, my parole officer Roman Bellini, cop who arrested me Easton Dorn, and Aubrey's attorney, Dean Bosley have all either lied to me or else chose not to tell the truth.

Tana Phillips and her NFL veteran husband Jack, had might not have lied, but I believe they lied by omission rather than a bald-faced untruth.

Cassidy Hammond didn't count. Neither directly nor indirectly, she was the only person I've spoken to since getting out of prison who had absolutely no connection to Aubrey Sinden Cabot.

There's something about her that makes me want to drop the

whole Aubrey search and concentrate on being with her. She'd jump-started my heart, and I fucked up badly—sexually. Not my fault, as I was forbidden that particular game for many years, but I knew I had to do something about it. If you were a quarterback a long time ago, and you decide to get back into the business of football after many non-playing years, trying a Hail Mary pass or taking the first snap yourself and running like hell for the first down is not a good idea. Won't do much good with your sixty-year-old legs and your sixty-year-old throwing arm.

I'm nowhere near sixty, but I am indeed out of practice.

Where is my new upstairs neighbor who is single, mature, drop dead beautiful, and came and knocked on my door with home-made chocolate chip-oatmeal cookies she just made herself as a way to welcome me to my new home? Where is my dear little sister with the best friend who is recently divorced, gorgeous, a lover of private eye fiction who's read every word I've ever written, patient as hell, and lonely just like me? But my upstairs neighbor, whom I have yet to meet, is apparently gay, from what Tana told me—and I don't *have* a dear little sister. I don't have a dear little anyone.

As for The-Aubrey-Who-Wasn't-There, I'd hit a dead end. More frustrating. I had no idea where to go from here. Gaylord Ogilvy wouldn't talk to me again, and everyone else has frozen me out, too. I Googled for background information on everybody I'd talked to. The more complete info was only for the old man, and it read like the biography of a long-dead movie star. His father was extremely rich doing the same thing his son is doing, and left almost everything to him rather than to his younger brother, who drank himself to death. Gaylord married Lilith many moons ago. No children.

I wondered then whether Ogilvy would have his billions buried with him, or burn them up along with his own cremation rather than leave it to anyone.

I was startled to hear the doorbell ring. I flipped on the

monitor, which showed whoever might be visiting via a hidden camera, shocked to see it was Detective Easton Dorn, along with a younger white guy who probably was his partner.

I buzzed them in. The skin on the back of my hands tingled with fright.

I waited until their feet stopped moving on the stairs and opened the door. "Hello, Detective."

"Reinert," Easton Dorn said. "This is my partner, Detective Delaware. Can we come in?"

I nodded. "If I said no, you'd kick down the door, anyway." I stepped back, and they came into the apartment. "What can I do for you, Detectives?"

"Nice place," Dorn said. "Different from where you were recently living."

"Yeah," I said, "but I really miss that small room I shared with another guy who snored louder than a rock brand, and whacked off every morning, where I could live and sleep and shit without hardly turning around."

"This place is a big step up."

"Because I put all my money where the state of Illinois couldn't get it."

"I think I heard that somewhere. Good job, Reinert, you're still rich." He took a moment to study me as though I were a dead insect in biology class. Then he said, "If you're not too busy, I wonder if you can come downtown to the precinct with us. There are a few questions we need to ask you."

"You can't ask them here? More comfortable than in your office?"

Detective Delaware was perhaps vocally challenged, because he spoke for the first time, just one word. "Protocol," he rumbled.

Now my skin was tingling all over my body. "Am I under arrest?"

"Not at all. We'd have you cuffed already if we were arresting you. This is just a quiet meeting to talk things over."

"A quiet meeting." I was suddenly aware of a stiff neck. "Shall I bring my toothbrush and a pair of clean underwear?"

"Aren't you silly?" Dorn said. He turned to his partner. "Isn't he silly?"

Detective Delaware spoke his second word. "Hilarious," he said.

I expected to be led to Dorn's office again, but they surprised me and put me in an interview room with a giant mirror on one wall I was certain was a two-way mirror. The entire police department probably gaped at me from the next room. That made me even more nervous.

Easton Dorn sat across from me, and Detective Delaware leaned against the doorway. I had no idea what his first name was, nor did I give a damn.

"So," Dorn said cheerily, "you want a coffee? Coke? Plain water?"

"We could have had coffee at my place, Detective. I had a whole pot brewing."

"Yeah, but it's so much more elegant where we are."

"True," I said. "And with an audience, too." I looked up at the mirror and waved. "Hey, guys," I called out, "and women too, if there are any. Get comfortable."

Dorn put a small pocket recorder on the desk. "I want to make sure I don't miss anything, Reinert. I hope you won't mind."

He switched it on and I heard the soft movement. I said, "Record what you want, Detective, but I don't sing."

"This is Detective Dorn with Detective Delaware. We're speaking with Russell Reinert." He gave the time and date, then looked at me. "Ready?"

"Fire away," I answered.

"Mr. Reinert, are you familiar with a man named Cole Cabot?"

"I am. I've met him a few times in the past week. Never before."

"Where did you meet him?"

"Twice on a park bench right by the Viking ship in Lincoln Park, and once in my home."

"What did you talk about?"

"Shoes and ships and sealing wax," I recited, "and cabbages and kings."

"Very amusing. Did you two speak about Aubrey Sinden Cabot? His wife?"

"Her name came up, yes."

"When was the last time you saw her?"

"Seven years ago. She visited me in prison."

"That's when you were incarcerated for involuntary manslaughter?"

"I'm sure," I said, "your buddies behind the mirror have my police record right in front of them. No problems, no demerits, no time in The Hole."

"The Hole?"

I made a face at Dorn. "Solitary confinement. Like *Birdman of Alcatraz.*"

"Have you seen Aubrey Cabot since your release from prison?"

"No. She's married, so there was no reason for us to get together."

"You were intimate at one time?"

"Is this going to turn into audio porn, Detective?"

"Don't be a smart ass."

"Then don't ask me who I had sex with seven or eight years ago."

"You know she's missing, don't you?"

I nodded. "Mr. Cabot informed me of that."

"Why would he find you, a complete stranger, and tell you that."

"Why don't you ask him?"

Delaware broke in. "We're asking you, asshole."

"Talk dirty some more, Detective. Potty-mouthed cops get me horny."

He broke away from the wall, eyes blazing, fists knotted, about to put me in the hospital, but Dorn waved him back. "Mr. Reinert, you told me earlier Cabot asked you to help look for his wife. Is that true?"

I relaxed against the back of the hard chair. "True."

"And the next day he changed his mind and told you to back off?"

"He did."

"But you continued to search for Aubrey Cabot by yourself."

"Yes."

"Why?"

"Because," I answered, "at one time, long ago, she was important to me, so I was worried about her and continued poking around, looking for her."

"But Cole Cabot told you not to."

"I don't give a good goddamn what he told me."

"Have you been intimate with anyone else since your release?"

"None of your fucking business," I said, anger flaring up inside my gut like too big a swallow of Mexican hot sauce. "Lock me up again and throw away the key, but it's none of your fucking business."

"Be cool," Dorn said.

"You, too."

Dorn pushed the pocket recorder a bit closer to me. "So you didn't see Cabot after that?"

"As I said, one more time, in my apartment."

"But you didn't part friends?"

"We never were friends."

"Then you parted enemies?"

"No, Detective. Not friends and not enemies. You aren't my friend, either, nor is Detective Maryland."

"Delaware," Dorn corrected.

"One state is as good as another, especially on the Atlantic Coast. Cabot and I are not friends, but not enemies, either." I shook my head. "I hope to hell we're not enemies."

"That remains to be seen."

"Snotty remark, Detective Dorn."

Easton Dorn warned, "This is an interview, not a pissing contest."

"Okay, I apologize. Now, will somebody tell me why I'm here?"

"Since Cabot left your apartment, you haven't seen him?"

"No."

"Talked to him?"

"No."

"You've heard nothing about him since then?"

"No. I've hardly thought about him. Why?"

The two detectives looked at each other, communicating with very subtle head movements, almost invisible use of their eyes. Finally, Delaware nodded slightly, and Dorn turned back to me.

"Why, Mr. Reinert? Because at eight o'clock this morning, Cole Cabot was found floating face down, dead, just off Navy Pier."

It was suddenly difficult for me to swallow. "What?" I tried to say.

Detective Dorn nodded brusquely. "That's right," he said. "His face looked like a body bag at a boxer's gym, three of the fingers on his right hand were broken. Whoever it was who bounced him around like a kick-ball finally got sick of it." He drew one finger across his Adam's apple and made one of those ghastly squawking sounds. "Then he apparently cut his throat."

CHAPTER TWENTY-TWO

The thought, accompanied by Dorn's gesture, made me want to vomit. Someone had tortured Cole before actually cutting open his throat, severing one or both of the carotid arteries that supplied blood to his face, voice, and brain. I saw quite a few attacks and a couple of killings while in the stir, but they were clean, quick kills—a homemade knife to the heart. Nothing like what happened to Cabot. I'll not fall asleep for a long time, thinking about it.

I didn't like Cabot. I only met him often enough to tell me he was a fucking dork, living off his wife who made a hell of a lot more money than he did. I even had the urge to smack him, though I didn't.

But torture? Throat-slashing? That changed everything. He was a human being, and did not deserve to die in such a horrible way. Forget my jury conviction, my records, my so-called personal history laid bare by most of the major newspapers in the United States. I felt I lost a friend—only one of the very few people I'd spoken to since I walked away from Joliet. I also feared I'd be thrown back in the slammer and put on trial again.

I wanted to run, wanted to hide—somewhere on the other side of the world. I wanted to leap from my chair and tell both these detectives what I thought of them—but that could get me shot and killed on the spot. My better sense wrestled with my bad temper—and won.

Instead, I remained seated in this interrogation room, with a glare and even a truculent nod to whatever cops lurked behind the window, and a quick, nervous glance at Detective Delaware. "Why am I in your precinct, Dorn?" I demanded, my hands turning into fists gripping the edge of the table. "Are you arresting me for murder?"

"If you were under arrest," Easton Dorn answered, "you'd be in handcuffs and leg chains. But you had difficulties with Cole Cabot this past week, and now he' s dead. You've already committed manslaughter, so…"

"I never committed anything, and you damn well know it. I served my time, even though I was innocent. You're going to hang this one on me, too?"

"You're here to talk, Reinert, and that's what we're doing. You're a 'person of interest' and we needed to hear your point of view. That's how murder investigations open up—and there's nothing we can do about it. Don't get your bowels in an uproar—we're looking in other areas as well."

"What other areas?"

"Areas," Dorn said, "that are none of your business.'

Detective Delaware chimed in—his first sentence. "Cabot's death is a homicide, which means it's our investigation, not yours. If you get in our way, we'll be up your ass sideways. Go home. Get a hobby. Collect stamps. Wear your ass out watching porn. Bet on football games. Get a cat. Write another book. Keep busy, Reinert, and out of our case. In Chicago you're as popular with the police as a decayed tooth needing a root canal."

I couldn't stop myself from saying, "Sheer poetry, Detective Delaware."

Dorn said, "Look at it logically. Cole Cabot came to you to search for his missing wife. Then he asked you to stop—but you didn't. Now he's dead. You'd even put this in one of your goddamn mystery books, right?"

"I'm not writing a book or looking for Cabot's killer. I'm trying to find his disappeared wife."

"Call me crazy," Dorn said, not really suggesting it, "but the two things are related, so you understand why you're on our list."

More than being a "person of interest" in the Cabot murder, my fear twisted all the insides of me into a throbbing ball of terror.

I rubbed my hand over my face as if I'd just walked into a spider's web. "Where did you find Cole Cabot again?" I asked. I heard my voice quivering and had to stop and swallow a few times before Dorn thought I was handing him myself on a silver platter.

"I didn't find him, somebody who works on Navy Pier did. Floating face down at about nine o'clock this morning. But rigor mortis had come and gone, so he'd been dead for at least twenty-four hours.'"

"I haven't been on Navy Pier for the last fifteen years, Detective."

Dorn laced the fingers of both his hands together and stretched them, his knuckles making the sound of castanets. "That won't help you, because whatever blood Cabot lost is now in the middle of Lake Michigan, so he was killed elsewhere. The medical examiner is doing an autopsy as we speak."

"I've never used a knife except for cutting steak at the Palm Restaurant."

"Rare?"

"What?"

"You like steaks rare?"

"Medium," I said. "Even medium well if it's a big steak like a porterhouse."

Easton Dorn blew out a chunk of air from under his lower lip and shook his head sadly. "One more reason why I don't like you."

"You prefer them rare?"

"Bloody."

"Me, too," said Detective Delaware.

I said, "Aubrey is involved with the businesses of the Ogilvy Corporation. Cabot was her husband. Check out the Ogilvys. You'll get a slightly better welcome than I did, in case you get tired of hassling ex-cons who could buy both of you with his pocket change. Just flash your badges at Mr. O. himself, boys— he'd love that."

Easton Dorn sighed once again and closed his eyes. Then he opened them again and looked not at me but at Detective Delaware.

"If you'd be kind enough to drive Mr. Reinert back home, Detective, I'd greatly appreciate it."

Delaware pushed himself away from the wall. "If I spend another half hour alone with this dickwad, you'll damn well buy me a dinner. A big, expensive one, too—with steaks that are bloody rare."

Gripping my arm above the elbow as tight as he could, Delaware led me out into the hallway, past the next door behind which I knew several other cops had observed me through the two-way mirror. I thought for a wild, insane moment to knock on the door and say goodbye to those mirror-peepers, but decided it was a poor idea.

In the car I'd been driven to the precinct, I was told to sit in the back with Dorn while Delaware drove. I thought that would make me feel like a white knight, going home in a limousine with my own driver, except the car was a four-year-old Chevy Malibu and the chauffeur wore a cheap suit, scuffed shoes, and smelled like old cigarette butts.

He reverted back to his monosyllabic vocabulary. Not a word out of him until he pulled up in front of my Oak Street brownstone. I got halfway out and my manners got the better of me. "Thanks for the ride, Detective. Much appreciated."

"Right," Delaware grunted, and roared off into traffic,

leaving tire skid marks on the street and me with a nose full of car exhaust.

After I got home, I took at least an hour just sitting in my recliner, hoping my hands would stop shaking and I'd once more feel relatively safe. After a jarring shot of fresh apple juice, I booted up the laptop and began searching for Cole Cabot. His wife disappears, and my first mission, I guess one can call it, was to set out looking for her. Then he's murdered. I obviously can't get caught up in finding Cabot's killer—it's a police matter and against the law. But you have to be a raving lunatic not to realize there is a definite connection—and Detectives Dorn and Delaware were not raving lunatics..

Not much information about Cabot on the Internet—certainly nothing on Twitter. I hardly knew how to use Twitter. I've never twatted.

I've never been a Wikipedia junkie. Anybody with half a brain for techno-bullshit can go onto anyone else's Wikipedia page and add or subtract whatever they chose to. I'm certain along with praise for my best-selling novels, any Wikipedia reader now knows I was seven years incarcerated for a killing I did not commit.

Odd, though, no stranger or longtime Facebook "friend" has contacted me since they freed me, to give their opinion of manslaughter of one's spouse. Let's hope no one ever will.

Back to Cole Cabot on Wikipedia, though. His birth date was announced, happening in Cambridge, Mass. Otherwise, he is a completely unknown and very distant member of the famed Boston Cabot family. I guessed when he was younger, he must have done something which got that powerful, political and high society aristocracy mad as hell at him, so much he had to exit Boston and never stick his nose above Mystic River water again.

Not much about his career, because he doesn't have one. He

has a job. So does almost everyone else in this country who is not in a so-called royal family and will not get a Wikipedia page. One sentence informing the Wikipedians he married Aubrey Sinden, listing the day and date.

As long as I was online, I clicked onto my own Facebook page. Not a bad photo of me that was at least nine years old, sitting on a big rock on the Lake Michigan beach up near Devon Avenue. A few threads looked interesting, and I figured out several of them were from Tana Phillips—just to keep my name alive. No one mentioned I was a convicted criminal.

So where could I go now? Aubrey's dry cleaner? Her podiatrist? Her window washer? Her gynecologist?

Fuck it, I thought—I've gone as far as I can. Where she'd gone to, nobody knows or cares. As for the murder of Cole Cabot, that's for the cops to investigate, not me. I was through. Finished. Move on to something else. Maybe my next book!

I clicked onto my Notebook. My ideas over the last seven years were damn near impossible to plow through. Some of them seemed logical, but most of them were snippets, and damn few were about people. In the old days I either carried a Spiral notepad or a pocket recorder to record whatever I saw, including strange-looking people. In my Joliet years, though, the only people I saw were hardened criminals—and I was damned if I'd write a book about prison. Why would I want to spend another year revisiting the worst period of my life?

I closed the laptop and stared at it for a long while, but it wasn't magic and it wasn't going to turn on again with the information I needed just because I wanted it to. I walked around a bit, then went into the kitchen, but there were so few dirty dishes in the sink running the dishwasher for them would be bizarre, so I washed them by hand. Then I sat by my living room window, looking out at busy Oak Street. There was plenty to do out there or in the rest of Near North, but doing them by myself would make loneliness and frustration ten times worse.

Maybe, I pondered, I should go out and grab an old lady's purse and run like hell, or steal a big tube of moisturizing lotion from the drugstore so I could get arrested and sent back to Joliet, where at least I knew a lot of people and could talk with them.

Bad people.

The decent ones like Denver Tolliver, mostly nerds and dorks who got railroaded into prison for having a bit more marijuana than was legal, or went six months without paying their rent because they'd lost their jobs and had no income, were fellow inmates I rarely saw or socialized with. They were usually locked up in a special area, a "neighborhood" all their own at the other end of Joliet with others like themselves—tokers and shoplifters—so they might not be attacked, mauled, raped, or even murdered by the bad guys.

The ones I lived with.

By the time I'd worn myself out examining the internet in vain, it was early evening and time to eat. I checked what was in the fridge, but nothing excited me. Besides, I needed some face-to-face conversation, even if it was only a waitress or a bartender. I did go out, strolled around Near North for a time, and found a restaurant I'd never heard of back when I lived in Chicago. It looked good. Not fancy, not suit-and-tie, but then that wasn't the kind of place I'd ever liked before. I went inside.

The waitress was probably a few years older than I was, but pleasant and cheerful, even though she had no idea who I was. I ordered a beginner salad, lamb chops and a baked potato. I also ordered single malt Scotch, straight up with only one ice cube, but they didn't have any single malt Scotch, so I had to settle for Makers Mark bourbon.

It was a few minutes after eight when I arrived back home—and a large, young African American man was sitting on the outside steps. Muscular, military buzz cut, medium brown, his look was uncertain but friendly.

"Are you Mr. Reinert?" He stood up. He was taller than me,

sporting a pull-over sweater over a pink shirt. He was more than twenty years my junior. "Mr. Russell Reinert?"

"Yes, I am," I said.

Then he smiled and stuck out his hand for a shake. "Great to meet you, sir," he said. "I'm Perwin Tolliver. My dad is Denver Tolliver. He called home a few days ago to talk to my mom and me. He says you're his best friend."

CHAPTER TWENTY-THREE

I've known for years Denver had a wife and child in Chicago, but he didn't talk about them much. I don't believe he mentioned his son's first name more than twice in all the years I hung out with him in prison. Now that his kid found me, as he sat in my living room drinking bottled water, I wondered where his first name came from. I've never heard of another 'Perwin' in my lifetime. "How did you know where I live?" I asked.

"My dad suggested I get it from the parole board downtown. I visited the office, but none of the parole bosses would talk to me, so I kinda turned on the charm with one of the receptionists. She was old enough to be my mother, or maybe even my grandmother, but I know how to bat my eyes and flirt, so finally she looked it up for me."

Interesting thought. He was young and quite handsome, and probably lots of women his own age melted with one look from those big brown eyes. He was a strong guy—not as huge and ominous-looking as his father, but large enough anyone might think twice before crossing him. "She deliberately went to the little girl's room and left the paperwork on her desk so I could copy the address. So—here I am."

"Here you are," I said. "Do you have a hot date set up with this grandmother?"

He laughed. "I didn't want your address *that* bad."

"I see your point. So—what are you doing with your life at the moment?"

"Sure. Second year at college—the East West University, right there on South State Street."

I'd never heard of East West University before. Maybe they were new in the past seven years—or maybe I'd had no reason to care about it before. At least I knew they didn't maintain a football team in the Big Ten.

"At the moment," Perwin continued, "I'm majoring in Business Administration and Computer Skills, but any time now I might change my mind and decide to be an actor—or an astronaut."

"An astronaut? I'm impressed," I said.

"Don't be. Partial scholarship. My uncle—my mother's brother—makes up the difference, and even more. He owns an independent company that supplies everything you might need in your bathroom, including plumbing." He grinned. "Everybody's got a bathroom, so business is booming."

"You live on the South Side?"

He nodded. "Mom and I have an apartment near Hyde Park."

We were quiet for a moment. He sipped at his water. Then he took a deep breath and got serious.

"My dad, you know—he thinks you're the greatest person he ever met."

"We like each other a lot," I agreed, "and I might not be sitting here now if not for him. During my first few days, he saved me from—some bad shit. After that, he became my non-registered guardian angel, and every other con knew if they wanted to mess with me, they'd have to go through Denver first. He's one tough son of a bitch," I said with as much affection as was in me. "He never fought much inside. He's so big everybody treated him with respect."

"He's a really kind man, Mr. Reinert. You can see the gentleness in his eyes—but he can also rip out your liver with his bare hands if you deserve it."

"I think he mentioned to me once he played football in high school."

"Right." Perwin's eyes got brighter, and he leaned forward, excited. "I wasn't born then, so I never saw him play, but let's face it. A man that size, wearing pads and a helmet that made him look even bigger, made other teams run a different route so they wouldn't smash up against him."

"That's your dad," I said. "Big and wide. Sometimes I felt like I was talking to an entire apartment building and not just one guy." I cocked my head, having a thought pop into my mind and then out through my mouth. "Did you also play football in high school, Perwin?"

"Everyone was after me to try out—the coach and even the principal. But I'm not like my dad. I don't think he ever felt real pain in his life, so it didn't bother him when three two-hundred fifty-pound linemen came after him on every play to try stuffing him into the dirt. But those football years for Dad are what made him so strong and tough and fearless."

"Are you strong and tough, too?"

"Not like him, Mr. Reinert. Nobody is like him. But I've gotten tough on occasion because everyone likes to try me out, so maybe they can brag they won a battle with a big guy like me." He shrugged. "Nobody's had to brag, yet."

"Good for you," I said.

"But," and Perwin Tolliver leaned even further toward me. The muscles that connect his lower jaw to the rest of his face jumped with tension. "That's one of the reasons I came. Look— I know Dad is in there for life. Cop killers don't get privileges. I see him whenever I can, probably about ten times a year. His birthday, Father's Day, the Christmas season. But he knows damn near everyone on the inside, even the ones, like you, who eventually get out. He learned a lot of stuff. One big thing is cons are treated almost as bad when they walk free on the outside as they did when they were serving out their sentence." He leaned back. "He told me on the phone, and now I'm telling you. I'm just a college kid—but if you're in a tough spot and fear is attacking your guts, if you find yourself at a dead end and can't seem to get past the goons who chased you in the first place—I'm here for you." He handed me three sheets of paper, folded in half. "My home address, my phone number, my cellphone, my college schedule—everything. Call whenever you want—twenty-four hours a day."

I was too stunned to say anything for a minute. He was indeed a good-looking kiddo, and he did have those eyes that drive women mad. But there was something else about him, too—something that reminded me so much of his father. Some danger sizzling under his skin. I figured he wasn't as mean and tough as his father—but he came pretty damn close.

I said, "Perwin, you don't have to do that for me."

"For you? I'm doing it for my dad. He told me, many times, you were his best friend. He can't do anything for you now, but I can because he told me to. I'm your linebacker, your wide receiver and your water boy, whenever you need me." One corner of his mouth lifted in a small smile. "Whenever you get into trouble."

"Now that you mention it, I am in a bit of a mess," I said.

"Wow. Tell me about it, Mr. Reinert."

"If you're my guardian angel, I think you better start calling me Russ."

"I'm kind of too young to call you by your first name, but I'll try."

"Attaboy!" I cheered. And then I told him what details I could remember of the happenings since I got out of prison, and related to him the story of the woman I was once in love with and who has vaporized into thin air without a trace, and why I'm trying to find her.

I guess what interested Perwin Tolliver most was, when Mrs. Lilith Ogilvy wanted to see me, she sent two tough guys to bring me to her home, whether I wanted to come or not. I didn't mention I might have taken one of them down, but not both. Telling him, I had to stop for a minute or two and think what the hell their names were.

Oh, right. Walter Yellen and Hayden Fantos. I didn't know there was anyone alive and tougher than hell named Walter.

I'm not certain Denver Tolliver taught his son to fight—but he sure as hell taught me.

"First thing is, kick 'em right in the stones," Denver told me. "Then go for the eyes, rip 'em out of his goddamn head. And no punching in the face—that's bone against bone and you'll break your knuckles. Overhead swing with the side of your fist. You'll flatten and disable anything you hit." He showed me, hitting me on the shoulder with an overhead smash. He didn't hit me more than ten percent of what he was able, but I still couldn't use my left shoulder for a week.

I wasn't blindfolded or anything when the muscle boys drove me there—that only happens in bad movies. I didn't check the street name, because that sprawling estate took up at least ten acres. I didn't know the exact address of the Ogilvy household—one of several, I learned—but I told Perwin Tolliver it was an enormous mansion on the west side somewhere, and he could easily look it up on Google.

"It didn't feel dangerous once I got there," I said, "but getting hauled off by two guys whose great grandfathers once worked for Al Capone and wouldn't take no for an answer seemed teetering on the narrow edge of trouble. *My* trouble." I waved it away. "I guess Lilith Ogilvy keeps them around just for the fun of it."

"Maybe—but they need watching." Perwin Tolliver cleared his throat. "She needs watching, too. I'll keep my eye on her."

"You'll do no such thing. You go to school every day, and I'm damned if I'll fuck up your education when I just met you."

"Yeah, but my dad owes you—"

"Your dad owes me nothing. I owe him everything—

including my life. And because I did live, and survive, he made my seven-year stretch as livable as possible."

"My dad," Perwin Tolliver, "owes you friendship. Big time. Before you got into prison, he had no friends at all. Especially the white guys hated his guts—like the white guys who tried to take advantage of you."

"I'm a white guy, too."

"That proves he doesn't hate all white guys. He gets news every day when anything happens in that joint, and he heard you were coming in. You're a smart guy, a writer, inside because DAs and governors and big shots had you in their sights. For some reason, Dad never believed you were guilty." He chuckled. His father's laugh was booming, overpowering, at times almost deafening. Perwin's laugh was nowhere near that, probably because I hadn't told a real honest-to-god joke. "He never said so right out, but he thought all guys who can write are pretty decent human beings."

"Most guys," I corrected him. "Not all. Not even Shakespeare. You can be the greatest writer the world has ever known, but at least ten percent of the people who read you think you're an asshole. It comes with the territory."

"My dad never read you. That's why you got to be great friends."

"He's always been my friend—and always will be."

"He feels that way, too," Perwin said, "but he won't walk free for the rest of his life. That's why I'm here for you. For him. I'm still a kid, but some people might think twice when they get a look at me. I'll always have your back."

We hugged before he left, which made it a real friendship. I felt closer to him because I only hugged his father, Denver Tolliver, once—and that was on the day I walked out of that prison.

Hopefully forever.

CHAPTER TWENTY-FOUR

It was not quite ten o'clock in the morning when my phone rang. My heart began beating faster, as I hoped it might be Cassidy Hammond. We were proceeding slowly, and the fragile understanding between us was I'd call her when I'd gotten my act together. But maybe she just couldn't stand not at least talking to me, so here she was.

But she wasn't. The photo on my cellphone told me it was Tana Phillips, my lawyer. Maybe she was just checking in, as I know she worries about me. But there is that little corner of her law firm she hadn't shared with me—one of her associates was the attorney of Aubrey Sinden Cabot, and another represented Cole Cabot. I have no idea what went on across Dean Bosley's desk, but it disturbed me Tana had not mentioned it to me.

After a few moments of chatting, I heard a change in Tana's tone. She said, "Is everything okay, Russ?"

"I guess so."

"You sound—I don't know, maybe slightly off center."

Defensibly: "Maybe I am."

"Want to share it with me?"

"Well—"

"Russ, your apartment and everything in it—your clothes, your furniture, your car, your location—you own it. And you're enjoying it right now because I spent the last seven years calling and cajoling and buying lunch for people who eventually got you out of prison. I know you better than anyone, including your former wife and your former mistress. I can't imagine you're holding something back from me. Come on, Russ, spit it out."

I sighed. "Why didn't you tell me Aubrey Sinden is one of your clients?"

"She's one of my law firm's clients. She's not mine."

"You own the firm, Tana."

"Fine," she said, "but I don't share what one client's problems are to another client—even if that other client is a millionaire mystery writer."

"But—"

"No buts about it. I don't know much about Aubrey, her business dealings, her needs. Drew doesn't share them with me unless it becomes a big deal—so I'm damned if I'll share them with you, no matter who you are."

I couldn't answer for a moment. I felt as if I'd just been sent to "time out" for sneaking an extra cookie from the forbidden cookie jar. And damn Tana, because she was right.

She saved me. "In case you're interested, I don't tell anyone, even my own staff, about you, Russ. They know who you are, they know where you've been, but your business dealings," and here a little humor sneaked into her tone, "and there aren't a hell of a lot of them at the moment—are nobody else's."

"Sorry, Tana. I get snarky sometimes."

"If I'd gone through what you've been through, I'd be snarky, too. I'm calling about something that might make you not so snarky."

"I sure as hell can use that, whatever it is."

"Okay. This might jangle you a little bit, but let me get through it," Tana said. "Most fiction readers today know what your last decade has been like. They know from TV and most newspapers in this country—and in other countries, too—that you're out and about again. They're huge fans of yours, Russ, and they love your stories. They love reading you."

I nodded, even though she couldn't see me. "Well, I love them back—and everything you bought came from the money they spent reading me."

"And watching your movies, too. But here's the thing, Russ. You have nothing published for the last seven years. You need to get your ass in gear working on another book. I know it'll take you months to write it, and probably another year after you get a publisher interested. Something came along yesterday that'll get the reading population talking about you again."

"A famous movie star—the gorgeous kind—is now in love with me?"

"Brad Pitt you ain't. Now listen—I got a call this morning that got me all excited, and I'm hoping you'll get excited, too. Do you ever watch the local news on TV?"

"Rarely," I said.

"Not Channel 14?"

"Not for the last seven years. Joliet Prison doesn't get local Chicago stations."

"One of their top field reporters," Tana said, "is Andrew Lim. He's Chinese, born and raised in Indianapolis. Went to college at Kent State, spent a few years in Omaha as a desk reporter, then moved over here. He's in his thirties, I think. Very sharp, very bright. He called me this morning. They want to do a live interview with you."

Something rumbled deep inside my stomach. "I don't want a goddamn interview. Is he going to ask me what it was like being locked up for almost a decade?"

"He'll ask whatever you want him to—and you can tell him ahead of time what you will and won't say on television."

"There's nothing I want to say on television except *get out of my face*."

Tana was quiet for half a minute. I could hear her breathing, though—the kind of breathing that happens when she got ready to lower the boom on me, and she was taking the time to make sure she didn't make a wrong step. Politicians, like lawyers, always talk about the danger of crossing "red lines," but every living human being has red lines that no one else dare cross.

"Russ," she said finally, "pay attention. This is important." Pause. "You've been a best-selling author, but you've been out of the publishing picture for seven years. No new work, no public appearances, no showing up at a bookstore, and everyone knocks themselves out trying to get your autograph. Your older books have sold all this time, but the royalties are much lower—and they'll get smaller and smaller, because your old fans will forget about you, and new readers have never heard of you."

"Eventually," I said, "readers always forget the great writers of the past. Who in hell knows Sinclair Lewis or Dashiell Hammett or even Pearl Buck? I'm not Shakespeare or Edgar Allan Poe. I'm not Dickens—and frankly, no one knows Dickens anymore except for Ebenezer Scrooge."

"Everybody knows Oliver Twist, Russ. Otherwise, they're all dead," she said. "You're alive—and you'll probably be alive for another fifty years. You need to keep writing." Now she teased. "I didn't spend fifteen hundred bucks on your new laptop just so you could spend all day watching porn."

"Watching porn is fun for about five minutes, and then it gets boring."

"I don't even give porn five minutes."

"That's because you've got Jack. Why should I write anymore, Tana? My agent and publisher sent me to writing Siberia. No one's on my side. I could write the best novel in history, and no one will get to read it."

"Your giant publisher is a behind-closed-doors covey of small-minded assholes—and so is your goddamn agent, who also happens to be a fudge-packer!" She lowered her voice. "Listen here, you. I have one of my law clerks examining the current book scene just for you. Making calls, making inquiries, studying this year's version of *Writers Market*. There are lots of smaller publishers who specialize in mystery fiction. They won't pay you the big advance your pub house used to, but their royalties are higher than usual, and the one who takes you on will bust his or her butt making the world know Russell Reinert is back and he's ready."

I swallowed hard. "Tana, that's—Jesus, I had no idea you were doing that. That could work great." I let my chin hit my chest. "The trouble is, I'm not ready. Not now."

"Then *get* ready! Get yourself out of this Find-Aubrey-Sinden mission. Ask yourself—quietly, when no one is bugging you one way or the other—ask yourself *What am I?* If your answer is anything other than *I'm a writer*, forget about it and spend the rest of your life searching for a woman who disappeared when you weren't even in town. And if your answer is *Jailbird*, then throw my phone numbers into the garbage, because I won't want anything to do with you."

I closed my eyes and let my head drift back, trying to process everything Tana said. I never had to think about things like that in prison, because every damn day was the same and there was nothing new under the sun. I took too long, I think, because she finally snapped, "Russ, are you still there?"

I jerked. "I'm here."

"So...?"

"I need time."

"How much time? Fifteen minutes? Half an hour?"

I licked my lips. "Three days, Tana. Give me three days. Then I'm digging through my notes and coming up with an idea for my next book. Three days."

"*...of the Condor?*" she finished.

I had to laugh. "Great movie."

"Well," she said, "I hope to hell *your* three days are a hell of a lot better than Robert Redford's."

* * *

I felt like an idiot when Tana and I ended our conversation. I'd asked for three days to discover what's happened to Aubrey Sinden, then realized I had no clue where I should look next. The murder of Aubrey's husband made it a dangerous search for me. No one yet knows why he was killed—throat cut and dumped into Lake Michigan near Navy Pier. But several people knew I was looking for Aubrey, too—and I just might be next in line to take a permanent swim.

Who else could I contact? For the better part of the day, I paced, trying to think of anyone else in Aubrey's life, or someone connected to Cabot.

I checked Cole Cabot first on one of those search engines on which, if you click often enough, you'll find out everything there is to know, including who wears boxers or briefs. What I discovered about Cole had crossed my mind earlier. It didn't reveal why he was so distant to his own family, nor why he no longer lived in the Greater Boston area, but I figured he was a black sheep of the clan. He probably committed no crime, but was not the kind of guy who kept up with a famous American family, and so found a different place to live.

I had no idea whether Aubrey Sinden's parents were still living, or if they might have moved to Azerbaijan or some other country no one knew how to spell or pronounce. She'd never introduced me to them during our time together, as I was married to someone else, and she didn't want to confess our adultery to her parents.

She probably didn't tell them her part-time boyfriend spent seven years in prison for involuntary manslaughter, either.

It took me more than half an hour to remember her father's first name, and when I finally recalled her telling me he was named Lloyd, I looked him up on that Google site, too.

Lloyd Stuart Sinden. Age 66. Married to Sara Jackson Sinden, age 63. One child, Aubrey Ann Sinden. They lived in the rather conservative suburb of Downer's Grove, west of downtown. I could have taken the train there, but what the hell—I have a new car.

I picked up the phone to connect with them, then thought better of it. They might hang up on me, which would bring my search to a screeching halt. They might never have heard of me, never knew of my connection to their daughter, or if they even knew she was missing or their son-in-law was dead.

I looked up driving directions and discovered it was a forty-minute car trip to get from my home to theirs. I wanted to go immediately, but figured one or both of them might work away from home, so I decided to wait until seven o'clock that evening.

I called Shaw's Crab House on Hubbard Street and made an early reservation. It's a Chicago classic, and I'd dined there often.Awfully fond of trout and mahi-mahi, I hadn't eaten a decent seafood dinner for the past seven-plus years. Going to Shaw's was like tiptoeing back into time. The hostess who answered the phone sounded surprised I'd be eating dinner for one. *Nobody* goes to an upscale restaurant alone—unless they just got out of a penitentiary and discovered most of their friends didn't give a damn about them anymore.

I spent the rest of the afternoon thinking about what I'd say to Aubrey's parents when I got there.

The home was large. Very large. About two steps below being a mini-mansion. I vaguely recalled Aubrey mentioning at one time or another she came from an ordinary middle-class family, but I doubted whether "ordinary" could afford a house like this. Maybe Lloyd Stuart Sinden won a lottery payoff or bet big on a 50-1 horse at Arlington International Racecourse who won the race by a nose.

Or he robbed a bank.

A woman—I assumed Aubrey's mother—opened the door. Many women in this day and age who were sixty-three actually looked as if they were in their middle forties. Sara Sinden looked sixty-three.

"Hello," she said—pleasantly enough, but there was a flicker of panic behind her eyes. It must have been unusual for anyone in this neighborhood to have someone strange knock on their door at twilight.

"Hi, Ms. Sinden. I'm sorry to bother you. My name is Russ Reinert, and I'm an old friend of Aubrey's."

'Pleasantly' disappeared from her face as if the word never existed. Her back stiffened, and her chin extended the way a bulldog's does when he's angry. "Reinert, huh? I know all about you. What do you want?"

She knew all about me, and I hadn't even realized it until this moment. Aubrey was called as a prosecution witness at my trial, and naturally her parents knew about that. Ergo, they knew Aubrey and I had been lovers.

"I was told by Cole Cabot that Aubrey disappeared about two weeks ago, and he asked if I'd look for her."

Her lips became a surgical slice on her face. One more angry change of expressions and she'd turn into a monster. "Cole is dead."

"I've heard that," I said. "If I could have a few minutes of your time...?"

A male voice from inside the house called out, "Who is it, Sara?"

Her eyes never left mine, but she called back over her shoulder, "You'll never believe it."

Lloyd Sinden came up behind his wife. They were approximately the same height, and both had gray hair, though his was thinning on top. His outfit did not look like that of a man who lived in such a house—old-fashioned denims and a faded cardigan sweater worn over a white T-shirt. He had a relatively small pot belly and walked almost with a waddle. He took one look at me and his expression mirrored that of his wife. "Christ Almighty! What the hell do you want?"

"I need just a few minutes, Mr. Sinden. I know Aubrey is missing, and I'm trying to find her. You folks could be my last chance." I sighed. "Please."

They exchanged frowns. She said, "I don't want him in my home."

Lloyd studied me like I was an animal corpse in a botany lesson. Then he turned back to me. "I think he's trying to help, Sara."

"He's a murderer!" she snarled, considering me the way she would if a rabid wolf just knocked on her door.

"I haven't killed anyone," I said. "I was framed."

"Bullshit!"

She hardly seemed the type of woman who carelessly used profanity, because her one-word curse at me sounded like someone speaking Lithuanian for the first time in their life. I continued, "Aubrey disappeared while I was still in prison. I know she's married now—or was until they found Cole Cabot. But I'll lways care about her, and if she's really missing, I'll be very disturbed until she's found. I'm hoping I can help. I'm hoping you know more about her than anyone, and that might send me off in a different direction." Another deep breath. "Please?"

For about twenty seconds, nobody moved an inch. We were like a painting of three people standing in the doorway of a magnificent home, looking as though we didn't belong there.

At length, Lloyd Sinden took a step backwards, not even meeting his wife's gaze. "Well, you might as well come in, then."

"Thank you."

"For ten minutes," Sara Sinden warned, "and not another second."

The inside of the house was not as impressive as the outside. There were no visible effects from a professional interior decorator. The furniture, though decent and relatively new, was probably on sale in big furniture stores all across the country. Over the fireplace, dominating the living room, is a large colorful oil painting of an Italian seaside village—obviously a paint-by-numbers.

Nobody asked me if I wanted something to drink. They didn't invite me to sit down, either.

"I have no use for you, Mr. Reinert," Sara said. "You were a marital cheat—and you went to prison for causing your wife's death so you could marry Aubrey."

"That's not true," I said. "I was stuck in a bad marriage, so Aubrey and I had a great relationship whenever we could. And my conviction was for involuntary manslaughter. Involuntary. That means I didn't try to kill my wife. The DA imprisoned me because I'm well known and made him more headlines. But I don't give a damn what you think about me, Ms. Sinden. I'm here to get help in finding Aubrey, wherever she is."

He said, "How would we know?"

"You wouldn't, sir. But if we both share what we now know, things might come together." Then I related everything I'd done in the past few days—not counting Cassidy Hammond.

Sara Sinden's mouth actually dropped open in shock. "You actually got an interview with Gaylord Ogilvy himself?"

I nodded.

Lloyd said, "Aubrey has worked for his companies for many years. Recently, though, she did most of her work at home."

"She didn't have a regular paycheck?"

"No. After her marriage, she didn't visit the office much. Someone would bring papers for her to sign and deliver money to her on odd occasions."

"Someone?"

He thought for a bit. Then: "Probably Ogilvy's second-in-command. Irving Greenfield."

That was a pretty big guy in the company to deliver checks and papers for Aubrey's signature. "Irvin," I corrected him. "No *G*." I'm finding out nobody likes that name without a *G*.

"Really? I've never heard of anyone named Irvin without the *G*."

"I had to go through him to get to the boss," I explained. "Welcome to the twenty-first century."

Sara, still fuming, walked to the bay window and stared out. It was growing darker and their outdoor lights had clicked on.

My cellphone in my pocket took on a nervous little jitter of its own to tell me I had a call waiting, but I ignored it. If I broke off this so-called interview with Aubrey's parents, I'd never got another word out of them.

I said, "What about Aubrey's personal friends—outside of work?"

"Probably most of them lost touch after her marriage—except maybe for Christmas or for someone's birthday. The only one she's talked about for the last few years is Amber Pollard."

Annoyed, I tried not shaking my head—but failed. "Ember," I corrected him again. "Not Amber. Ember."

He looked embarrassed. "People get strange names these days. I can hardly remember any of them."

"Who gives a damn how people spell their names?" Aubrey's mother snapped from across the room and moved toward us like an infantryman charging at Nazis across the sand at Omaha Beach. "You really think one of my daughter's friends killed her?"

"I never thought anyone killed her, Ms. Sinden."

"And why, pray tell, do you believe that?"

"Because she's done nothing wrong that it would cost her life."

"My god, Sara." Her husband gently touched his own face with his fingertips.

I suggested, "Can we please get back to Irvin Greenfield?"

"I was at her home a few times when he showed up," Sara grudgingly admitted. "He generally gave her an envelope, which she never opened in front of me. I assume it was a check inside, along with some pretty important papers, but I never knew how much." She bit her lip, then went on, "Aubrey would peek inside the envelope and smile, so I'm sure it was a pretty big check, too—not a regular salary. It was always for something special.”

“What about the papers Mr. Greenfield brought for Aubrey to sign?”

“I have no idea what they were—but it wasn’t one or two pages. More like a hundred.”

“Were those papers on Ogilvy Corporation stationery?”

“How the hell would I know?”

“Sara—” her husband said softly. We both ignored him.

I said, “Did she sign those papers in front of you, Ms. Sinden, or did she wait until you left?”

She shook her head. “Always signed them right away so Greenfield could leave with them.”

My mind was racing. After writing so many mysteries, I was trying to make clues—if that’s what they were—come together for an answer. But I was running out of questions until the last one popped into my head. “Ms. Sinden.” I broke my ass trying to make this last query not sound all that important. “When Mr. Greenfield visited Aubrey—at least the times you were there—was it during the day, or was it perhaps later, after his office closed down?”

She got defensive again. “How am I supposed to remember that?”

“Just wondering,” I said. I doubt if I sounded as airy as I tried to be.

“Well, usually between five and six in the late afternoon,” she finally said, “because we’d often go out and have dinner together.”

“Just the two of you?”

“Aubrey and her mother,” Lloyd Sinden said. “Sometimes I went, too.”

I thanked them both profusely for allowing me into their home to ask things about their daughter I never knew before. Lloyd Sinden was polite enough saying goodbye, even shaking my hand with both of his. Sara, however, warned me never to come near them again—or she’d shoot me.

Driving home, I pulled into the first gas station I could find, took out my cellphone, and checked the call I couldn't take during my meeting with the Sindens. It was Andrew Lim—one of the head news guys on local Channel Fourteen. I looked at my expensive-but-not-a-Rolex watch and saw it was closer to nine p.m. than eight. I figured I'd return the call in the morning.

This was the first time I'd driven in the dark since before my conviction, so I played it very carefully. No speeding, no changing lanes, no stupidly running over a pedestrian I hadn't noticed.

Aubrey was earning a hell of a lot of money from the Ogilvy Corp—so much she probably picked out the home in which her parents live, and put down a handsome down payment, despite her living with her husband in a middle-class apartment. When she took her parents out to dinner, she was the one who paid the check and tipped the waitstaff.

She was making a hell of a lot more money than ninety-eight percent of Ogilvy employees, and she hardly ever had to go into the Merchandise Mart offices. So—what the hell was she working on at home?

And, why did Irvin Greenfield always visit her in the late afternoon or early evening? And what were those hundred-page contracts—or whatever they were—she signed without really looking at them?

CHAPTER TWENTY-FIVE

It's nearly impossible to say no to Tana Phillips. She's a high-powered lawyer and knows just about anything worth knowing. But I was in no position, no situation, and no mood to do a local TV interview less than a week past my long vacation in Joliet when I was still trying to learn where were the neighborhood drugstore, the butcher, and the dry cleaners. Nothing was done to me in the past seven years that wasn't a crock of shit, and I had no desire to relive it by discussing it on television.

When, after four cups of coffee and two bagels with cream cheese, I returned Andrew Lim's request call to Tana. Since I'd been elsewhere the night before, I didn't get to see his news show, so I had no idea of what he looked like. I suppose I could have found his photo on the Internet, but I didn't give a damn.

Using my cell phone with the speaker cranked up high, I told Andrew Lim after the *hello-how-are-you bullshit,* "You're catching me off-guard. I have no idea why you'd want to interview me."

"Because you're a famous author, Mr. Reinert," he answered.

"Being famous was yesterday. No one remembers who I am anymore."

"Carl Sandburg. Nelson Algren. Studs Terkel," Lim recited like a seven-year-old conquering the triumphant moment reading a book aloud in front of the class. "They're all immortal Chicago writers, and they've been dead for many decades, but they're revered here, and people still read them all the time. Everybody knows who you are, and not just in Chicago. All over the country. All over the world." Then he lowered his voice as if telling a secret. "I'm with a local news show, Mr. Reinert, but networks often pick up and re-run my interviews country-wide, which will do you a hell of a lot of good selling your work."

"I'm not dead," I growled, "and I don't have anything current to talk about to the rest of the world, which makes me boring."

"You'll never be boring. I'd never let you be boring. That's my job."

"You want me to talk about the killer fights in the prison dining room between two guys who sharpened spoons to be lethal at close quarters?" I kept my voice level. "Lethal, Mr. Lim, means one of those fellow diners leaves the dining room on a stretcher, with a sheet covering his face."

He sounded appalled. "Nothing like that—certainly. Not at dinnertime."

That interested me. I was worried he'd be on TV at two o'clock in the morning. "You mean you're on the six o'clock news?"

"Five nights a week. Trust me, Mr. Reinert. I'll have great questions."

"Not about prison, Mr. Lim. Not one fucking word about prison. I lived enough of those days to not talk about it anymore. Do you understand me?"

He hurried to make me feel better. "I won't even mention prison. I'll just say you've been away for a while and ask you if what used to be great in Chicago in the old days is still great, and whether what's new in the present is great, too—or not great."

"You mean the Chicago Bears, who haven't even been in a

Super Bowl since I was a teenager?"

I heard a short chuckle over the phone. "I don't talk sports on television, Mr. Reinert. I report news."

"I'm not news!" I insisted. "I've just returned to my roots, that's all. At best, I'm a Prodigal Son." Despite my not wanting to show up in his studio for this few moments of emotional torture, Andrew Lim was getting on my last nerve. "You want everyone to know where I live? Make sure to take a picture of the front door with the numbers over it."

I heard his heavy sigh of frustration. "You're right, Mr. Reinert—Russ—-is it okay if I call you Russ? Well, you are the Prodigal Son, whether you realize it or not, and that, my friend, is news. Maybe I started this conversation off all wrong." The tone of his voice became professorial. "You're an addict, Russ. You're addicted to writing."

"Everyone," I said, "is addicted to something. Drugs, booze, gambling, eating a pig, sex—no matter what kind of sex it is. Chocolate, coffee, teenage girls doing gymnastic splits in bikinis, binge-watching Seinfeld…"

"I really want you to come on, talk to a Chicago that still loves you, tell how happy you are to be back in town, and say what your next novel is about."

I nearly hung up, totally annoyed. An only child has no siblings who love and support him, nor family members who grind your guts with irritation and stupidity and allow you to take out your temper on them and still be loving. As for Lim, I had no clue what my next novel was going to be. I had pages and pages of ideas while behind bars, but not one of those ideas were standing tall and shouting *Do me! Do Me!*

Andrew Lim was about to drive me crazy.

Then he said, "You might've lost your luster a little, and you need to get people on the edge of their seat for your next work. You'll get hundreds of Facebook memes every day asking you when it will be ready, how far into it are you, and how much will it cost in the bookstores—and eventually they'll be right,

they'll buy your new one, and you're famous all over again."
He cleared his throat. "And the money will start pouring in."

"I don't need the money," I said. "I'm already rich."

"Then give it away."

"Is there a charity for Chinese news reporters?"

"It's Chinese-American," he told me, getting serious. This time, he took my retort to be racially offensive. He was correct. "My mother's maiden name was Wilson, and she married a Mr. Lim Bojing, who was also born in Indianapolis. In my own small way—mostly local, right now—I am kind of famous. You used to be, and this is a first step toward you getting famous again."

I felt all the starch go out of me. I know news reporters. They won't let up until you give them what they want. I made a mental note to watch Lim carefully this evening. If he continues to piss me off, I'd recant my agreement.

"Come to my apartment and interview me, then, Mr. Lim— and if you step over the red line and bring up my arrest, conviction and imprisonment, then you are going to be famous, too—as the first TV interviewer who had his camera shoved up his ass—live!"

An only child is always aware of what that made them. There were moments they missed having a large family. Thanksgiving and Christmas and even Easter Sunday, when everybody found relatives with whom to celebrate, even if they didn't really get along. Those holidays, especially New Year's Eve, often heightened their feeling of aloneness.

I also felt nostalgia for the non-existent family who might have ticked me off but were there for me to bitch at. For seven years all my fellow cons were upset at the same things as I was—-prison stinks, no matter where you are. There was no whining involved. One learned that pretty damn early—-and if not, one winds up dead in the shower room at three o'clock in the morning.

I'd deal with Andrew Lim and his possibly vicious interview all by myself.

The television crew—smaller than I expected—arrived at my apartment just after one in the afternoon of the following day. Andrew Lim, a pretty good-looking guy, taller than me and wearing slightly tinted blue glasses that gave him the air of an Asian John Lennon, accompanied by a fussy TV and audio guy whose name I didn't quite hear because he mumbled, and a female producer who was in high school when I went to prison. We were introduced, but within ten minutes I forgot her name. If it's not Mary or Barbara or Karen, it doesn't stay in my mind for more than thirty seconds.

She was the one who gave me all the hints how to sit, which way to turn my head, and what to do with my hands. Her job, apparently, was also to plaster my face with make-up, promising me I won't look feminine, over-theatrical or clown-like. I didn't get a chance to check myself in the mirror after she was through. I could feel the make-up on my face, and hoped like hell she didn't make me look like Ronald McDonald on meth, or anything else except a writer. She also said she was glad I was growing my hair out a little bit.

Her boss——if that indeed was how he was considered——was pushy to the point of being obnoxious. I held short shrift for people whose first effort was to overwhelm you. "Glad to meet you, Russ," Andrew Lim said, shaking hands and slapping me on the back. "I'd never read your books, but a few days ago when I got the idea of putting you back on television, I thumbed through the most current one. It's terrific."

Thumbed through? My attention went scurrying under the sofa, never to be seen again—like a cat's favorite toy. First of all, my "current one" came out during my first year in prison. Second, one does not "thumb through" fiction and decide whether it's terrific or just plain boring. I'd never been a dedicated watcher of Channel 14 news, but I'm sure some other on-air reporter was not quite so thoughtless. Ah, well.

I wore a sports jacket with a shirt open at the throat. Lim said, "Don't you think you'd be more comfortable on camera wearing a suit and tie?"

"In my own living room?" I replied. "Why don't you take your tie *off*?"

"Whatever," he said, and I fear I hurt his feelings.

The TV guy set up two lights, pointing at me in my lounge chair, moving me around a bit so that the window, looking out on Oak Street, wouldn't be so bright as to make silhouettes out of both of us. He clipped a small microphone onto the collar of my shirt and made me count to ten so he could set the audio. Finally, endlessly, we were ready to shoot.

Lim's introduction of me was so short I only had time to nod my head and give the viewers one of my better smiles. I also attempted to sit up straight so I didn't look like a homeless man the crew had found on the street. Then we got right into it.

"Now that you're back on your home turf, Russ, you've been a Chicago legend for a long time," he said to me. "How does that make you feel?"

I thought to keep my head raised so as not to call attention to my nascent double chin. "I'm no legend," I said. "I can give you a long list of writers who are. I'm just glad a lot of people here and elsewhere are reading my books."

"Tell us about your next one."

"I haven't started it yet. I'm trying to decide what I should be creating."

His eyebrows climbed toward his hairline. "When we spoke on the phone the other day, didn't you tell me you were addicted to writing? In that case, why haven't you jumped right into a new book? What's the deal?"

I swallowed hard. I'd also told him via phone I'd shove his camera up his ass. His tiptoes were getting dangerously close to the edge. "People are addicted to Diet Pepsi, too," I said, "but they don't walk around with a can of it in their hand twenty-four hours a day."

"You can't even give us a hint?"

My first impulse was to tell him and his viewers *the butler did it*. I changed my mind, thinking it a bad idea. I said instead, "It's about murder."

Lim laughed. "All your books are about murder."

"Did you think I'd write a book about the sex lives of three-toed sloths?"

"No, I didn't think that," he said. He was more used to his interviewees being well-behaved, answering his remarks with a pleasant smile. He shrugged. "But you're famous all over the world, certainly more so in Chicago. Even if you did write about three-toed sloths, everyone here will read it."

"Everyone but you, Mr. Lim. You'll just thumb through it."

That one rubbed Andrew Lim the wrong way. His perennial on-camera smile disappeared, to be replaced by a granite face just two steps shy of anger. He glanced over at his female producer, who gave him a Marcel Marceau mime hand signal to wind things up. He did so very quickly, and he and his crew left with little more than a thanks-and-goodbye.

I was certain when they found their way back to the studio, they'd get into the editing room and cut out my last remarks.

When I watched the show that evening, I was pleased to know I'd guessed correctly.

CHAPTER TWENTY-SIX

I didn't watch the show by myself later that day, because shortly after the Lim crew left, Cassidy Hammond called me. Just checking in to make sure I was okay and had not jumped off a pier after my ridiculous performance in the sack? At least, she didn't mention that on the phone.

But when I told her I'd just been interviewed by Andrew Lim for the evening's six o'clock news, she had a great suggestion.

"I'd hate for you to watch that all by yourself, Russ. Why don't I come over there and we can watch it together? If you love it, terrific, we can celebrate. And if you wince and shudder and wish Andrew Lim had never heard of you, I'll supply a shoulder for you to cry on."

My heart beat more loudly than usual, and gut-deep terror swept over me like a tsunami of ice water. It took me several seconds to catch my breath before I answered, because I didn't know what to say to her. All I came up with was, "You really want to watch that with me?"

"Sure. Then I won't have to call you up and give you notes. Maybe afterwards we can watch an old movie. Do you have Netflix?"

"I don't even know," I said. "I haven't seen a new movie since…" I stopped. They never showed a new movie in Joliet in all the time I was there. No cops, no criminals, no westerns, no guns, no sex, not even passionate kisses. Most of them were films older than I was, and simple comedies were the weekly deal there for a coterie of convicted criminals—-Van Johnson, June Allyson, Esther Williams swimming, Abbot and Costello clowning, Fred and Ginger dancing, Nelson Eddy and Jeanette Macdonald singing to each other like third-rate opera singers. Singing, for crysake!

Those were only movies we watched in prison, over and over and over again. In seven years, I think I had to sit through "Ma and Pa Kettle" at least twice each year. However, it was indeed a reprieve from staying in my cell all evening with the Supreme Jerker Offer.

"One more thing you'll have to catch up with, Russ," Cassidy reminded me.

I just sighed.

Cassidy giggled. "I didn't mean—-*that!* You're so out of touch with everything new. Look, I'm coming super-casual, which means jeans and a flannel shirt, so you be casual, too. I'll drink whatever you have there—and all I want otherwise is some cheese and crackers."

"Uh—-"

"Don't tell me, Russ. You don't even have cheese? You don't have crackers?"

"I—-don't know," I protested. "I think I have cream cheese. But other kinds? When you live in an eight-by-ten cell for seven years and then move into an elegant apartment furnished by somebody else, the last thing you do is check what's in the pantry. I looked in the refrigerator but I didn't see any cheese."

Cassidy said, "You're like that little kid in Kipling's *Jungle Book*. You don't know anything exists because you were raised by wolves."

"I was almost *eaten* by wolves—-every day. Thanks to the best friend I've ever had, not much ever happened to me in Joliet."

"Aww! That sounds so nice, Russ. Why don't you invite him

over to watch the show with us?"

"Life with no parole for cop-killing, Cassidy," I told her, and there was real sorrow in my tone. "He's—otherwise involved tonight."

"Shit!" Cassidy nearly whispered. "I stuck my foot in it again. I'm sorry."

"You didn't know. Besides, I wasn't expecting extra company tonight."

"Gee, how can I make it up to you for that?" she wondered.

"Stop off in a grocery store on your way here," I said. "And bring some crackers and cheese."

Three different kinds of crackers, including Triscuits—and three different cheeses, Brie, Gruyere and Feta. Cassidy Hammond shops very well. She also brought wine, something she felt would make the cheese seem even more delicious. I've never been much of a wine-drinker, but I felt obliged to drink her visiting gift.

When she arrived, the hello kiss was just that. Romantic, sort of—better than how you'd kiss your maiden aunt hello but wouldn't make the movie love scenes between Burt Lancaster and Deborah Kerr thrashing around in the surf boring. Cassidy *did* have grocery bags in both hands. She dressed casually, jeans and a Northwestern University sweatshirt, making her look like a high school senior.

"I hope you'll tape *this* TV interview," she said.

"Why would I do that?"

"Because you'll hate it at first viewing. Everyone hates seeing themselves on TV. Your nose looks too big, and your triple chin is showing, and your moles and pimples show up like a Renoir painting. Or you look fat. It's not true, though, and when you watch it again two weeks from now, you'll realize how fabulous you looked."

"You're prejudiced," I said.

"If I were prejudiced, I'd never stop to talk to you on North Avenue Beach. You're smart, too."

"I'm only a genius on the tips of my fingers," I told her, wiggling them.

"I knew that before I ever laid eyes on you." She'd put out the food after searching for cheese and crackers plates, as I had no idea where they were. Finally, all done, she sat next to me, looking serious. "Speaking of which…"

"My fingertips?"

"I know you're still getting your sea legs, Russ——"

"You mean my *free* legs, along with the rest of me."

"I know you haven't started writing again. It's probably too soon. But do you have an idea for the next book?"

"I have more than two thousand ideas, one for each day I spent in prison. But not one has jumped off my notebook to bite me on the ass."

"Probably not. But you should start writing something—anything. Keep a journal," she suggested.

"That'll be fascinating. *'Today was nice. I fell in love with a cheese maven.'*"

Cassidy sighed. "Fascinating. Here, start with the brie. You'll love it."

"I've eaten brie," I said. "But seven years of hot dogs, Spam and egg substitutes made me forget about it. Besides, I'm kind of on a mission."

"You said something about that before," Cassidy reminded me, "but it wasn't very informative. So, are you going to tell me?"

"If I tell you, you'll want to get involved, to help, and you'll just get yourself into all kinds of dangerous trouble."

"You mean somebody's going to get mad and yell at me? Or am I going to wind up a dead body on the front page of the Chicago *Tribune?*"

"Probably somewhere in between." I looked at my watch. "It's one minute to six, Cassidy. We don't want to miss my ugly puss in all its glory and just get the sports scores."

"Fine. You know how to make a copy of this to watch later?"

"I didn't get arrested during the Roaring Twenties," I told her. "I actually think I can work a TV set."

I switched on the TV with my Universal Remote, set it to *Record,* and opened the wine. Within seconds, a loud cacophony introduced the Six O'Clock News show as if it were the beginning music of an old RKO movie about World War Two. The title panel faded to Andrew Lim, sitting behind his desk. He'd put on a different suit for his live appearance and changed his white dress shirt for one of blue. He was looking down, as usual, and then suddenly looked up at the camera as if surprised to be on the air.

"Good evening, Chicago. I'm Andrew Lim for *Fourteen News*. Let's see what's going on in our community."

I just looked at Cassidy and raised my eyebrows. That was his every-night opening greeting. I didn't care what went on in our community, but I knew I wouldn't be the first story on his program, so I busied myself putting the different cheeses on my crackers and eating while he spoke.

She'd been correct. I liked the brie best.

After several local news stories, a commercial, traffic and weather reports, and another commercial, Lim came back on. He was smiling—-but the smile looked smug. I'm sure he knew I was reluctant to give him a chance to chew on me a little bit, and he seemed completely tickled he'd won the tug-of-war. I wanted to slap him upside the head before he continued.

"We have a special guest this evening. You all remember him. A best-selling author, a prize winner. He hasn't been around for a while, but now he's back in town—-and *Fourteen News* got him. He and I chatted at his beautiful new apartment in Near North. Here he is, after a long absence—-Russ Reinert."

When Lim said "long absence," my stomach felt as if I'd swallowed a shot glass full of strychnine. No, he didn't mention prison, but he hinted at it well enough everyone who did remember me knows where I've been.

Cassidy quietly muttered, "What a prick!"

I slumped back against the sofa, but she learned forward, elbows on her knees, until it was over, and Andrew Lim was back on-screen, live. He'd slightly edited our interview, managing to get out of the clip before I insulted him on air. I couldn't really blame him for that, but instead, he added comment of his own when I wasn't face-to-face with him to hear it.

Once again live, he said, "Russell Reinert is back in town, and we're all glad he's home again. It's been seven years since his last novel was published. Will he ever write another one?" He winked at the camera. "Watch this space," he said, and *Fourteen News* went to another commercial. My second choice was to click off the TV, but my first thought was to put my foot through it.

We were silent for about half a minute, not looking at each other. My whole body was cramping, and I noticed both my fists were clenched.

I finally said, "Sneaky, back-stabbing son of a bitch! This time it won't be involuntary manslaughter for me. It'll be Murder One."

"Don't worry, honey," she said——and the fact she called me "honey" took much of my pain away.

I said, "Everyone will remember this for the rest of their lives."

"Everyone will forget about it two days from now."

"I won't."

"Of course not, Russ——but it's about you, not about the rest of the people who watch the six o'clock news while they're eating their fried chicken and washing it down with a beer or two."

"I should have turned him down when he asked for me."

"Not really. Nasty and sneaky as he was, he reminded everyone who reads you that you're back and writing again——and that's a good thing."

"I'm not writing again!" I protested.

"You will. I know you will. You're going to write a book all about me—-but you'll change my name and call my character Hortense."

That made me laugh, which surprised me. For a while there, I thought I'd never laugh again. "You drive me crazy," I told her.

"Thanks. That's been my goal."

"Ever since you met me?"

"Before I met you," she said.

"An ex-con who can't even write his name anymore and is a lousy lay."

"You're just out of practice," she said. "On both counts. It'll take time for you to get back in the groove—-to where you were before."

"I wonder if that will ever happen."

"It will. Start believing in yourself."

"Now," I said, "you're sounding like one of those women who write books about taking control of one's own life and winds up plugging them on *The Today Show* while they whip up some obscure recipe for spaghetti sauce."

"I don't make my own spaghetti sauce. I open a jar."

I shook my head sadly and slumped even lower on the sofa. "That sounds like one hell of a future between us. Spaghetti sauce in a jar! Just—oh, hell! Make me another cheese and crackers, will you?"

Cassidy stood up slowly, then reached down and took a firm grip on my hand, pulling me toward her. "Didn't you ever hear that wise old warning, Russ? Nobody eats crackers in bed."

Have you ever lost your car keys? You look all over the place, forgetting where you put them. The longer you search, the more frustrated you get. You check the pockets of everything you wore yesterday, you search in the refrigerator, you look in the cookie jar, you lie flat on the floor and check under the sofa, you run out to your car at least three times, thinking you left them there the day before. Maybe you dropped them on the car floor as you were climbing out.

And then—-you find them! They were in the same place you put them every day of your life, but you couldn't locate them because, for some reason we'll never understand, your brain literally stopped functioning that day. You feel proud of yourself because you have accomplished a major victory.

Cassidy Hammond came to my apartment that evening and watched with me being given the Third Degree by Andrew Lim, which for me was a major victory! Speaking figuratively, anyway—I found my car keys.

And I took no crackers to bed with me.

Cassidy just lay there for a while afterwards, trying to catch her breath, but she was smiling. "God, Russ," she said, "have you been practicing without my knowing it? Or did you read a book?"

"The last time…" I began.

She corrected me. "The first time."

"The first time. I guess after seven years of celibacy, I was terrified."

"Of me?"

I nodded—-as best I could with my head resting on a pillow. "More scared of you than I was of the serial killers and rapists I was locked up with."

Her brows knit into a frown. "Scared? What did you think I'd do to you?"

"Laugh," I said. "I'd hate if someone laughed at me after sex."

"That's worse than a serial killer. I'd never laugh at you." She took my hand and squeezed it. "Unless you tell me a really great joke in bed. In the meantime, Russ, I understood. You're having to learn again to live like everyone else. And if your—

problem happens again, I'll understand that, too."

I rolled over and kissed her, hard. "Cassidy, you're a keeper."

"It's a damn good thing, because my next job is getting you to write again."

I snaked my arm under her head, and she snuggled against my shoulder. I confessed, "Right now, that's easier said than done."

"You haven't got one good idea?"

"I've got thousands of them. But at the moment, something's standing in my way. Something from my past."

"'Splain, Lucy," she ordered.

"I'm afraid to tell *you* about it."

"Because…?"

"It involves a woman from my long-ago past. Someone I haven't seen or heard from in seven years. Please don't get jealous, she's married to someone else. The relationship is way, *way* over."

She took a deep breath. "I'm not jealous. Yet. Why are you preoccupied with her?"

"She's missing," I said, "gone without a trace for more than two weeks. The day I got out of prison, her husband approached me and begged me to find her."

"Why you?"

"Because in my books, private eyes can find anything."

She pulled away the slightest bit so she could see my face. Softly she said, "Tell me about this secret mission."

Before I began, she suggested we get out of bed and put some bathrobes on, which seemed like an excellent idea. There was nothing at all romantic about what I was going to tell her when we were both naked. We also moved out into the living room. The remains of the cheese and crackers were still on the coffee table, having been there untouched for the past two and a half hours. I rushed them into the kitchen, out of sight. There was still some Burgundy left, so I refilled each of our wine glasses before we took our positions at either end of the sofa.

Her smile at me was sincere, but somewhat uneasy. All she knew at this point was it involved one of my old girlfriends. I wriggled around, pushing a few cushions behind my back, worrying as I had been for the past five minutes of how to begin. When I got around to speaking, my opening statement was legendary.

"My marriage sucked," I said.

CHAPTER TWENTY-SEVEN

"I don't understand," Cassidy said when I finally finished my long story. "You weren't even in Chicago when your house exploded. How the hell could they even try you and convict you?"

"Ask the District Attorney," I suggested.

"He's not the District Attorney anymore. In fact, he's not anything. He ran for governor about four years ago and got his clock cleaned in the primary. I think he's back in private practice."

"I don't think I'd hire him. He thought convicting a nationally famous person would put stars in his political crown."

She moved close to me. Tana had bought me two nice bathrobes, but Cassidy got the prettier one. "Russ, there are so many people in this town—and in lots of other places, too—who never believed you were guilty."

"You never believed, Cassidy?"

"Not for three seconds. I told you I was in love with you from the first time I ever read one of your books."

"You weren't really in love. You never saw me in person. You didn't know. I could've been fat, which don't show in my head photos on my books. I could've had bad breath. I could've been a mean, nasty son of a bitch. There's lots of famous writers who aren't too nice in person."

"Oh, yeah?" she challenged. "There are dozens of movie stars and big-time athletes, politicians, pastors or rabbis or even priests who are nasty, miserable bastards, and people seriously and completely fall in love with them every day." She giggled. "Besides, Brad Pitt was taken."

It took me almost an hour to get through the whole retelling of my life. Rarely, Cassidy would jump in to ask a question or for a qualification, and made me repeat each name so she'd remember them, including the fellow inmates I learned to live with during my long incarceration. As for the two main females in the story, Aubrey Sinden and my late wife, Dayna, she never asked for further information. She didn't care whether they were blond, beautiful, fantastic in bed or endowed with a spectacular rack—and after the long evening was over, none of that was important to me, either. She was more interested in the relationships Aubrey Sinden had with Gaylord Ogilvy, Irvin Greenfield, or her late husband, Cole Cabot—and was chillingly fascinated with Cabot's murder.

She also wanted to know all about Denver Tolliver, the lifelong friendship I'd developed with a convicted cop-killer. She seemed interested, too, in Denver's son, Perwin, who showed up in the middle of what she began referring to as the Search for Sinden.

"Perwin has nothing to do with any of this," I told her. "His father is the best friend I ever had. He suggested Perwin look me up, too. I trust him as much as I trust Denver."

Cassidy said, "That's great. But Gaylord Ogilvy is mixed up in this somehow, and I don't think Perwin can help you on that count."

"True. But it's a good feeling to have two best friends at the moment."

"Who's the other one?"

"You, knucklehead."

She put her hand to her chest, feigning surprise. "I didn't know I was a best friend. I thought we were just casual hook-ups."

"Casual cheese and crackers hook-ups, right—because we've yet to have dinner together. So just keep thinking that way, Cassidy."

"I have another thought, Russ. It's relatively late, and I have no class to teach tomorrow until ten o'clock. Would it be permissible if I stayed here for the night?"

"Hmm," I said. "I don't know about that."

"I can sleep on the couch," she offered.

"The bed is more comfortable—but if you stay, you'll have to pay rent."

"How much is the rent?" she asked.

I didn't have to think twice. "It's negotiable," I told her.

We made love three times that night, with a two-hour break in between two and three. We did it again in the morning before Cassidy drove off toward Northwestern University in Evanston. I figured my awful performance of a few nights earlier was a quickly forgotten freshman fuck-up. After she was gone, I dumped the leftover cheese and the now-stale crackers into the trash can and quickly washed the plates and glasses, wondering at the time if I would ever use my dishwasher.

I toasted and ate a bagel, then sat by the window with my second cup of coffee, looking out at busy Oak Street. It relaxed me; I was getting used to living Near North, even though the neighborhood had changed considerably since I was a kid.

Everything changes, though, doesn't it?

I also replayed the night before, regaling her with my current and uncomfortable history. What stuck with me the hardest was her advice for me to start writing—anything.

Maybe I should begin a novel entitled "Hortense," which will drive her crazy. Not a good idea, though. Even though I was totally enchanted with her, and after just three meetings was falling in love with her, I really didn't know much about her—-certainly not enough to make her a central character in a book. She admitted she was not a virgin—a logical background for a beautiful woman in her thirties—but I had no idea if she'd been very promiscuous before I met her or if she'd had a long-standing love affair that ended painfully.

Besides, I still worried about Aubrey. I hadn't been *in love* with her, and in almost seven years, I hadn't laid eyes on her. But she was a loving part of my history, and now she'd disappeared and her husband murdered. I wouldn't give up finding her, dead or alive, but I honestly had no idea where to turn to next.

My phone rang, so loudly it startled me, as I was just sitting quietly and chewing on my problem. Being a Luddite, I had no way of setting incoming calls to be accompanied by music. If so, perhaps a cool, quiet jazz, though I really prefer classical music. I'm mostly a Tchaikovsky fan, as I find Russian music more emotional than the Germans.

But before I clicked the phone on, I read the Caller ID, and was hazy and confused when I saw who was calling.

"Hi, Mr. Reinert. I hope I'm not disturbing you. This is Perwin Tolliver."

My short meeting with him was just that, I thought. Short and in person, as he waited for me on the front steps to the brownstone where I lived. Now, I concluded, he was calling because Denver Tolliver told him of our friendship, and he wanted to go out of his way a little bit. Hearing his voice again so soon threw me off-center. All I could come up with was a lame, "Hi there, Perwin."

"Man, it was so great meeting you yesterday. A really special moment, sir—no kidding. Y' know, I've got two great buds here at the college, and when they heard I know you personally, they went ballistic. One's a computer tech major, and the other one majors in American literature. They told me if I didn't invite you to come downtown and have lunch with us, they were going to kill me." He laughed. "Slowly."

He sounded happy, if nothing else, but the invitation closed my throat. I didn't even know my neighborhood yet, and I've barely opened my new laptop. What would I be doing having lunch with kids twenty years younger than me who'll spend more than an hour telling me how wonderful I am.

How wonderful I *was* is closer to the truth.

I grew up believing real writers *write.* I did that every day of my adult life, even when I was out of town or vacationing somewhere, but I hadn't done that in Joliet for seven years.

I rubbed the bridge of my nose between the eyes to stave off what might become a full-blown headache. I said, "Sounds good, Perwin. What time?"

Seeing the East-West University for the first time surprised me.

It still looked "downtown." The building is large, imposing, sprawling, and seemed well-cared for, at least from the street. I took a long look but was supposed to meet Perwin and his buddies at the Yolk restaurant on South Michigan Avenue. It's a breakfast and brunch place, but our lunch would probably begin and end before they closed down for the day at two o'clock.

They were assembled by the time I got there. Perwin made introductions to his two best friends.

The American Lit major was freckled and redhaired Cory Yancey, originally from Springfield, where Abraham Lincoln made his debut. He came to Chicago because he assumed that's where all the good stuff happens, whether art, literature, entertainment of big-city sports. He was probably right about city fiction, as his favorite author was the late Chicagoan Nelson Algren. Still, he'd read all of my books and was properly impressed, or maybe he just wanted me to think so. Blue eyes that jumped out and bit you in the ass if he so chose to, and an intensity for a guy who reads volumes of novels every month.

The Computer Tech guy, Ariel Rickman, was a few years

older than the other two, possibly mid-twenties. Light-toned skin, grayish green eyes, taller than me, pretty good-looking, and pointed in his questions and comments. He carried his laptop with him wherever he went, and that included a lunch meeting. I found out fairly quickly he'd been born and raised not two miles from where we sat.

Of course, they wanted every scrap of information about my life, and the first half-hour was rapid-fire questions. They stayed away from my recent history, as Perwin asked them to, but they both knew about my police record.

"I told them about my father," he'd said to me on the phone, "so I didn't think you'd mind if I said you and he were best friends."

Fine, I supposed, though I didn't want to walk around with my prison history stamped on my forehead. Maybe that's why they wanted to meet me in the first place. It's rare anyone meets a long-time convict head-to-head if they aren't expecting danger.

After we all ordered brunch, the meal immediately became an interview. Cory Yancey began it with his question.

"Where do you get all your ideas, Mr. Reinert?"

My answer was always the same to people who didn't write for a living, as I do. "Well, there's this elderly Jewish guy in New Jersey. Every so often I mail him twenty-five bucks, and he sends back five ideas."

The young man laughed. "I'm sorry, that was a stupid question."

"It's a question I used to hear five times every day. I didn't mean to be rude." I shifted in my seat, as we were at a square table in the middle of the restaurant. I'd checked out all the other diners before I sat down, and realized more than half of them were eating eggs. I said, "My ideas just pop into my head, Corey. Maybe from a newspaper story, maybe something happened to someone else I can turn into a murder mystery." I was unsure whether they'd chuckle at this next, but it came out anyway. "Maybe one about three college guys who were trying to figure out how to stage a jailbreak to free one of their fathers."

Perwin laughed loudest. "I checked that out for Dad a few years back," he said. "There's no way to bust out of Joliet short of a nuclear bomb."

Ariel queried, "Have you started to write again?"

"Only a few days home, Ariel. Not ready to spend eight hours a day flat on my ass at my laptop. I've got too many other things to think about."

"You've had several years to think but not write. How does that work?"

I shrugged. "If they'd let me have a laptop—or even an old falling-apart typewriter—I would have written damn near every day. I made lots of notes in longhand, stepping stones to new novels, but my handwriting has always been so damn unreadable I couldn't remember what I was thinking." I didn't mention Tana had one of her office people decipher my scribbles, type them, and put them into a folder and put them in Word on my new laptop.

All quiet for a moment, and I guess it was me to keep things going. I said, "I do have a project I'm working on that has nothing to do with my work."

Now all three grew quiet, leaning forward a bit so as not to miss a word. I continued, "When I got out, the husband of a woman I dated years ago met with me and said his wife had gone missing. He asked me to help find her."

"Wow!" breathed Corey Yancey.

"And then," I went on, "that husband was murdered and thrown in the lake. They found him floating just off Navy Pier—with his throat cut."

Ariel Rickman immediately opened his laptop and hit a few strokes. "Go on, Mr. Reinert. I don't want to miss a word of this."

"You're taking notes, Ariel?"

"I realize you're not up to snuff about the internet," he said, "but I might hear something you said, and check it out on my own laptop. It might help you." He shrugged. "Or not."

Corey Yancey chimed in, "We won't talk to anyone about this—but because you're who you are, this might be the beginning of your next book."

"Really? And what if this missing woman I was once in love with turns out to be dead?"

"Eew!" Previn exploded. "Worse, you've got time served you're hauling along with you. You'll be the first guy the cops will look at. Maybe if Ariel learns enough stuff after he hears the whole story, it just might keep you out of prison again."

Corey said, "Listen, Mr. Reinert—I've waited a hell of a long time for your next book, and meeting you at lunch today is a highlight of my life. If Ariel can help you find this Aubrey person, maybe you'll be able to start writing again."

"Besides which," he went on, "I plan getting my masters and my doctorate in American literature, and I'll want to use *you* as my subject."

That set me back on my heels. "My god," I said, "it never occurred to me anyone would care that much."

Perwin said, "You'd be surprised. You were a best-selling author, and you and my dad were best friends in the most stressful circumstances."

"That goes into my doctoral thesis, too," Corey said.

I closed my eyes for a moment. "Let me get this straight, guys. One of you is the son of my best friend from prison, and you all want to be friends with me, too. One of you plans on getting a doctorate in American Literature by examining me, inside and out. One is going deep into the Internet right now to help me find a missing woman. You're all at least twenty years younger than me—and you're buying me lunch. Have I got this straight?"

"Well," Perwin pointed out with a wide grin, "you're here, aren't you?"

CHAPTER TWENTY-EIGHT

The last thing I wanted to do that morning was have lunch with three guys who still wore teeth braces and had high school acne. None of them had families who could afford even one semester at someplace like Loyola or Northwestern, which was why they wound up at bargain-basement East-West. I figured Perwin Tolliver and the two guys he hung out with were probably Trekkies, too, and went to the conventions dressed as characters from the old TV shows. I guess they loved pop music I'd never heard of before and spent at least one Saturday per month getting together at one of their homes to binge all three Lord of the Rings movies.

But they surprised me. Even driving home that afternoon, I hadn't the first hint of what would come out of that meeting, but by the time I finished the eggs, I was somewhat dizzy with these three collegians who were dignified, clever, and smart as a tack. One guy getting his doctorate writing about me, another one tracking down Aubrey Sinden with his magic internet fingers which would make me seem like an idiot, and young Perwin, who wanted to be best friends with me just like his father when we were both in prison.

I had no idea what would come of all this—with me in the middle—but I felt pretty damn good.

The eggs Benedict was terrific, too.

I was haunted, though. It was strange, getting out of Joliet and only having two real friends—Tana Phillips and her husband Jack. She was one of the busiest lawyers in town, and Jack was an NFL superstar making his own fortune nowhere near Soldier Field where the Bears play. Neither much had available time to be great friends, even though they took the entire day off to meet me joyfully as I passed through that iron gate and hauled me home to my classy new apartment, but one day was enough for them.

There was Cassidy Hammond, of course. She first rose out of the surf like Venus de Milo—even though it was on the sandy sidewalk of North Avenue Beach, she was glistening wet with perspiration rather than sea water, and unlike that famous statue, she had both her arms. She quickly became a brand-new lover—sexy, kind, funny, tender, and generously understanding of a long-time celibate taking a chance again.

But as crazy as I was about her, there was no indication the two of us might be in it for the long haul. I had no idea if she was free on evenings she didn't spend with me, which roiled my insides. Another guy, maybe—not someone who spent seven prison years for killing his wife. She also had a full-time job teaching at Northwestern University—and an associate professor can't always just put in a nine-to-five day.

But my new East-West buddies, Perwin Tolliver, Cory Yancey and Ariel Rickman—all half my age—were making me feel pretty good.

That lasted until I got home at about two-thirty and saw the message light on my phone blinking madly red. I made half a pot of coffee and kicked off my shoes before I pressed the playback button.

"Mr. Reinert, this is Dean Bosley—Aubrey Cabot's lawyer? Call me back ASAP. Do you have my number?"

I naturally know the number, you jag-off moron, I thought but did not say. It was also Tana Phillip's central office number. I returned his call. "What do you want to see me about, counselor?"

"I don't want to see you at all," he said, "but someone does."

"And who might that be?"

"The sister of the late Cole Cabot," he said, then added if he thought he was speaking to an imbecile, "Cabot was Aubrey's husband. He was murdered."

"Does she think I did it?"

"If she does," he said as if he were growing tired of the entire conversation, "she'd show up at your home with a homicide detective, four armed guys from the S.W.A.T. team, and somebody pretty high up in the prosecutor's office. But she's coming here instead. And I can't arrest you, Mr. Reinert. I don't have a badge."

"Are you Cole Cabot's lawyer, too?"

"As far as I know," Bosley replied, "he didn't have a lawyer." He cleared his throat, and I heard him shuffling some papers. "Can you meet with her in my office tomorrow at three in the afternoon?"

"May I bring my own attorney with me?"

"I ran this by Tana. She said you probably wouldn't need her here. Nobody's going to sue you." He took a breath. "As far as I know."

"Does this woman have a lawyer, too? Just in case?"

"You'll have to ask her, Mr. Reinert."

When I arrived at the reception room, two stories lower than Tana Phillips's elegant law firm at two minutes past three o'clock, dressed in another suit I'd never worn before and one of my Jerry Garcia ties that were a bit out of fashion at a law emporium, I was escorted by a gorgeous young woman in the sprawling reception area, not to Dean Bosley's office where I'd been before, but to a small conference room. The windows in there did not overlook the dancing fall sunlight skipping over

Lake Michigan's waves as they did from Tana's office, but staring due west. The West Side of Chicago was heavily industrial, and for the most part, not much to look at. Relatively unimportant people were ushered into this particular room.

People like me.

Dean Bosley sat at the end of the long table, hands folded in front of him. I think he was trying to look like Citizen Kane. To his left were the people I think wanted to see me. Bosley introduced us.

"Russell Reinert, meet Skyler and Lyric Poston. Lyric is the late Cole Cabot's sister."

Let's see, I thought silently. Lyric Cabot—melodic first name and historically moneyed last name—marries Skyler Poston—Skyler with a *K* and Poston a name undoubtably Episcopalian. Cole Cabot marries Aubrey Sinden. Aubrey, who had an adulterous affair with a married man who got locked up for killing a wife named Dayna. What the hell ever happened to people named Dick and Jane?

"I'm sorry for your loss," I said to Lyric Poston. She didn't reply, and neither offered a "Glad to meet you" or some such nicety, but after an awkward silence, Lyric began with "When you were having an affair with Aubrey Cabot, you murdered your wife and went to prison for it. Did you not?"

"Her name was Aubrey Sinden back then, Ms. Poston, and to my knowledge, she'd not met your late brother. My marriage was falling apart, but I had no reason whatsoever to kill my wife. It was involuntary manslaughter, and I was more than a hundred miles away when it happened. A prosecutor who loved the idea of taking down a famous and successful man like me convicted me. But yes, before that, Aubrey and I had a romantic relationship for about a year and a half. We didn't go to many upscale events—because I was married."

What I remembered stuck in my guts. I wondered whether both Aubrey and Cassidy were at that signing at the Chicago Book Store so long ago? Funny, but I couldn't recall either of them there. Aubrey usually kept in the background for turnouts like this one, and Cassidy said she stood amongst the crowd, just looking but not approaching. Then again, there were two hundred persons attending, so—

"You were working for my brother when he was—when he died. Looking for his missing wife."

"I wasn't working for Cole Cabot," I replied. "He hired me one day and fired me the next. But I kept searching for Aubrey on my own. No pay."

"Why is that?"

"Because at one time she was a main cog in my life. If she's disappeared without a trace, that makes me uneasy. I'm looking for Aubrey as hard as I can, mostly because your brother hadn't the foggiest notion of how to search for a missing person."

"Why would he ask you?"

"Because I write mystery fiction, and my fictional detectives find missing people all the time. Cole assumed I could do that in real life, too."

"You actually turned down a paying job?" she said, feigning surprise. "How could you, just out of—well, you haven't worked in a long time, so—"

"Ms. Poston," I said as kindly as I could, "I'm nowhere near as wealthy as the Boston Cabots." Her husband, sitting next to her with the personality of a box of hair, had his lips pressed tightly together as though he were fighting off a humiliating attack of diarrhea. "Sorry, I'm not that familiar with the Poston legacy. But I assure you, I own ten times the money I'll ever be able to spend."

Skyler Poston frowned slightly. Very slightly. It would take a microscope to see it. But it was his wife who spoke.

"You didn't like my brother, did you?"

"I didn't like him and I didn't dislike him. We had a few meetings, and all we talked about was finding Aubrey."

Lyric Poston uncrossed her legs and then re-crossed them. Of course, I couldn't see that, as she was sitting at the table, her legs out of sight, but that soft, sensual *zip-zip* noise nylon-clad legs make when they are crossed is unmistakable. Her tone became angry and questioning, but she didn't lean forward the way most angry people do. The iron pipe running from her ass up through her backbone to the top of her head made such a change of position impossible. She said, "Is Aubrey still in love with you?"

"I doubt that much. She broke up with me—rightly so—many years ago. Then she married your brother."

Now she pointed a long, slim index finger at me. Her red-tipped manicure must have cost at least two hundred dollars. "She was rich. She was rich, you know?" She turned and looked at Dean Bosley, and he shrank three sizes before she even addressed him. "She was rich, wasn't she, Mr. Bosley?"

"I can't discuss a client's financial affairs, Ms. Poston."

"Forgive me for pointing this out," I said, "but until there's an official report from law enforcement Aubrey is no longer alive, she's still your living, breathing client, Mr. Bosley. And Ms. Poston, she might still be your sister-in-law."

She turned to Bosley. "When can we read her will?"

"That's against the law, Ms. Poston. For all we know, she's having an amazing time in Jamaica or the Virgin Islands right this minute—possibly with a friend. She's only been missing for two weeks. We can't possibly read her will now. As her attorney, I'd read it first, and then gather any people she'd mentioned, possibly those she remembered."

"But she must be dead!" Lyric's chin quivered with anger. "If she were alive, she'd have at least called Cole and told him where she was."

"Ms. Poston," I said. "Amelia Earhart was gone for eighteen months before being pronounced legally dead. Two weeks isn't going to make it."

Drew Bosley said, "I think Mr. Reinert has a point."

"I know why you're sticking your nose in this," Lyric gnashed at me, barbed wire wrapped around each word.

"Aubrey left you money."

"I haven't seen, spoken to, or corresponded with Aubrey for seven years. I imagine she left everything to her husband."

"And he's dead!" She didn't say it sadly. She hadn't shown the smallest amount of grief at the loss of her brother.

Now Drew Bosley was right in there, swinging away. His wimpy personality morphed into tough guy with a sharp accusation. "Do you think Cole Cabot bequeathed everything to you, Ms. Poston?"

She said, "I didn't know if he had a lawyer, or even made a will."

"Then why," I asked, "are you involving me in looking for Aubrey?"

"If Aubrey is—" She paused, looking for a word other than dead, as she'd used it less than a minute earlier. She eventually chose a somewhat kinder word. "If Aubrey is deceased—and if she left all she owned to Cole—"

I interrupted her. "And since Cole is also deceased—and you're his only living relative, you're hoping I keep looking for Aubrey and find out she's dead. That makes you rich." I turned to Drew Bosley. "Am I on the right track, counselor?"

Lyric Cabot Poston snapped her head back as if she'd just been backhanded across the mouth. "That's a shitty thing to say."

"Is it? Then why am I here?"

Bosley jumped in. "Let's not all get bent out of shape. Aubrey Cabot was a close friend of yours, Mr. Reinert."

"*Is,* counselor. Until further notice."

"I apologize. Aubrey *is* a friend of yours—and she is my client. And Cole is Ms. Poston's closest living sibling. That's why we hope to get this finished as quickly as possible."

Lyric uncrossed and crossed her legs again. *Zip. Zip.* That time, her husband actually looked down at her knees. She said, "I don't want Mr. Reinert anywhere near this so-called search."

"You can't fire me," I said. "I don't work for you, and I

didn't work for your brother. I don't want to be involved in this, but I can't just sit in my apartment all day. Mr. Bosley is not my attorney. Here's my opinion, for what it's worth. I don't think Aubrey ran off with another man and left Cole alone and wondering. She has too much class for that. I don't think she's having an affair, but if she were, she'd do it quietly. I don't think she was murdered, but I think Cole was killed for their relationship, especially because he told me he didn't want the police involved. As for kidnapping, it's been two weeks and there has been no contact asking for a ransom. If there is a reward, I imagine Aubrey would have paid it off herself. Someone has her for some reason, and that's what I've been trying to find out."

Finished, I sat back in my chair, and the room was quiet. Then Skyler Poston opened his mouth for the first time since I entered the room. "Mr. Reinert." His voice was that of a man who made money. "You're an interesting human being. I hope you start writing your next book very soon."

CHAPTER TWENTY-NINE

I spent the rest of the afternoon at home listening to my favorite jazz pianist, the late Bill Evans, on three of the CDs Tana Phillips kept for me and then put them back in my new home, reminding me my adoptive parents didn't much give a damn about music of any kind. My mother, however, bought me a *Charlie Parker with Strings* album, even though she hadn't the foggiest notion what it was all about. That album turned me into a lifelong jazz freak.

I thought Lyric Cabot Poston had either kidnapped or murdered her sister-in-law, Aubrey. She could have executed her brother, too, except even a humorless, arrogant ice-cold monster like Lyric couldn't cut her own brother's throat and dump him into Lake Michigan.

But if Lyric was guilty, I was at a dead end once again. I talked to so many people and gone nowhere. My stomach was doing Olympic-style gymnastic triple-twists of frustration. Should I have stayed in prison for all ten years? At least behind bars, I never felt like a loser, even though locked away for a crime I didn't commit? As Navy guys often say about a shore leave, I was screwed, blewd, and tattooed—but it wasn't my fault.

Now, though, I felt like a five-year-old kid trying to swing a baseball bat at a slow-pitch ball for the first time in his life, but the whole thing turned dangerous when Cole's body turned up in the lake. Now my existence is staring at a brick wall and hoping somewhere there was a door or a window.

The only light at the end of my dark tunnel was Cassidy Hammond, and I was stupefied to know that after my long, *long* incarceration, the first woman who showed any interest toward me, the first woman I had touched in nearly a decade, was someone I was beginning to love.

Just after seven o'clock, when I was feeling depressed and thinking dangerously of getting drunk as a skunk, someone rang my doorbell.

I dragged myself out of my chair and made it over to the speaker. "What is it?" I growled like a highly annoyed grizzly bear.

"It's Perwin Tolliver and Ariel Rickman. Can we come up?"

"I'm not much in the mood, Perwin."

"Sorry, but Ariel was on the internet for hours, and what he found out may just surprise you."

I'm not sure I said "Oh, fuck!" aloud, or just thought it. In either case, I pressed the 'come in' button, reluctantly turned off Bill Evans, and steeled myself for another round of praise and affection from two kids I hardly knew.

Ariel Rickman seemed more bowled over by the grandeur of my apartment than Perwin when he first saw it—or at least the living room. He probably had too much dignity to ask to see the bedroom, which was a good thing because, of all the domestic chores I had to do each day to keep my place in order, the one thing I totally despised was making the bed. Or maybe he was too jazzed just being named after a famous Shakespeare character in *The Tempest*.

"Sit down, guys," I said. "Make yourselves comfortable." They both wore autumn jackets and kept them on. Ariel had his laptop tucked under one arm.

"We hate to bug you, Mr. Reinert," he said, "but I was awake all night doing research for you—and most of today, too.

You need to know what I found out—and I hate to screw up your evening, but I think it's important. If you don't, just kick my ass out of here, and I'll never bother you again."

For about thirty seconds, I was unable to say anything. This intense young man, who had never heard of me until yesterday's lunch, had twisted his brain and worn out his fingers, typing—and all for *me*. I took a few deep breaths and tried not shaking my head to get my thoughts in order.

"Ariel, you've worked to help me look for a missing woman?"

Perwin said, "Cory Yancey and I would've been working for you, too, but Ariel is ten times faster than us."

Ariel grinned, then said, "You had a meeting with Gaylord Ogilvy, right?"

I nodded. "He didn't tell me a thing. Did you find something?"

He said, "Sit next to me on the sofa so you can see," he suggested, and flipped open his laptop.

For the next hour and a half, he told me more about Gaylord Ogilvy than I'd ever known before. Since I hadn't watched local TV news shows from jail, I had no idea a tough political reporter, beautiful and relentlessly truthful African American journalist named Angela Damron, who appeared on Channel 6 almost every night, had a long affair with Ogilvy. The adulterous romance lasted about two years, until she moved to Florida for a news anchor job about the same time Ogilvy Company put up a magnificent, towering building right on the Florida west coast, near Naples. Ground floor and mezzanine were all retail, plus two high-end restaurants. The next four levels were business offices, including an Ogilvy headquarters which took up an entire floor. Angela Damron became the CEO for all Ogilvy buildings in the state of Florida. The next twenty-seven floors were residential. And Gardner lived in the penthouse. Ariel found two photographs of her on the Internet—one with Gaylord Ogilvy and one by herself, the photograph that got her the TV news job in the first place.

Perwin studied the photographs and remarked, "Mr. Gaylord has fantastic times with beautiful women."

Ariel answered, "He looks like a geek."

"He's much more beautiful," I said, "when he stands on his wallet."

I wondered whether Ms. Damron—the kind of woman who enters a large crowded room in which all go quiet staring at her—was in a relationship in Florida with Gaylord when Aubrey was seeing me at the same time she was his Chicago mistress—or one of them—and the multi-billionaire didn't seem upset about that.

Ariel Rickman apparently found a few more photos of beautiful women who shared a small slice of their lives with the richest man in Illinois, mostly candid photographs snapped by Chicago paparazzi when no one was looking.

Ariel then switched to a photo of Ogilvy with Aubrey Sinden, the two of them together at a booth in some restaurant. They were not bestowing each other with mooning love-faces, but from Audrey's glamorous dress, it was obvious that it was—well, does anyone still call this a *date?* The setting didn't look familiar, but it might have opened within the last seven years. That made me feel a sliver better—Aubrey had worn that dress a few times when she was out with me.

"This is the woman you're looking for?" Ariel asked. "She has fast company." He tilted the laptop closer to him and did miraculous things with his fingers. Then he pushed it back toward me and said, "Here."

Aubrey Sinden Cabot—Wikipedia used all three names. It listed her birth date, her parents' names and location, her university experience—business degrees, both bachelor and masters at Case Western Reserve University in Cleveland, which I never knew about because I never asked her if she'd gone to college. The bio celebrated her current business activity—vice president in charge of international operations for the Ogilvy Company. Her disappearance had not yet reached Wikipedia.

It also said she owned several major land properties in foreign countries—Saudi Arabia, Austria, Thailand, Portugal and Russia. Wikipedia reluctantly admitted they didn't know how much money she had in the bank but guessed at least sixty million dollars in foreign properties alone, which would probably increase twenty-fold when those locations begin constructing profit-making buildings.

I shook my head in disbelief, looking away from the screen and directly at Ariel Bowen. "This isn't possible," I said. "Aubrey Sinden Cabot worth sixty million dollars? In a pig's ass!"

"She doesn't have that much money in a bank, Mr. Reinert," Ariel said. "It's what those properties are worth—and she owns them."

"Where the hell would she get money to buy them?"

Perwin said, "She's a vice president at Gaylord Ogilvy."

"Even if Aubrey was his sometime girlfriend," I said, "there's no way Gaylord would pay her sixty million bucks."

"Mr. Ogilvy has so damn much money," Ariel Rickman observed, "he doesn't give a damn where it goes. I looked him up for hours. Apart from all his building in other cities and countries, even though his main headquarters is in the Merchandise Mart, he owns seven different properties right here in Greater Chicago, and some of them are empty buildings."

"Empty, hell!" I found myself yelling. I hadn't raised my voice in seven years—and for damn good reason. Somewhat softer, then. "He's probably staffed one of them with perverted hookers, one with a bookie joint that takes in millions every day, maybe a special place where he has people executed."

"Executed?" Perwin's eyebrows strained toward his hairline. "Who would actually get executed?"

"Aubrey Sinden's husband—Cole Cabot. He got his throat cut," I said, once more with heat, "and they threw him in the lake."

"Jesus," Perwin breathed. "You think the Ogilvy people did that?"

I replied, "You call it execution if you want to, Perwin. I call it murder."

In this day and age, it's astonishing to realize if someone does hours and hours of research on what interests *you,* it's as easy as one-two-three to transfer all his research to your laptop. That's what Ariel Rickman did for me, transferring much of what was on his laptop into mine. When he and Perwin Tolliver eventually went home, I was overwhelmed by all the information he'd left me.

Aubrey Cabot seemed to be the owner of a great many land deals all over the world, but all Ariel was able to discern is which countries they were in. More informative was which unused buildings Ogilvy and Company controlled all over Chicago and its suburbs. What I would make of all this hidden news, I had no idea.

Did Aubrey's lawyer, Dean Bosley, have knowledge of this? If so, he didn't share it with me. Did Aubrey make a will? Did Cole Cabot? What has his sister, Lyric Poston, to do with all this besides outright greed? And is Detective Easton Dorn actively investigating Cole's ghastly death?

I couldn't close my eyes that night. I sat at my desk, scrolling through the internet. I even made myself a half-pot of coffee, making sure it was very strong. If I wasn't able to sleep, I wanted to be awake and alert.

I'd run out of people to interview, at least for the moment. But after several hours of thinking, scratching my head, drinking all the coffee, I figured the only thing left for me to do was to probe some of those real estate properties Gaylord Ogilvy owns right here in the city.

I showered, shaved and shampooed, then dried off and combed my hair. For whatever reason, my hair *never* looks as if it had been combed, because I have a cowlick in the front, I guess I was born with it, and have never been able to do anything with it. No matter what the rest of my hair looks like, that fluffy cowlick in front makes me resemble Shirley Temple. While in Joliet, I stuck to a crew cut until a month before I was released. After seven years, that damn cowlick still hadn't gone away.

I waited until ten a.m. to leave my apartment. Chicago freeways are a twenty-four-hour traffic jam, but especially awful in the morning. I chose streets instead. The first address I looked for was about six blocks from the southern border of the city.

It used to be an office building, faded yellow brick and now looking a total wreck. It was four stories tall, its windows completely boarded up. I had no idea why the Ogilvy Company owned it. The street was nearly deserted, so my walk around the building trying all the doors was unobserved. Everything was locked up tight, one of the hundreds of ancient buildings in Chicago that had outlived their usefulness. The main door was made of steel—dented, attacked, but strong and sturdy. I think I made a long drive southward for nothing.

My second stop was a building not too far from East-West University, about five stories high, and this one was partially occupied. A tiny advertising agency, a photography studio, a company on the first floor that sends out part-time workers to businesses who temporarily need them, and a small unit that takes orders for T-shirts that are created elsewhere. Inside the main entrance was an ancient brass sign, probably mounted a century ago, reading "Welcome to the Shovel Works." I doubt anyone there made shovels anymore.

I went into the temporary hires office and asked if there were vacant spaces I could rent in the building. The woman, who was alone in the room, told me there were a few empty offices and said I'd have to call Ogilvy Company and ask for someone in Irvin Greenfield's office who can help me.

Irvin Greenfield. Chief of Staff? Vice President of everything? Guardian of the Gates—-and he's busy renting out small, useless buildings to those who can't afford to do business elswhere? He gave me a headache—or more accurately a pain in the ass.

I didn't want to open an office in the first place. I was only picking up scraps of a vague idea of what had happened with Aubrey Sinden. Irvin Greenfield was a scrap.

Traveling west, then, not too far from what used to be the largest stockyard in America. My next address, thanks to Ariel Rickman, was an actual house. A very nice house. Not a mansion, not even a mini-mansion, but a nice house, circular driveway of oyster shells, two and a half stories, three gables, and my guess, a large pool in the back, a guest house in which to shower and change clothes, a tennis court, and an enormous propane grill that could cook enough food at one time for a hungry Republican congress caucus.

I wondered who lived there and was about to find out because an elderly gentleman who looked Latino was trimming the elegant bushes that surrounded the house. He waved as he watched my car enter and then roll to a stop.

"How're you doing there, young man?" he said. His accent, whatever it might be, was slight. I climbed out of the car. *Young man.* I guessed thirty-eight was the new twenty-three.

"This is a beautiful house," I said.

"I work here full-time, six days a week. It's the best job I ever had." He put down his hedge clippers. I thought he must be in his late sixties, if not older, but beneath his overalls and T-shirt, his body seemed to be in great shape.

"I'll bet it is," I said. "I'm looking to buy a house in the neighborhood, and this one seems prettier and more upscale than the rest."

He nodded. "Afraid you're out of luck, young man. The house isn't for sale."

"Who lives here? A large family?"

"Nobody actually lives here. It's owned by a huge company, and they use this when important people come to town and don't like staying in hotels. We've got a full-time housekeeper and cook, and—well, nobody calls them butlers anymore, but there's a guy who's worked here for about ten years. He doesn't wear a butler's suit, but he's really kind of the boss, and he makes sure the visitors who stay here for a while get whatever they want or need."

"You have current guests at the moment?"

"Nope. Probably not for another few weeks."

"I'm wondering," I ventured, "if I can talk to this butler guy?"

"Desmond Prival?" The gardener reached under his cap and scratched his head. "I don't know, sir. He doesn't usually see uninvited visitors."

I tried not to look snarky, but I was frustrated. "Maybe tell him I'm kind of a famous guy?" That turned me into a narcissistic asshole—similar to other famous guys. "That might get his attention."

"Famous? Sorry, but I don't recognize you. What are you famous for?"

Confessing I was a recent ex-con didn't seem like a good idea—but I did tell him a truth, albeit an old one. "I'm a best-selling author," I said, and recited my name.

He looked embarrassed, scuffing the oyster shells with one foot. "Sorry, sir, but I'm not much of a reader."

"No, but you're one hell of a gardener. Look, can you tell this Mr. Prival I'm here and would like to talk to him?"

"Well..."

"How about I just knock on the door?" I asked. "Will he answer, or will the housekeeper? I just need a few minutes."

Now the old man looked nervous, almost frightened, and he kept turning his head to make sure no one was at the front windows, watching him. "No, let me talk to him, sir. What was your name again?"

I pronounced carefully, "Russell Reinert. I don't need much time—"

He sighed audibly, and tugged on his gardener's overalls and attempted to finger his hair into a relatively neat appearance. Then, as if using the last mile in a Dead Man Walking death house corridor, he made his way to the house and fearfully rang the bell.

A black woman who, from my distance, seemed fairly young opened the door. No maid's uniform, but instead what they used to call a housedress. Her head was wrapped in a red bandana, so I had no idea what her hair looked like. She and the gardener whispered to each other for more than a minute. Then she went back inside, leaving him staring at a closed door. He turned back to me with a weak but embarrassed smile.

I raised my eyebrows in a silent question. He answered, "She's telling him you're here."

I waited for five minutes, perhaps more, until finally, the door opened, and Desmond Prival stepped out into the daylight. Indeed, he was not wearing a butler's uniform, but gray slacks and a white tennis sweater over a black sport shirt. His sunglasses practically hid his eyes. He walked toward me.

"Mr. Rinehart?" he queried.

"Reinert. Russell Reinert. And you're Mr. Prival?"

He didn't extend a handshake. "I'm afraid you've come on a fool's errand, Mr. Reinert. This house is not for sale."

"I'm sorry to hear that. It just caught my eye because it's such a great property. Do you live here?"

"I work here."

"I see," I said. "May I ask who owns it?"

"A very large company with headquarters in Chicago."

I knew the answer, naturally, but I played along with it anyway. "Like Boeing?"

"No."

"United Airlines?"

"No."

"Hyatt Hotels? Swift Meats?"

"Now you're guessing."

"Is it a secret, Mr. Prival?"

His nostrils flared which made them seem as if they no longer supported air. "Hardly a secret. It's owned by The Ogilvy Company."

"Ah, yes—I should have mentioned that first." I took a healthy breath. The air out here was cleaner than where I lived, in Near North. "That's interesting. I know some people who work at Ogilvy. Irvin Greenfield, for instance."

Prival nodded.

"And Aubrey Sinden—or should I say Aubrey Cabot?"

"There are more than six thousand people working for Ogilvy right here in Chicago," he said. "I don't know all of them."

"Don't know Aubrey?"

"I don't know Aubrey and I don't know you," Prival said coldly.

"I write mystery novels—or I used to, anyway. Aubrey Sinden never visited here? Even maybe for just an afternoon? Or evening?"

"Mr. Rinehart," he said, and this time he deliberately meant to screw up my name, "You have the balls of a bull elephant! You don't want to buy this house! You're here asking questions—and I'll be double goddamned if I'll answer any more of them. Take a hike," he ordered, "or I'll call the police and have you carried out of here."

He spun around and headed back for the front door where the Latino gardener stood, hopefully out of the way. But Desmond Prival stopped in front of him. "Stupid idiot spic!" he hissed. "Don't ever do this again!" Thus said, he delivered a sharp slap across the gardener's mouth, marched back into the house, and though the door was heavy and too large to slam, he tried it anyway—and failed.

My face felt as if it were on fire. I wanted to bang on that door again and pay Prival off for the slap to the old man's cheek, but I had to think better of it. During seven years in Joliet State Prison, I was in enough fights to know I can handle myself if I had to. I could have ripped off one of Prival's ears and make him eat it, but then I'd wind up in Joliet again—and nothing was worth that!

I moved over to the gardener, who stood as small as he could, wishing he could disappear. I wanted to do something for him, but I couldn't give him money. I couldn't offer him a better job because I didn't have one to give. I couldn't hug him—I didn't even know his name.

I clamped both his upper arms and just half-whispered "Sorry," and got out of there as quickly as possible. This took more out of me than I'd imagined. I was finished running down Ariel Rickman's internet listings until another day.

I didn't even have an empty can to kick down the road.

CHAPTER THIRTY

My most recent trip, the psychological head-butting with Desmond Prival, and the ice-water shock of humiliation the arrogant house manager bestowed on the old gardener left me more than shaken—so I decided not to have a drink with my dinner. Upset as I was, I knew one shot of whiskey would turn into quite a few more, and my system had grown unused to heavy hitting. All I had in the refrigerator to eat were the deli meats Tana bought before I moved in, along with some excellent rye bread and an obscure bottle of mustard. I figured I'd soon have to go to a regular grocery store. One cannot live on pastrami on rye for their entire life.

Of course, I still had a few bagels with cream cheese left, and that was my dinner.

After I ate, I watched the MSNBC Nightly News, then stretched out on the sofa, kicked off my shoes, and called Cassidy. I missed her. We were not yet at the every-night portion of our relationship, as we'd only known each other for a week. But I'd been much bothered my back-and-forth quarrel with Desmond Prival.

More times than I can remember, I witnessed one prisoner in Joliet hitting another one in the face, more than once a week, and often for something as trivial as sneaking an extra piece of bread for dinner or asking someone at the other end of the table to please pass the salt. Noses broken sometimes, or the violent loss of a front tooth or two, and sometimes a down-for-the-count knockout, leaving the attacked with a concussion who only mumbled bounding silliness for the next few days. But a slap—in public? That was pure power cruelty, an overseer publicly punishing a peasant.

My urge to rip out Prival's throat was overwhelmed by my fear of winding up in Joliet again, this time with a longer sentence—so I did nothing.

But I needed to talk about it, and at the moment the person whose voice I desperately needed to hear was that of Cassidy Hammond. As I dialed, it amazed me I'd already memorized her number.

When I recounted my ghastly experience of earlier that day, her first response—not at all surprising—was "My god, Russ. What kind of man is that? What kind of household?"

"I never saw anything like that," I said. "It nailed me right in the heart."

"It would have messed up my thinking, too," she said, and took a deep inhale, the kind one might suck in before beginning a major speech. I wasn't sure I wanted to hear what was coming, but I waited anyway. "Russ, I know you're on a big search for your ex-girlfriend, and I understand that. I really do. The past is the past, so I'm not even a little bit jealous. But you've only been out of prison for a few days. If you keep this up, you might run into real danger that will surprise the hell out of you—and either you'll get hurt, or you'll hurt someone else and find yourself behind bars again because no Chicago cop or DA will believe you. It's also possible this woman might not be with us anymore, and you're running yourself ragged. Your heart will be permanently broken and your personality totally crushed." I heard a subtle sniffle. "You have to quit this search. You really do."

I had to struggle for a moment to breathe, as though a hippopotamus was sitting on my chest. I finally said, "Aubrey might be alive, too—and in terrible danger. It's not my busi-ness—but her husband was murdered, she's vanished, and nobody else I know seems to give a damn. I'm the only one left, Cassidy."

"Russell," she said, her voice quavering, on the edge of tears, "you're an ex-convict! You spent seven years in prison for involuntary manslaughter! Every cop in Chicago, the state police, the Justice Department, and for all I know the FBI are all out looking to catch you doing something illegal so they can lock you up again. I waited for you seven years, and you didn't even know I was alive. But we know each other now, and I won't wait seven more. She might still be alive—but you're risking your future, your whole life, looking all over town for her."

That hole in my chest where my heart used to be started throbbing again. Cassidy and I were still strangers, but my feelings for her could possibly be love. Now I felt her pulling away from me.

My mouth was dry again. While I was still able to talk, I said, "Let's make a deal, Cassidy. This is Thursday—Thursday evening, so that's really the end of the day, and it's too late for me to go out and poke around again. Give me three more days—Friday, Saturday and Sunday. If I don't find anything by then, I'll stop. I promise you. No more Aubrey, no more jail time, and Monday morning I swear I'll sit down and begin working on my next book. Deal?"

"How in hell are you going to stop?"

"Because," I said with difficulty, "I'm making you a promise. Dead or alive, I'm nowhere near in love with Aubrey. I'm not sure I ever was in the first place—so I'm promising."

Now Cassidy waited for a long moment. She was thinking it over, too. She finally said, "If you keep that promise, Russ, call me on Sunday night and tell me so. If you don't?" Long pause. "Then don't."

After we said our stiff, awkward goodbyes, I couldn't sit still anymore, but paced like a zoo-captured animal. I poured a brandy and walked from room to room, window to window, peering out at Oak Street, listening for the faintest of noises. Did I just louse up what might have become a very serious relationship? Am I crazy chasing after a woman I hadn't seen in seven years? And for the exception of Ariel Rickman's list of Chicagoland places owned by the Ogilvy Company, I didn't know where else to go or who else to talk to.

Just past nine o'clock, the phone rang. I couldn't imagine who was calling. The only people who knew my phone number were Cassidy, Tana Phillips and whoever in her empire she chose, and my so-called parole officer, Roman Bellini, even though I am not on parole, but free and clear—or so I've been told.

"Is this Mr. Russell Reinert?" a female voice wanted to know. A strange voice I never heard before, but her lilt and her pronunciation of only a few words told me she learned how to talk in the American south.

"I'm Russell Reinert," I confessed. Then her reply knocked me right out of my socks.

"Mr. Reinert—I'm Kalinda Tolliver. Denver's wife—and Perwin's mama."

"After you and Denver became good friends," Kalinda Tolliver said, "I always wanted to meet you in person—but I only got one visitation per month to Joliet, and if I had to pick between you and Denver, I'm sorry but I always chose him. I'm really glad they let you out. He always believed you were innocent. He said you were a kind man. He knew you'd never kill anyone."

"He was the kind one, Ms. Tolliver. He saved my life more than once."

"He really loved you as a friend, Mr. Reinert. I don't think he ever spoke about anyone else like he talked about you. You did so much for him."

"It's just Russ, please. All I did was talk to him whenever we could get together. We told each other things the other never knew about. But he saved my life at least a dozen times. Pretty soon the whole prison knew if they wanted to hurt me, they'd have to go through him, first. Damn, Kalinda—I hope I can call you Kalinda—I'd give anything if they'd let him out, too."

She sighed, and the sigh had a little jump in it, as if she were ready to cry.

"He killed a policeman. He'll never get out." Then her tone got a bit brighter. "But I have Perwin to remind me. He's like his dad, only more gentle. He's so thrilled he got to meet you. So did his pals, Ariel and Cory."

"Ariel. I didn't ask, but isn't Ariel a girl's name?"

"It was in Disney's *Little Mermaid* movie. But in ancient religion, it was a man's name, particularly in Hebrew. Ariel was embarrassed a mermaid shared his name, but now he's used to it, and likes it a lot."

"Smart guy," I said. "Good for him."

"Him and Perwin stayed up most of the night checking things out for you on the Internet because you're looking for someone you used to know."

"A woman I knew very well a long time ago went missing, and her husband approached me for help to find her. Then someone murdered him and threw him in the lake."

I could almost hear her shudder. "What a terrible thing! What you do is dangerous, Russ."

"Denver taught me how to fight in prison. God knows I'm nowhere near as tough as he is—or as big, either—but I learned how to take care of myself. I'm not worried."

She was quiet for a while, until I added, "Well, maybe a little bit worried."

She said, "You've got help. Perwin isn't as tough as his daddy, either, but almost as big, and Denver schooled him to take care of himself." She snickered. "I learned a few things, too. I'm no Denver—but if you come after me, you better be carrying a gun and can kill me from fifteen feet away. Otherwise, I'll take it away from you and shove it so far up your ass everyone'll believe there's no such gun anymore."

The steel in her voice indicated she was not exaggerating. I said, "I won't try to shoot you. I've always written about good guys and bad guys, but I never fired a handgun in my life."

"That's good to hear," Kalinda said, "but don't forget you've got a whole team behind you. Perwin, Ariel and Corey. That's Team Reinert, my friend. And I'm that team's mascot, too."

I felt almost starry-eyed. "Kalinda—when this is all over, I want to take you to dinner. There's nothing I could do for Denver, but I can start making it up to him with you."

She actually chortled. "Just don't forget, I'm only the mascot. Denver's a whole lot bigger than me—but I'm no Barbie Doll, either."

I said, "Now that means you're my best friend in the world. Ever."

"In that case," she said, "I'm going to worry about you."

"Only worry until Sunday evening," I assured her. "After that, I'll be safe."

CHAPTER THIRTY-ONE

I woke up early the next morning before the time I'd set my alarm. I stayed under the shower water for twenty minutes. It was hotter than hell, but I was enjoying the privilege of taking a shower whenever I wanted to. I made half a pot of coffee, strong, and ate the last of the bagels Tana had bought for me, then watched the TV news and ignored the commercials.

Going to my laptop, I booted up the information Ariel Rickman had researched for me. Several buildings owned by Ogilvy companies were listed by street address, including ones I visited yesterday. Two were dreary wastes of time. One of them was difficult but did not seem particularly criminal.

That left four to go.

At a few minutes past ten, I went outside and walked to my garage, where I was again greeted by my car valet, Rollo, as though I were a long-lost relative, and set out, driving through The Loop and continuing southward.

The first address was a sprawled-out commercial building. The street level presented several retail stores, plus a high-class coffee house, the drinks expensive imported coffees.

I talked to the manager—not the owner, a young African American woman who didn't look much past twenty-two. I asked if there were any spaces open for rent. She assured me they were completely full.

"What happens upstairs?" I asked. "More businesses?"

"Oh, no," she assured me. "People live upstairs. There are four one-bedroom apartments. I've been to two of them. They're very nice. But again, not for rent right now."

"Do you know who owns the building?"

She looked flummoxed. "I have no idea, sir. I manage this shop, but I have no connection with the building's owner."

"Well," I said, "thank you for the information." I turned to go.

Her eyes twinkled as she said, "May I offer you a cup of great coffee? On the house?"

I only hesitated for a moment. I'd bolted down half a pot for breakfast and certainly didn't need more—but the offer by a pretty girl of a five-dollar cup of coffee caused me to thank her, sit down at a table, and enjoy.

Half an hour later, I headed west. Cicero, a close Chicago suburb, is probably best known for famed gangster Al Capone moving his outfit from downtown Chicago to a town that began as a complete Caucasian enclave in the nineteenth century. One hundred years later sported a Hispanic majority, along with blacks and Asians. Now there are office buildings, a commercial section and even a mall.

I've hated malls since I was a small child. I always wished for privately owned retail stores my parents used to tell me about, where one gets to personally know and like their clothing clerks, bakers, milliners, and owners of stationery stores. Back in that day, there was no such thing as a supermarket or shopping mall—just grocery stores—and there were no "chains" of restaurants, numbering in the many hundreds. Now you can go to an Applebee's in Chicago, for instance, then travel to Spokane, Washington and eat in a restaurant that looks exactly the same and has the identical menu.

Cicero looked the same as almost everywhere else in the country, but it had changed over the last century. There was much racial hatred in Cicero over the years, but it had more or less calmed down by the time I paid my first visit in search of the whereabouts of Aubrey Sinden Cabot.

According to Ariel's research, I was to look for a large Ogilvy-owned house on a short street. Carrying my laptop, I could access maps that would show me the way, but I've always been lousy at reading maps.

I drove around the city—or town or village or whatever the hell they call it these days—for about twenty minutes until I found what I was looking for. It was a dark-painted square-shaped ranch home on a small hill, all one story, set back from the street and approximately fifty feet on each side from the homes next to it. Across the street there were no residences, only a half-assed park no one had yet figured what to do with it. No gazebo, no playground, no baseball or soccer field—just a scattering of half-grown trees, shaggy bushes, and grass that hadn't been mowed for at least three weeks.

I parked about thirty yards away. There was no sidewalk, so I trudged along the curb, then turned and worked my way up the driveway to the house.

It was uncomfortably quiet. Chilly and windy, it was past the season for birds to be singing loudly. No sound from inside that I could tell. I rang the doorbell, hearing a soft *bong* on the other side of the door. I waited.

I buzzed again.

I waited again.

Then I knocked on the door, hard enough to bruise my knuckles. No answer. Was it possible no one was home?

I walked to my right. There were large windows in front, but someone had heavily draped them so no one could get a look inside.

I almost shouted, "Hello. Anyone home?"

I moved further in the same direction. At the top of the driveway was an iron gate with spikes at the top on which to eviscerate medieval usurpers, supposedly leading to the back-yard. I called, "Hello! Anybody home?" and then carefully opened the raspy squeaking iron gate and almost tiptoed through.

For such a large house, there was nothing behind it except a short stretch of pavement ending at the rear entrance. It didn't look like anyone else's kitchen door. Heavy solid wood that would take more than a hefty cop's kick to open it. Though it was turning cold in Chicagoland, as it does each autumn, there was no outdoor seating at all, the kind where everyone sits around a fire pit, wrapped in blankets and drinking cognac and toasting marshmallows. Here, I saw no fire pit or campfire area, no barbecue oven or a swimming pool. Nothing. The rear windows were also heavily curtained.

I didn't bother calling out again.

The three-car garage was not connected to the house but was about forty yards further from the house itself, backing against a stand of trees that seemed to be some sort of mini-forest.

I sauntered back toward it, lifting my shoulders against a sudden stiff lake breeze, hugging the entire east end of Chicago. It was no whim nicknaming us "the Windy City."

Visit anytime.

I was certain the garage was locked and the doors only opened via remote control. Still, there were small horizontal slits of windows. I stood close, up on my tiptoes to see.

There was only one vehicle parked inside. I squinted into the relative dark until I saw it was a black Cadillac Escalade—the same car in which Walter Yellen and Hayden Fantos drove me to and from the home of Lilith Shadburn Ogilvy several days earlier.

I couldn't give it much more thought, because something hard lashed against the back of my head. The day rapidly became the darkest night as I fell forward, scraping my forehead against the garage door.

I don't remember anything after that.

* * *

It could be I was struck by lightning—or maybe there was a massive earthquake and a giant tree had fallen on my head. More probably I was run over by one of the "L" trains that circled the loop, and it crushed my skull. But when one is out cold and begins nibbling on the edge of reality, weird things start happening from the inside.

When I began regaining consciousness, everything I could see at the moment was blurred, a badly-developed video no one bothered to check. I immediately thought I was back in prison and someone—or some *ones*—finally got past Denver Tolliver and attacked me, setting the back of my head on fire. Not one of those awful moments to wonder why anyone would set fire to my head, but then fighting your way back into awareness did not lend itself to realistic thinking.

Slowly, almost painfully, everything seemed to be working toward a focus. I was lying on a floor, on something relatively soft, and from what I could make out, I was in a basement somewhere. It took more than a minute to realize in what house I was waking up. I didn't know whose house. Whoever it was felt peeking through the small window of a garage was trespassing.

I was on a thin mattress. No pillow, no sheets, just a bare mattress with old-fashioned stripes on it. Who decided years and years ago to put stripes on a mattress no one else sees? I was covered with a lightweight blanket that, frankly, smelled of dog.

For the first three weeks or so in Joliet, I'd wake up each morning terrified, not remembering where I was, or why. Eventually that went away, mostly thanks to Denver Tolliver, but in seven-plus years I never felt completely safe. It was, after all, a high-security state prison, and a cell that looked like every jail cell in every movie. No one felt completely invulnerable in there, but that's why they designed the whole system in the first place—to make everyone scared shitless.

With great effort I turned my body a bit to check out the

surroundings, and was shocked to see another human being across the room, curled up on a similar mattress and covered with a blanket. Thunder exploded in my head, and I fear I groaned loudly and rolled back to my original position. I drifted into blacked-out one more time.

I don't know how long I was out, but I awoke to soft, gentle hands on my face and forehead, and a familiar voice that was little more than a whisper. "Russ. Wake up, Russ. Are you okay?"

I opened my eyes, fought to focus them. When I was finally somewhat sentient, I took a gulp of stale basement air and our eyes finally met. I said with fear and wonderment, "Aubrey! I finally found you!"

CHAPTER THIRTY-TWO

The last time I saw Aubrey Sinden was on her third and final visit while I was in Joliet, when she told me she just couldn't wait that long. I didn't blame her. If she was the prisoner, I wouldn't sit around celibate and lonely for ten years, either.

Now, in this dank, cold basement, I could only get a good look at her by moving her directly below the sixty-watt bulb that hung from the ceiling. She hadn't changed much. Her hair looked the same, though it was all mussed up. She had only her fingers with which to comb it to since she disappeared—and I noticed two fingers on her left hand had been broken, recently, as they hadn't been straightened. One side of her face was swollen and turning different colors of blue and purple. She had one black eye, the other eye nearly shut. Her lower lip was cut open some days earlier and now a crust around the wound had formed. Traces of blood at her nostrils told me she'd had a recent nosebleed.

Or several of them.

Her long-sleeved white blouse and blue slacks were wrinkled and soiled, with dried blood on her blouse. She'd obviously gone through some tough times in this dank, shitty basement— and when I said tough times, I really meant torture.

I wondered why.

I was glad she wasn't a prisoner of the CIA, though. Slapping and punching weren't even a beginning for them. I reached up and softly touched the side of her face that was not swollen and bruised, and said, "What are you doing here, Aubrey?"

She paused, searching for the right word. Then she just shrugged. "I've been kidnapped, Russ."

"Who's hurting you?"

She put her hand up to her swollen eye and then looked away. "They want me to do something I won't do." With the good corner of her mouth, the one not as badly wounded as the other, she gave an almost invisible smile. "They'll have to kill me first." Deep sigh. "They probably will, anyway."

"They? Who is 'they?' What the hell is going on?"

"Long story, Russ."

"Neither of us is going anywhere. Just tell me."

"This is awkward," she said. "We'll have to go back several years, way before you went to prison."

"It'll be awkward for both of us."

She took a moment to get her thoughts together, then began. The first thing she told me, with embarrassment, that when she'd been my mistress, she was also the mistress of Gaylord Ogilvy.

"I didn't know that at the time. I was married," I reminded her, "so there's nothing to confess."

She nodded. "After you went to prison, I met Cole Cabot. He's a nice man, kind of fun to have around, and when he asked me to marry him, I decided my affair with Gaylord was approaching past tense, so I said yes. We drove to the house of a justice of the peace in Whiting, Indiana and got married there."

"How did Mr. Ogilvy take that?"

She nodded her head. "Gaylord was decent about it. I had a job with his company—a stay-at-home job that earned me quite a lot of money."

"That's the nicest thing I ever heard about Gaylord Ogilvy."

"Where did you hear about him and me? And what the hell are you doing here, anyway?"

My heart moved rapidly and excruciatingly from my chest to my throat. This might be the most difficult moment of my life thus far. I pulled myself up into a sitting position and tried to ignore the pain in the back of my head that went all the way through to my eyes. I started as softly as I could. "The day after I got released from prison, Cole Cabot approached me."

"Why?"

"He said you were missing, told me all about you and Gaylord, and hired me to find you." I shrugged. "My private eye novels apparently turned him onto me. I tried convincing him I was no private eye—but he was rather insistent."

She took a gulp of air and blew it out through her lips. "I had no idea he'd do anything like that. I suppose your personal P.I. tricks led you here to me?"

"Sort of."

"Good. Then you've been reporting to Cole every night?"

There it was. I had nowhere else to go but the truth. I stammered, "Uh—no. Aubrey, this rips me up. Cole—is dead."

She gasped, whatever white skin still showed on her face turned pale, and for about twenty seconds, she stared at me as though I'd just spoken to her in Farsi. Then her eyes filled with tears that rolled down her bruised cheeks. She put her head down and sobbed for a while. I took her hand and squeezed it gently. There wasn't much more I could say.

She pulled her hand from mine eventually, and wiped her tears away. "What happened to him?"

"Someone—killed him."

That brought more tears, and a growl that sounded nothing like a whine. Then she whispered, "Monsters. Fucking *monsters!*"

"Who are they?"

"Cole was—a decent guy," she said, shaking her head. "I wasn't desperately in love with him, and I know he more or less lived off my money for our whole marriage, but he was a good—companion."

"Do you have any idea who killed him?"

"Sure I do—but what's the difference? They'll murder me, too, when they get what they want. They think I'm either too stupid or too smart to give in, no matter what. And they'll kill you too, my friend, just because you're here." She tried to smile, but failed. "Bad move to show up here, Russ. Really bad move."

I had to agree, if only in my mind. I tracked her down, stupidly showed up here to rescue her, and was probably going to die with her. I said instead, "Who are this 'they' you keep talking about?"

Aubrey waited for almost a minute, her chin down on her chest once again. Then she said, "I'd better begin at the beginning."

She struggled to sit up straighter. She'd been batted around a lot, and the least of her physical troubles now was a horrendous headache, and soreness all over her body. She touched both hands to her temples and pressed. I gave her all the time she needed.

"Going back ten years ago, almost eleven years," she eventually said. "I was still a kid in my heart. I needed money, but what twenty-something doesn't? When summer rolled around, I went to one of those temporary job finders downtown. They placed me at Ogilvy Company for approximately eight weeks, part time. I wound up on the executive floor, filling in for Irvin Greenfield's secretary, who was home having a baby. Ogilvy saw me the third day I worked there, and that was it. He came on to me like a fully armed destroyer, waving promises and expensive gifts most temp office workers never heard of. I tried giving that stuff back, but he wouldn't hear of it. What the hell? I'm not a hooker, but I figured I'd get rich quick with one of the wealthiest men in the world. I became his mistress—or one of them, anyway."

"My god," I said, "how rich could you get?"

"I've got jewelry in my safe deposit box you've never seen, Russ. An eight-thousand-dollar necklace. A diamond ring so big it was uncomfortable just to raise my hand while wearing it. Diamond earrings, brooches, a pearl bracelet—real, honest-to-god pearls." She made a valiant effort to shrug. "I figured eventually I'll sell all of it and never get off my ass for the rest of my life. The other good news was, Gaylord Ogilvy was pretty dull in bed, so there was nothing kinky or horrible for me. Boring, if you want to know the truth, but I had to go through it, anyway. I don't know about the others—or care. But it only took him about a month before he realized I was smart, too, and not just sexy."

"I always figured you were smart, Aubrey," I told her. "That's why our relationship was so good. I could never get a divorce, or I'd have wound up begging for change on State Street for the rest of my life. But I thought you and I would stay together—for a long while."

"What's a long while, Russ?"

I rolled my head around trying to chase away the pain, but mostly because I had no answer for that. I told her so. "I was just happy the way it was, and I thought you were, too."

"I was happy on my days and nights with you," she said. "The other times were—I guess you could call it working hard."

I nodded. "That bad? No fake orgasms?"

"For him," she said. "Not for you. Anyway, he gave me an actual job, and it was no way a secretary. I had to do tons of research from home, mostly about foreign countries and their capitals. If he thought about buying properties in Europe or The Middle East or South America, and wanted to build on them, were they a good idea? A decent price, most in the multi-millions? In a great location? If so, who would he talk to, or send someone high up to talk to them? Of course, that turned out to be Irvin Greenfield."

"Chief of Staff, isn't he?"

She nodded. "I still had to sleep with Gaylord occasionally, even after I started seeing you—but I became vitally important to his business, too."

I rolled over on my back and studied the ceiling. "I'm glad you never told me before, Aubrey. Now, all these years later, I can't get upset being jealous."

"There's more to tell," she assured me. "Eventually, right before I told Gaylord I was engaged to marry Cole, Irvin started bringing papers to my house—maybe every six weeks or so. They were hundreds of pages long, and he actually stood there just inside the doorway, never even taking off his overcoat, watching me like a vulture until I signed them. Then he'd take them away with him. I did notice they were all documents for foreign land purchases. He told me that, on paper, I was the owner of these properties, but they really belonged to the company."

I said, "That's because they won't want any other company to think they were the real owners. The bigger a corporation is, the bigger their secrets."

"Things continued like this until about two months ago," she went on. "The company wanted to sell one of those properties to somebody else, and make a handsome profit."

"You held these properties for how long?"

"This particular one was for more than three years. In Brazil."

"What did Ogilvy want to do in Brazil?"

She looked ceilingward. "I have no idea. Irvin always refused to tell me."

"You only dealt with Irvin?"

She bobbed her head in a yes, then grimaced at whatever was going on inside her brain that was hurt by the nod. "Legally, Russ, I owned those properties. I don't want to be selfish, but if Ogilvy Corp. was going to make a huge profit, I wanted some of that profit for my own. That's what I told Irwin."

"My guess is that made him unhappy Why didn't you go directly to Ogilvy?"

"Because," Aubrey said, "Mr. O stopped having anything to do with me when I told him I was getting married and wouldn't fuck him anymore. After that, we'd see each other accidentally and wouldn't exchange much more than a nod and a grunt. Whatever happened after I became Mrs. Cabot, he didn't want to know anything about it."

"And Irvin?

"He worked on me for weeks. Pleaded with me, cajoled, threatened, even begged. He even offered me twenty thousand dollars—cash! No record to the IRS, and I'd get that money—all in twenties—just if I'd sign away that property in Brazil."

"A lot of cash."

"Yes," she said, "but I figured Brazil was worth close to a hundred million bucks. Twenty grand didn't excite me at all."

"How much would have made you smile?"

"I asked for four million—but I would have accepted three."

Now I was getting a genuine headache, too, to match the ache where somebody had slugged me unconscious. "Aubrey— you owned all those other properties, too. If they gave in to you once, they'd have to, again. That would mean even more millions in your pocket."

"I wanted more," she said sadly. "Much more."

"So—?"

She closed her eyes again. "One morning a few weeks back— Christ, I don't even know what day it is anymore—two guys knocked on my door, one clamped a handkerchief full of chloroform or some other kind of knock-out drops that put me to sleep immediately, and when I woke up, I was here."

"Two guys. What were their names?"

"We weren't formally introduced," she snapped. Then she gently touched the fingertips of one hand to the dried blood at both nostrils. "I think one of them busted my nose. It hurts like hell, and I can't breathe very well."

"They hurt you."

"They hurt me every day." Her head jerked spasmodically

and her voice, quivered badly. "I can't even tell you some of the things they did to me."

It nearly made me cry. But I don't cry anymore. After being the only kid in the household, and then spending seven-plus years locked up with a bunch of killers, rapists, chicken hawks and Christ knows what else, there's not much left bad enough to make me cry. "They never said their names, Aubrey?"

She lifted her shoulders up toward her ears. "I don't know. Once, maybe, I think I heard one of them call the other one—Wally."

Wally, I thought.

Wallace.

Waldo.

Walt.

Walter…

Walter Yellen.

Walter Yellen was one of the tough guy punks who dragged me away from my apartment to a ten-minute meeting with Lilith Ogilvy. He and—what was the other punk's name again? Harvey? No—Hayden. Hayden Fantos.

"These two guys," I said hesitantly, "they work for Mrs. Ogilvy?"

"I don't know who they work for, Russ. They come in here every morning with that paper signing away the Brazilian property. They spend ten minutes arguing with me to sign." She shuddered. "For the next hour or so after that they try different persuasions."

I held her hand again. "Oh, Aubrey—"

"If they kill me, it'd be a waste of their time, though."

"Why?"

"Because if I die, according to my will, most of what I own goes to my husband." She began crying again, more quietly. "That's why they killed Cole, too. Fucking stupid bastards!"

"Why stupid? Wouldn't those properties wind up with them, then?"

"Maybe," she answered. "After ten years or so. Every property I own—on paper—are in foreign countries. It'd take at least a decade for big-time lawyers and foreign lawyers to figure out who owns what."

I licked my lips. "I'd imagine the State Department will get involved, too."

"That's why they'll keep me alive as long as possible." With her other hand she rubbed her bruised eyes very gently. "People can live under torture for years and years, Russ. Look at American slavery. Starved, kicked, raped, whipped, sold down the river, as they said, and then whipped and raped all over again—"

"Sign the papers, Aubrey. For crysakes, sign them."

"Sure—and they'll keep me here forever until they want me to sign away some other contract I own. I'll die in this fucking basement." Her whole body heaved as she filled her chest with half the air in the room, and then blew it out through her damaged mouth. "So will you, Russ. So will you."

CHAPTER THIRTY-THREE

A few hours later, I heard the door at the top of the cellar stairs being unlocked. Walter Yellen and Hayden Fantos arrived, walking carefully down the stairs. Each of them carried a tray of food and a bottle of water, and put them on the floor near where Aubrey and I were lying. Aubrey's body stiffened a bit, beyond her control, but she was damned if she'd wince in fear. Other than mattresses there was no other furniture in the basement. Off in one corner was a very small bathroom—toilet and sink, with a roll of paper towels serving for both hand-drying and toilet paper. Not exactly the Waldorf Astoria.

"You're a pain in the ass, Reinert," Fantos said. "Now we gotta worry about two meals for you instead of just one."

I looked at the meal. McDonald's hamburger with lettuce. No cheese. No ketchup. A scattering of potato chips. Yellen said, "This is all you get for breakfast." He jerked a thumb toward Aubrey. "She always looks forward to our morning visits. Don't you, cunt?" His smile turned into a mean sneer. "Sometimes, though, she doesn't enjoy her breakfast so much."

"Why doesn't your boss come and have breakfast with us?" I said, sitting up straight on the mattress. "Whoever the hell your boss is."

Yellen stared at me for about fifteen seconds before his backhand slap across my face knocked me over sideways. "We ask the questions. Otherwise, keep your fucking mouth shut. Talk to her, not us. We ask her questions every day—and she pretends she doesn't know the answers." He shrugged. "You can only pretend so long."

They went back up the stairs and locked the door behind them. We were silent for a while. Then Aubrey said, "Did he hurt you bad?"

I rubbed my cheek. I felt good about it, because I think he aimed for my mouth. "I'll live. Are they going to hurt you again?"

"Right after breakfast," she sighed. "It's their ritual."

"I'm going to get you out of here," I said.

"Magic words? Or is there a machine gun hiding in your back pocket?"

"I'll think of something."

"Don't rush. Tonight, it's probably a spicy chicken sandwich again."

"If they try to injure you, I'll—I don't know what the hell I'll do."

"Not much you can do besides just watch," Aubrey said. "There are two of them against one of you, and they both have guns. And knives. They bring down papers they want me to sign to give up all the deals they've allowed me to own on paper. And I'll be damned if I'll do that."

"They'll just keep torturing you."

"It's an everyday thing, now, Russ. Nobody ever hurt me like this before, and I didn't think I could stand it—but I can. They eventually stop beating on me when they think I'll pass out. It gives me time to heal—as much as I can. It gives me lots to think about for the next twenty-four hours."

"This can't go on, Aubrey."

"It will for as long as they want it to."

"Then I'll figure something out. But here's my question. These two meatheads won't be the owners of these properties if you sign them over. Who are they working for? Who's telling them to beat cooperation out of you every morning. Is it Ogilvy?"

"I doubt it. If he's mad at someone, he hurts them by ruining them financially. He's got security people all over the place, but they're all retired Chicago cops and they're all bonded. I don't think Wally and the other guy even work for him."

Wally again, I thought.

"But it was Irvin Greenfield who kept in touch me with about these properties, he was the one who came to my house all the time. These two guys took me away forcibly, but they're hardly the kingpins of this operation."

"Then it's Greenfield!"

"He's rich, too."

"Think about it, Aubrey," I said. "Sure, he makes a great salary, and sure he has stock options up the yin-yang. But he works for one of the wealthiest men in America who treats him like shit. I know, I was there when Ogilvy did it. If he can get those properties back from you, that means one percent of the people in the world who are down-and-dirty rich. Even if Irvin lives another hundred years, he'll never get richer than Ogilvy, but those big-time millions could make ninety-nine percent of us happier than a pig in slop."

Another sigh. She was growing tired.

"My—" She stopped, gulped, shook her head, and I could see the tears beginning again. She wrestled with another crying fit, her whole body shaking. This time, she won. She leaned back on both elbows. "I didn't think Irvin had the balls to do something like this."

I leaned forward and stroked her face—the good side that wasn't discolored by violence. "Maybe he's involved with someone who does. We'll find out for sure, Aubrey—and we'll get him," I promised. "We'll get 'em all."

She slowly lay down flat, her eyes closed, and after a minute or so, I believed she'd fallen asleep. I sure couldn't blame her.

I lay back, too. Closing my own eyes was easy, as the back of my head still throbbed, but I couldn't seem to get to sleep until Aubrey Sinden Cabot rolled over on her stomach and crawled several feet between her mattress and mine. She pressed her body against mine as hard as she could, her face buried in my neck. "Hold me, Russ," she almost begged. "Please, just—hold me."

I held her until Walter and Hayden came back. Then Hayden held a gun to my head while Walter slapped her around for at least twenty minutes. Her nose began bleeding again, and so did her mouth. She screamed in pain, screamed at the degradation that was going on in front of me. But it was one violent punch in the stomach that knocked her off her feet. She crumpled onto the floor, gasping for breath.

Walter stopped, obviously tired. "You ready to talk now, Aubrey? Jesus, why do you go through all this punishment every day? You like having your friend watch, now?" He took a handkerchief from his back pocket and mopped his sweaty face with it. "It was easy today, right, Aubrey? Tomorrow it's gonna be real bad again—like before. I'm gonna bring some interesting toys, new ones—only this time your pal here will watch—until he barfs all over at what he's seeing. How much fucking humiliation will you put up with? Sign the papers and you're out of here." He pointed at me with his chin. "Him, too."

The two men headed for the stairs. Hayden stopped and looked at me, his nasty smile a sneer. "Fuck her if you want to, Reinert," he suggested, "but I don't think she's gonna like it."

As soon as they were gone, I rushed to the bathroom for some wet paper towels to wipe away most of the blood on her face—but it took almost half an hour until she could speak again.

"They're going to kill me," she managed to whisper.

"Sign the papers, Aubrey, whatever they are, and they'll stop hurting you. You can't go on with this much longer."

"Russ..." She shook her head sadly. "When I sign those papers, they're going to kill me anyway—and now they'll kill you, too."

I woke up early—five o'clock in the morning. I suppose while I was out cold, the two punks frisked me, but didn't take anything except my cellphone, leaving my watch, keys and wallet. They didn't even take my Swiss Army knife, which in hand-to-hand combat, was more or less superfluous—-so in a way, I was damn lucky. It was still dark of night, but there were no windows down here in the basement except one, and that had been boarded shut from the outside. The only light was a sixty-watt bulb on the ceiling, which was never turned off, and another one in the bathroom.

Aubrey had been relieved to see me, even though I was carried in, totally out of it, and dumped on the floor. She figured we were now both prisoners and would probably die soon, though she had no clue what I was doing in this basement with her. She had fallen asleep, her entire body shivering, with her head on my shoulder and arm, and hadn't moved since. I didn't move, either, for fear I'd wake her, but when she wasn't quite slumbering yet, I managed to snag the thin blanket from her mattress and half-ay covered both of us. Still, it had been a damn chilly night.

I wasn't going to let either of us spend much more time in that basement, though I knew whatever I do might get me injured. How badly, I suppose, would be up to our two musclebound hosts.

I carefully extracted my arm from under Aubrey's head, sat up and took a good look around the basement, as my seeing her, alive, took up all my attention when I first emerged from a night-night smack from behind. There was a furnace in one corner, and a water heater, both installed to make living upstairs more comfortable, but at the moment, neither was turned on. However, disconnecting the too-heavy water heater and hitting both guys on the head with it as they came down the stairs seemed a foolish idea. There was nothing else in the room, not even a broom or a mop. You can't disable too huge muscled villains by hitting them with a mop.

Twenty minutes later, Aubrey stirred, thrashed around on the mattress for a few seconds, and then opened her eyes, wide with fear and terror. Then she saw me and groaned softly.

"Hey, kiddo," I said.

She sat up, grimacing from pain. Then she closed her eyes again. "Russ. Oh shit! I'm so sorry."

"For what?"

"For getting you involved in this."

"You didn't get me involved. You haven't seen me until last night. I came looking for you because I wanted to."

"Because Cole asked you to. I'm sorry anyway," she said, "because now we're both going to die. Even if I sign away that real estate, they'll kill me anyway. You're just—collateral damage."

"Maybe not. I'll figure something out."

She reached up her hand and I took it, pulling her to her feet. She grunted again, touched herself across the middle. "I'm really fucked up, Russ. They concentrated on my stomach yesterday—the punches and kicks. Now I can hardly breathe."

I moved to hug her, but she pushed me away. "No, don't touch me," she said. "It wasn't nearly as bad yesterday as other days. Christ, how long have I been here, anyway?"

"Almost three weeks."

She put both hands over her face for a moment. "It feels like half my lifetime."

"You've got a long life ahead of you, too."

"Sure—until three o'clock tomorrow afternoon when they decide we're both too much trouble." She moved toward the bathroom. "Oh, well—torture or no torture," she said over her shoulder. "I have to pee."

She closed the door, leaving me to worry all by myself.

During my long stay at Joliet, there were a few occasions when I wound up in physical combat at a time when Denver Tolliver was nowhere in sight to save my sorry ass. He taught me plenty about prison fighting, but I was nowhere as big or as tough as he was to perform them with accuracy. Still, I learned inmate-to-inmate combat was nothing like a Saturday night barroom fight, but often even life survival. The first thing Denver suggested was to knee the testicles of my opponent, or even grab them and squeeze. If that were not effective, go for the eyes—not punching, but gouging, possibly causing permanent blindness.

Naturally most convicts knew those tricks, too, but I was at least their equal because I had learned to be fast. I never got around to gouging out someone's eyes, but a few of those attackers retired from the scene walking funny and clutching their gonads.

What were the fights about? I hardly remember. Once, a particular inmate decided he hated my guts because I wrote books and made money from them. Another—second-in-command of the biggest and toughest black con war army in Joliet—evidently loathed all white people, and I was his brand-new victim. A third, almost as big and strong as Denver, desperately wanted to turn me into his one and only love. Denver hadn't yet gotten around to breaking his head open. I suppose some thought Denver and I were indeed lovers, but that is flat-ass untrue. He made me his good friend, talked about his own pre-prison life, listened when I spoke about mine, and fought for me whenever he could.

I learned a great deal from him about surviving as a convict, and he learned a lot about living a classy and productive life on the outside, even though he knew he'd never leave prison alive. I found out a few days before I left those iron gates festooned with barbed wire that there was much he understood about the world in which I lived, and passed on to his wife and, hopefully, his son, if only by telephone.

After a few minutes, Aubrey emerged from the bathroom, trying futilely to straighten her wrinkled and dirty clothes she'd worn for about three weeks. "God damn them," she said through clenched teeth, "leaving us to use paper towels in there is almost worse than the beatings." Her face turned slightly green as she continued, "Not some other things."

"I'm giving a lot of thought to busting out, Aubrey."

Her eyes brightened. "How?"

"I'm not sure yet." I managed to stand up and headed toward the bathroom. "My turn," I said.

The seat on the toilet was down. Not a surprise, because Aubrey was the only one to use it in the past three weeks. As most males, I preferred it to be up during urination. When I finished, I put it back down, washed my hands in the tiny sink, and started drying them with a paper towel, looking around for anything at all I could use to get the two of us out of our illegal imprisonment. There was no way I could overpower one or two men twice my size by obliterating them with a roll of paper towels.

And then it hit me.

I had no idea whether it would work or whether Yellen and Fantos would kill me immediately without another thought. But I was marked for death anyway, whether that day or two weeks from now, and whether or not Aubrey Sinden Cabot signed those property documents, she would certainly be killed, too. Weapon or no, I was not about to sit around and wait for it to happen.

I took my Swiss knife from my pocket, opened up the ridiculously small screwdriver, and knelt down beside the toilet.

It took me more than fifteen minutes to do what I wanted to do. In the middle, Aubrey knocked on the door and called, "Are you okay in there, Russ?"

"I'm fine," I answered.

"What's taking you so long? I thought you fell in."

"A man's gotta do what a man's gotta do."

She mumbled something under her breath and then walked away, back to her mattress, giving me more time to unscrew all the screws and remove the toilet seat from its usual position.

When I was done, I went back out into the big room, getting a kick of the shock on Aubrey's face when she saw what I was carrying. I said, "Don't even ask."

"Are you nuts? That toilet seat is the only way I can sit down in the last three weeks. What the fuck are you doing?"

"Aubrey, I've been an atheist all my life, but right now I guess what I'm doing is praying." I sank down onto her level. "I don't guarantee anything, but if you just sit and be quiet, it might help." I stuffed the toilet seat under my mattress and sat so it was near my right hand. "Desperate times need desperate measures."

Aubrey said, "They covered my face while they brought me here, so I don't even know where the hell I am."

"I tracked you down, so they caught me while I was prowling around outside. We're in Cicero."

"Cicero?" She laughed, but there was little mirth in it. "Is this Al Capone's old house?"

"Al Capone had a nicer house than this one," I told her.

"Too bad. Okay, so the toilet seat will save our lives. How will we get out of Cicero? Walk?"

"I parked my car near the gate—which is probably a few blocks away."

"Let's hope both of us will be able to walk a few blocks." She ground her teeth loudly as she shifted around, changing positions. "What do we do in the meantime?"

I flexed my hands, squeezing them to wake them up. "What we do best," I told her. "We wait."

CHAPTER THIRTY-FOUR

It was only a few minutes before nine o'clock in the morning. My stomach was rumbling. In prison, we got lousy food, but there was a lot of it, and I grew accustomed to having three meals a day. The yummy-good breakfast they brought both of us on my first day was something I wouldn't feed to a stray dog. Aubrey had eaten whatever they brought her in the past three weeks, just to stay alive. I supposed keeping her in hunger pain all the time was another form of torture. They'd either decided not to use waterboarding on her to make her sign, so minimal food did the trick as well. I wasn't sure how many more days of brutality she could stand.

It was chilly in that basement, and she kept wrapped in a blanket most of the time, so when Walter Yellen unlocked the basement door and came down the stairs, once more carrying a food tray, she did little more than lift her head. Walter wasn't wearing a jacket this time, nor a tie. He had on Dockers, a dress shirt open at the neck, and a cardigan sweater, and this morning his handgun was under his belt—no holster. He probably thought of himself faster than Clint Eastwood or Steve McQueen or John Wayne, but if he tried to draw it faster against one of those movie cowboys, he'd probably shoot off his own dick.

He put the tray down on the floor next to Aubrey's mattress, then straightened back up. "Whattya think, bitch? Changed your mind—finally?"

She just sneered at him and gave him the middle-finger salute.

"That's just gonna make it worse. Look, Aubrey—we're getting tired of beating the shit out of you every day. Give us all a break, okay? We'll both be back with those papers. Sign 'em, and then no more hurting. We'll all be best buddies again."

I said, "Best buddies? What a lying jag-off you are!"

"You shut the fuck up!" Yellen hollered. "That's one reason why you don't get any breakfast!" He kicked at my head, but I turned to one side, and his foot hit the side of my face and scraped off some skin. taking some of the pain on my left ear. Then he turned to Aubrey again.

Yellen said, "You know what we'll probably do today, Aubrey. We're gonna smack this prick around—slow and steady and keeping him conscious like we do to you—until he dies right in front of you. Maybe that'll get you to be a good little girl and do what we tell you."

He took another swing at me, but this time I was ready. Ducking, I pulled the toilet seat out from under my mattress and smashed his left kneecap with it as hard as I could. I can't tell you how satisfied it was to hear the knee bone crack.

He almost shrieked in loud agony and collapsed on his side right next to me. I took one more swing at him, this time at his forehead, and he went down for the count, blood spurting from over his left eye.

Walter Yellen didn't notice the bleeding, though, because he was unconscious. Knocked senseless. Out cold—the way I was the previous afternoon when either he or his muscle buddy practically took off the back of my head. Among the many things I learned from Denver Tolliver in Joliet prison: Forgive— but never forget.

I jumped practically on top of Yellen and snatched the handgun from under his belt. My grin at Aubrey was more of a snarl when I said, "Now at least we're even."

"Are you okay, Russ?"

"Just look at the other guy."

She did. Who knows what terrible things he and Hayden Fantos did to her in the past three weeks—I figured from the way she talked without being completely open that violent rape and god knows what else might have occurred, but she couldn't help worrying my toilet seat blow to the head might have killed him.

"He screamed pretty loud," she said. "I bet the other guy heard him."

"He'll be here any minute now," I said, and started upstairs, toilet seat still in hand, now blood-stained. Then I stopped, cocked my head and listened. Voices—upset voices. "There's somebody else up there with him."

"Another guy?"

I nodded. "It sounds like an angry guy."

"Oh, shit!" She let her head sag, chin almost touching her chest. "It's going to be really bad again today, Russ. Probably for both of us."

The voices stopped, replaced by a couple of loud thumps and then a crash of some sort. I backed down the stairs to the bottom, making sure the safety of Yellen's weapon was off. I pointed it up the stairs to the cellar door, making sure I could shoot quicker.

Then a dragging sound, and the top door flew open. Hayden Fantos was framed in the doorway, his head bobbling a little bit, hanging onto the wall. Then he came flying down the stairs, landing with a thump at the bottom that knocked the breath out of him. His mouth was bleeding from the left corner, looking as if someone had just punched him in the mouth before throwing him into the basement.

Then the top doorway was filled again with someone who looked healthier. In his hand was Fantos's gun.

"Is everything okay, Mr. Reinert?" Perwin Tolliver asked.

"Did they hurt you any?"

Aubrey managed to clamber to her feet. "Russ, who the fuck is this?" she asked.

"A friend, thank god," I answered. "I'll explain it all later."

Then I moved over to where Hayden Fantos had wound up, leapt high and landed right on his chest with both knees. I still had Yellen's gun in my hand and I pressed the muzzle against his left eye.

"Be a good boy, Mr. Fantos—or I'm going to break your nose all over your face, and then I'm going to open up your goddamn head."

He still didn't have control of his breathing, so he just whimpered instead. I waited until I figured he could talk—and then *my* questions began.

"You and Yellen are just pawns, Hayden. Unimportant, expendable chess pieces. I can bash your goddamn brains in, just like I did to Yellen. Save your ass. Tell me who you're working for, and maybe—just maybe—I'll let you live."

"You gonna hit me with that goddamn toilet seat?"

"I don't have to, Hayden. I have your gun." And I pushed it hard against his cheek, just below one eye,

He struggled to get out from under me, as he probably outweighed me by eighty pounds or so, but after whatever fistfight he had with Perwin, who was almost as big and twice as tough as he was, and his fast head-over-heels trip down a long flight of wooden stairs, left him in no condition to fight any further. He did have enough breath in his lungs to tell me to go fuck myself.

I'm always a man of my word, so it won't surprise you I flattened his nose with one downward stroke of the gun, just as I'd warned him. I wasn't fast enough to get out of the way of the spurting blood, though, and knew I'd have to burn all my clothes, but it made me feel amazingly good.

In any event, I was halfway getting even. I said, "I spent seven years in prison, Hayden, so I can take care of myself—and if I have a problem, my good friend, whom you just met, will step in and mop up the detritus. God, your nose looks like roadkill. Bad memory there, Hayden? You need another little nudge so you can remember?"

"No, please," he blubbered. He didn't quite make a clean *s* through the blood all over his face and in his mouth, but it was a brave try. "Please, no more. I'll talk. I'll talk."

"Glad to hear that. Go right ahead."

He begged, "Can you get off me?"

"Talk first."

I told Aubrey to find a telephone, and call the police, figuring that even though she was unsure of the address, 911 would know where she was. I didn't think until later the Cicero Police Department might not have that advanced a 911 system. She was thrilled to go. She hadn't been out of that basement for three weeks, and had been abused in a dozen ways every day, so even going upstairs was a magical moment for her. Besides, she wouldn't want to witness what Perwin and I might do to Hayden Fantos to get him to open his mouth. Now that she was free, all she had on her mind was revenge.

It took Hayden about two more minutes to get his shit together—and I kindly waited until he did. Then—he talked.

I listened. Perwin talked, too, telling me he'd checked out all the Ogilvy-owned buildings, saw my car parked nearby, and got in touch with the Cicero Police, who arrived minutes later. Perwin warned them there had been a kidnapping. He couldn't believe two middle-aged white cops had listened to and followed a young black man who didn't even live in Cicero. No, cancel that. He looked stunned out of his mind.

"Sorry, you missed half the fun, Perwin," I said to him, still perched on Hayden Fantos's chest watching the blood that spurted out of his nose with every breath, "but you're about ten minutes late."

* * *

Once Aubrey and I got back to downtown Chicago, I didn't even bother going back to my apartment, nor did I call Tana Phillips to tell her what I just went through. Instead, we went directly to the office of Chicago Detective Easton Dorn. He's the cop who arrested me the first time, and with my criminal record, I wouldn't normally walk in there alone to report a kidnapping. But the Cicero police had Hayden Fantos and Walter Yellen in custody already, and they wrapped their yellow police tape around the entire house and back yard so no one else can get in. Still, I made sure Aubrey came with me to corroborate my story.

Dorn spent a good bit of time interviewing Aubrey, but he naturally knew about her husband's murder and wanted as many details as he could get. After thinking about it for a while, he told us both to stick around.

"I'd like to go home, too," I told him. "But Ms. Cabot was in that basement for three weeks, and I was only there less than twenty-four hours. Both of us just want to go back to our apartments and sleep for a week."

"You drove your car here," Dorn said, "so you can leave if you want. But you served your time, Mr. Reinert, and now I'm thinking you might have gone to prison for something you didn't do. I arrested you because that was my job—but I never judged you, even back then."

"That's okay, Detective. It was just a seven-year long vacation."

"Vacation from what?"

"From life."

"Ouch. And Ms. Cabot, according to what you shared with the Cicero Police, you'll make this a lot easier for all of us." He took a swallow of coffee from a cardboard cup and made a painful face. Coffee in police stations is always ghastly, not just in Chicago but in every police precinct in the world.

"I'll stick with Russ Reinert," Aubrey said, "because I didn't see or speak to him for seven years before yesterday, so we have to catch up. We're old friends."

"I understand," Dorn said, then turned back to me again. "You write about crime and murder and stuff, and I'm sure you rubbed shoulders with some pretty scary people in Joliet. But if you want to hang out with me for a few more hours, you might learn something about a real arrest."

I knew a lot about real arrests from when he'd banged on my house door and cuffed my hands behind me. He figured when he made today's capture, we could help him out with some of the finer points, but I think he felt sorry for Aubrey and me, and letting us tag along with him on this particular day was sort of a make-up favor.

Aubrey and I rode in the back seat of Dorn's personal car. Dorn was in the front passenger seat, and his partner, the nearly silent Detective Delaware, did the driving. Aubrey had washed her face both at the Cicero Police Department and this one in Chicago-proper, but after three weeks of physical abuse, her face was in terrible shape, and she'd had no chance to repair the look.

Following us in a marked squad car were four uniformed officers. A lot of people, I thought, to make a takedown of an unarmed man, even though the cops were not carrying helmets, shields and military assault rifles like the guys on S.W.A.T. Just handguns.

It's always difficult to get past the huge front desk in the lobby of the Merchandise Mart building unless you'd been invited, but six well-armed cops weren't even polite to the downstairs security guys, so we got in with little argument, and commandeered the private elevator that took us up to the executive offices of Ogilvy Company. I'd been there once before, recently, so I showed them the way to the private office of Irvin Greenfield. His secretary didn't recognize me from a few days earlier, but she sure recognized the badges, and was too discomfited to buzz him and tell him we were coming.

When the six cops blasted into his private office with me a

few steps behind them, Greenfield leaped up from behind his desk and said, "What's the meaning of this?" Frankly, he knew damn well what was *the meaning of this,* and his eyes bulged out with terror. "What are *you* doing here, Reinert?"

"Reciprocation," I said at almost the same time Detective Dorn said, "Mr. Greenfield, you're under arrest."

Greenfield looked hard at the telephone so he could call his lawyer, but the police didn't let him near it.

Dorn stepped aside so one of the uniforms could twist Greenfield's hands behind his back and cuff him. Then he told Greenfield, "This is for the murder of Cole Cabot and the kidnapping of Aubrey Sinden Cabot."

Detective Delaware, who rarely spoke at all, stepped in front of Greenfield and recited the speech he'd already given hundreds of times before. "You have the right to remain silent..."

Irvin Greenfield looked stunned, shocked, almost unable to speak. He'd never been arrested before, never had his hands cuffed behind his back. I just nodded at him. Been there. Done that.

Dorn began opening desk drawers and fumbling through papers. "Let's see what else we've got here."

"I've done nothing wrong," Greenfield said, in what sounded like a five-year-old's whine. "Take these cuffs off me. Do you realize who I am?"

"You're a kidnapper," I said. "A mastermind of torture, gang rape, and me getting the shit kicked out of me. You probably ordered a horrible murder and throwing Cole Cabot into the lake, too. That's who you are, Irving."

"It's Irvin, goddammit!"

"It's whatever I say it is, asshole. And thank these police officers I don't punch your fucking teeth in right now. I owe you big-time."

"You're the murderer!" he almost screamed. "Not me!"

Dorn warned, "Don't bring up someone else's past, Mr. Greenfield—because you're currently wallowing in deep doo-

doo yourself."

"I want my lawyer."

"When we get you down to my precinct and talk to you for a while, you can call any lawyer you want."

"This is outrageous!" he sputtered. It *was* outrageous, naturally, but it wasn't up to me to make him feel sorry.

There were seven of us in Greenfield's office, but it was a large one, so no one felt too crowded—until Number Eight walked in. That's when everybody got quiet, even Detective Easton Dorn. Everyone in Chicago feels small and unimportant when Gaylord Ogilvy shows up, whether it's a theater play, a football game with the Chicago Bears, or standing just behind the mayor who owes him his whole life. Even cops. Even the governor and the two senators. That's because he's richer than all of them put together.

"I assume, gentlemen," Ogilvy said quietly, "that you're kicking up a shitstorm at my company right next to my own private office—which disturbs me. I don't like being disturbed." He perched on the edge of Irvin Greenfield's executive desk. Greenfield, already terrified of the police and of Aubrey and me, nearly fainted when his employer came that near to him.

"As far as I know," Ogilvy continued, "this organization is not secretly selling weapons of mass destruction to international enemies, nor stealing funds from innocent people's internet bank accounts or sex-trafficking pre-teen children. Everyone here has already screwed up a thirty million-dollar phone call, except Ms. Cabot, of course. I respectfully request someone explain all this—like fucking *NOW!*"

CHAPTER THIRTY-FIVE

As she was obviously the star of the show, Aubrey did most of the talking—a kidnap victim for three weeks of torture and unspeakable sexual abuse, her husband brutally murdered. I was only kept in that scummy basement for less than twenty-four hours, attacking one of the bad guys with a toilet seat and kickstarted the big escape. That made me little more than a movie extra.

Irvin Greenfield tried interrupting Aubrey several times until Detective Delaware walked up behind him and did something strange to the back of his neck that made him shriek out loud. Delaware told him one more word from him and his mouth would be duct-taped.

Gaylord Ogilvy didn't seem to belong there, but he listened intently, sometimes putting his thumb under his chin and his pointing finger against his lips, mostly frowning, nodding, or glaring at Greenfield with in-house hatred. When Aubrey finished, he stood and walked over to her, reminding me again she was his mistress at the same time she was mine.

His speaking tone to her, though, was gentle, or as gentle as he was able to talk. "Aubrey," he said, "these documents you signed, making you the so-called owner of these foreign properties. Did you read them?"

"They were all hundreds of pages long," she answered, shaking her head. "I usually read the first two or three pages to find out where these properties were. Argentina, the United Arab Emirates, Romania—"

"And you were told during the last few years you signed these ownership documents so it wouldn't seem like my company owned them?"

She nodded. "That's what Irvin told me."

"Did he indeed?" Ogilvy didn't even glance at Greenfield. "But I had no idea these so-called properties even existed. When he told you to sign back these properties to make him sole owner, you refused."

"I knew I wasn't the real owner, Gay," she said. "I put my name on those properties because I thought you wanted me to. Irvin offered me a damn pittance for my signatures, and I didn't think that was nearly enough. I wasn't figuring anything close to two hundred million bucks—I'm stupid, but I'm not *that* stupid. Still, I think I deserved something more. I told him the company would have to come up with a better offer. He argued with me for a few weeks, and then he had me kidnapped and tortured so I'd give in. Beaten every day. Kicked. Burned—and some other things I won't mention." She straightened her back and tried to smile through her bruised lips. "I didn't give in, though, even though eventually he'd tell those two hoodlums who hurt me every day to kill me." She shook her head sadly. "I didn't think you'd let this happen, Gay, because if I died, it would tie your properties up in limbo for years—decades."

"You think?" Ogilvy asked.

"I think."

"Then why do you all suppose I'm here listening to this?"

I finally piped up. "Because you want to figure out a way to come away from this with your skirts clean."

He stared at me for a moment as if I were a perfect stranger. Then he said, "Mr.—Reinberg, is it?"

"Reinert."

"Mr. Reinert, then—shut the hell up, you don't know a

damn thing about this." He turned to Detective Dorn. "What is this man doing here anyway, Detective?"

"He's involved, Mr. Ogilvy."

"I am not, Detective."

"What?" I said.

"Involved. Put simply, gentlemen and Ms. Cabot, I have never in my life allowed an employee or anyone else to sign their name as an owner to an expensive property owned by the company. And these countries Ms. Cabot mentioned? I have no property deals with any of them. I believe whoever made a deal to buy them was scamming the shit out of her—and me." Then he turned and psychologically destroyed Irwin Greenfield with a piercing stare from the depths of hell.

"Irvin," he said carefully, as if he was reciting a bible verse, "you have an annual income of two hundred seventy thousand dollars. Impressive to some—but you don't have enough money to make down payments of all these international real estate deals. Who came up with the big cash up front?"

All eyes went to Greenfield, but handcuffed as he was, he was too terrified to answer, until Gaylord said, "Never mind, Irvin. I'm pretty sure I know."

Less than an hour later, Aubrey was driven home by two uniformed officers, and I was once again invited to accompany Easton Dorn and his Partner Delaware to one more address, but not before Gaylord Ogilvy warned me, "You'll turn this into one of your half-assed novels, Mr. Reinert. But if you create a fictional character who completely resembles me and bears my name or anything close to it, police or no police, I will personally have you killed."

CHAPTER THIRTY-SIX

"I'm not surprised to see you again," said Lilith Shadburn Ogilvy. She stood in the doorway of her magnificent mansion, one hand cocked prettily at her waist, one knee slightly bent. Ten thousand per day fashion models knew how to pose that way. "But I didn't think you'd bring the entire police department with you."

"This isn't a social call, Ms. Ogilvy," I said.

"The last one wasn't either. Won't you come in, gentlemen?" She stepped aside and the five of us—Dorn, Delaware and the four uniformed cops—I never did find out their names—filed past her into the magnificence of the palace she and Gaylord Ogilvy call their primary address. She was dressed today all in varying shades of blue—cobalt blue scarf, baby blue blouse, cornflower blue necklace, sky blue stockings, navy blue draped slacks, and one I didn't have a name for. In my head I thought of it as *blue* blue.

When we were all seated, she said, "My husband phoned to tell me you were on your way, so no surprises here—so far."

Detective Delaware started with the Miranda rights but she cut him off. "I watch movies, Detective, and I've heard that one more often than *'Now I lay me down to sleep.'* I don't have an AR-15 hidden in my slacks, so I won't kill you in the car and run away and hide forever, so I'd really appreciate it if you didn't put handcuffs on me behind my back and make me sit on them all the way to wherever you're going to take me. Naturally my lawyer, or my husband's lawyer, will be there before us."

Easton Dorn frowned, studying her carefully as though she were an Italian statue in the Art Institute. Then: "We have some questions, Ms. Ogilvy. We can ask them here in your home in relative comfort or take you down to the police station and ask you there."

That wasn't what Lilith Ogilvy was expecting, but she shook it off like a home-run hitter who was just struck by a pitched ball. She asked if any of us wanted coffee, tea, or since it was late in the afternoon, something stronger. We all hemmed and hawed a bit before we said no, and we all sat in the parlor in chairs and on sofas which probably had cost four or five grand apiece—all except Dorn, who remained standing, dealing himself the alpha male position for the afternoon.

"Ms. Ogilvy," he began.

"Lilith. Call me Lilith. Everybody calls me Lilith—except the people who work for me."

"Lilith," I said, "is a she-devil in Judaic mythology."

Dorn said, "She-devil is pushing it a little bit. But you're ready to be arrested, Lilith, even though you worry about handcuffs. Let's talk about why."

She shrugged. "I'm not nearly as obscenely rich as my husband, Detective, but I'm pretty damn wealthy on my own. When I married Gaylord Ogilvy, I thought together we'd be invincible—or more invincible than he is now. I respect the hell out of him, and actually like him—sort of. No love there, of course, but you know what they say? Money is the root of all evil? Well, when you're rich, money is the root of everything."

"I see," Dorn said, but I don't think he 'saw' at all. I, however, was beginning to.

"He gives me a generous allowance," Lilith continued, "and pays for my shopping trips and clothes, but he didn't allow me to cash in on his goddamn billions. I had to think of another way—and I did." She winked at Easton Dorn. She actually winked. It startled Dorn so much if she mooned him right there in the living room, he wouldn't have been half as shaken up.

Delaware spoke again, which convinced me he could speak English when so desired.

"You did what, Ms. Ogilvy?"

"Lilith," she corrected him. "Well, I realized I wouldn't get financial help from my husband, and I had no authority whatsoever at his vast companies, so I turned to the man who was closest to him, a man who was making a pittance compared to Gaylord."

"Irving Greenfield," Dorn suggested.

"Irvin. With no G."

"Yes, ma'am—with no G."

"Gaylord told me Irvin has already been arrested today—along with Hayden Fantos and Walter Yellen." She put one hand up near her throat. "Those two men work for me, not for the Ogilvy Company, by the way. They're my bodyguards."

"Where were they guards before that?" I interrupted. "Auschwitz?"

"Keep quiet, Reinert," Dorn snapped at me, then turned back to Lilith. "Are you also aware of Aubrey Sinden? Aubrey Sinden Cabot?"

"I'm aware, Detective—naturally. She works for Ogilvy Company, making too damn much money—and for a long time she was my husband's number one piece of adulterous ass."

"She was my—" I couldn't repeat that even if I wanted to. "Aubrey was my girlfriend during part of that time, too."

That made her happy. "Oh, you're the one. Now I remember. She testified at your trial a long time back. It didn't help. They locked you up anyway."

"I think your husband was aware of that," I said, "even when I wasn't aware of him."

"My God, aren't you the dumb bunny?" she sneered.

Dorn said, "Let's just talk about Aubrey Cabot, shall we? Do you know she owned several valuable pieces of international real estate, thanks to your husband?"

"Gaylord Ogilvy doesn't know a damn thing about it. It was Irvin Greenfield's idea in the first place."

"How could Greenfield afford the down the down payments on all these?"

"I gave him the money. We couldn't let Gaylord know either of us had anything to do with it when the time came, so we made sure only this Aubrey person's name was on it."

"Why, Ms.—uh—Lilith?"

"To take something from Gaylord he never had before."

"But," Dorn said, "he's got fifty times the money he'll ever need."

"True, Detective, but—look, I know he fucked around on me from the very start. I knew before we ever got married. No great love affair from the beginning, but hopefully when you take those vows, a shred of decency comes with them. Trouble is, decency is one of those rare words Gaylord never knew how to pronounce."

Lilith Shadburn Ogilvy stood up, wandered around the edges of the room and stopped at the vast picture window that looked out on a garden rivaling the one at Versailles and which probably cost more. She continued, "Oh sure, I got back at him. I've probably had more adulterous afternoons and evenings than he ever did—famous men, blue-collar men, both my bodyguards, alone and together—and Gay probably knew about them because he has private security that tells him every single thing about me, including whenever my menstrual period begins—to the very hour. But he didn't care. He only cares about money.

"When Irvin Greenfield, who had the same yearnings Gay does but wasn't smart enough or tough enough to make them come true, came to me with ideas he'd discovered while being my devoted husband's chief of staff and right-hand snot-licker. Good thought, wasn't it? That's why I gave him the down payment money and he got Aubrey Cabot to sign the property papers so if it all got exposed, she'd take the blame and not us."

"And when Aubrey wouldn't give the properties back—"

"It's beginning to look like Argentina, for one, is ready to move forward, so we wanted this bitch's name off all of them. But she decided not to sign them back to us unless she got a gazillion chunk of money. We offered her a halfway profitable payoff, but she wanted to get rich. *Big* rich. So my two muscle boys kidnapped her and kept her out of sight until she changed her mind. I hear she was too damn stubborn, so they had to hurt her a little bit."

"A little bit," I mumbled. Dorn waved a hand at me as though I were a mosquito in his bedroom in the middle of the night, so I shut up. Again.

Lilith shrugged. "I'm glad she got through it."

"Maybe she'll tell you about it," I suggested.

"Fine," Dorn said, "except for her husband, Cole Cabot. He got his throat cut and thrown into Lake Michigan. Were you responsible for that, too?"

Lilith frowned, lowering her head for half a minute. Then she said, "I didn't know about it until Irvin told me. I never laid eyes on the man, but Irvin said he was lower middle class. If his wife got her hands on several million dollars, he'd be on a free ride for the rest of his life. Aubrey, for whatever reason, was crazy about him, and Irvin thought Cole would talk Aubrey into holding out."

"So?"

"So—Irvin sent Yellen and Fantos on a midnight mission."

Then she stood up straight, head up, shoulders back, and extended her two hands toward Easton Dorn. "You might as well cuff me now, Detective, before this all ends?"

Delaware moved to her, cuffs dangling. Easton Dorn said, "Cuff her hands in the front, Detective. She's a pretty famous lady around here."

"Damn right I am," Lilith snapped. "It'll cost Gaylord a few million dollars—but I'll be out of jail before nightfall—and I'll never go to trial. And if I do, the verdict will be Not Guilty." Then she turned toward me and winked. "You made a good living typing your little fingers off, Mr. Reinert, so you must know—that's what money is for!"

CHAPTER THIRTY-SEVEN

Skip ahead in this story for the next three weeks, because nothing exciting happened anyone would care about. The weeks were busy as hell for everybody involved, but it would be wearisome to write about it and deadly dull to read about it.

Here's the news, short but sweet: Irvin Greenfield went up before the grand jury, which indicted him for kidnapping, sexual abuse, fraud, theft, and murder after the fact. Walter Yellen and Hayden Fantos never really stole anything, but were rightly charged with kidnapping, sexual abuse and rape, and murder of Cole Cabot.

Easton Dorn testified, as did I, along with Aubrey Sinden Cabot. She talked longer than I did—several hours—and was frank and open about what her captors did to her by Yellen, Fantos and Irwin Greenfield during her three weeks of captivity, trying to get her to sign over the documents which would otherwise put approximately four hundred million dollars into her very large piggy-bank. Some of the grand jury was shocked out of their socks by what happened to Aubrey during those three weeks, and even more jarred by that amount of money.

It's damn near impossible to shock a grand juror, but both Aubrey and Lilith handled it with aplomb, and were even a little amused by it.

Those seven real estate documents will probably be taken

away from Aubrey, possibly by the federal government as opposed to the state or local law enforcement, and possibly by Gaylord Ogilvy himself. The hassle will go on in court for years, possibly decades. Ogilvy had retired Aubrey as his mistress many years before, but now felt sorry enough for her he put her on an allowance from his regal offices, probably worth a million bucks a year—more to keep her quiet than anything else. It also shut her off from any further contact with the Ogilvy Companies and their subsidiaries.

A million bucks a year for not doing a damn thing is a pretty neat job.

Lilith Ogilvy was to be charged for every crime also leveled at Irwin Greenfield except those having to do with forced sex, as she never visited that house while Aubrey was kept there. She did get out of jail on bail until the trial, her bail money at half a million dollars, fifty thousand of which was payable before they let her loose. Gaylord advanced her the money after she spent two days in a downtown women's lock-up, along with a divorce demand that would strip her of just about everything except the outfit she was wearing at the time of her arrest, including the jewelry.

Eaton Dorn, the cop with a badge who got there first, was promoted to Detective Sergeant, which made him a total maven hero in his own precinct. Aubrey got her mind-bending allowance which will keep her comfortable for the rest of her days. The last time I spoke to her, she told me she was looking for a bigger, better, nicer apartment that wouldn't remind her of her murdered husband every day.

I got a great big thank you from everyone.

While the topsy-turvy world was at a temporary slowdown, I threw a dinner party—a small one, consisting of Tana and Jack Phillips, tough young guy but kind and relentless Perwin Tolliver and Kalina—his mother and Denver's wife, a charming woman, gifted with a loving heart, a great sense of humor, and probably fifty pounds too many.

Of course, Cassidy Hammond was there, too. She's spent almost every night there since I returned from my short but violent kidnapping, as I was recalling bit by bit all the things I used to do in bed with a woman, and even learning a few new ones from my brand new GFF.

I wasn't remembering much about my cooking skills pre-Joliet—too many years living on prison-kitchen slop—so I hired a Japanese chef Tana had suggested to me, as she and Jack used him frequently when she invited big shots, important clients, political powerhouses, and potential targets to their beautiful home in Evanston for a magnificent meal that often changed the minds of some guests between entrée, dessert, and Armagnac—my favorite of all the brandies in the world. When he arrived in mid-afternoon to get the dinner started, the super-chef delighted me when he commented on all the glistening new cookware Tana had purchased for my return. She must have had me confused with Martha Stewart.

Well—Martha Stewart and I both cook, and we're both ex-convicts.

"This is such an amazing party, Mr. Reinert," Kalinda Tolliver said, sipping on her Armagnac, her eyes opening in surprise at how magnificent it was. "I'm so honored you invited Perwin and me."

"Perwin and Denver both saved my life at different times," I said, "and they are your family. You're welcome here anytime. And while you're at it, just call me Russ. Everyone else does."

"We're all *your* family," Tana added.

"Especially Tana," her husband added, "and for the longest time. She's not only the city's best lawyer, but she looks great in the shower."

Jack Phillips' raunchy remark got its uncomfortable laughter, and he got an elbow from Tana, but Perwin did a quick glance at him and then away. Jack played for the Chicago Bears—and for any local kid, that meant almost idol worship.

"For me," I said, "there's no such thing as family. I was

adopted, my real parents are unknown, my adoptive parents had no other children, not even distant cousins. When my wife died, I went into the slammer for killing her, so I was completely alone. Except for Tana, no one visited me. Of course, without Denver Tolliver, I wouldn't be sitting here today enjoying with my friends."

"Mostly new friends," Cassidy observed. "You've only known the Tollivers and me for about a month. You're good at making friends, Russ."

"My husband thinks you're the greatest human being in the world since maybe Jackie Robinson or Muhammad Ali," Kalinda said. "When you were still—uh—*in,* I guess, Denver told me all about you every time I visited."

I shook my head. "I don't know what he saw in me, Kalinda. He saved my ass without ever knowing me, and after that we spent as much time together as we could. I almost hated getting out and having to leave him there. For all those years, Denver was my only real friend. He's still my friend, always will be." I fiddled with my brandy glass. "I'd go see him, but as a convicted felon, I'm not sure they'll let me get back into Joliet as a visitor."

Perwin said, "I'll tell my dad I saved your life, too, even if I really didn't. I just took one guy out of the running, that's all."

I shook my head and then gazed at the ceiling. "I'll never understand why he gave a damn about me—but I'm eternally grateful."

"Here's why he gave a damn," Kalinda said. "You actually got him to read books. Before you, I don't think he ever read a book in his life, not counting schoolbooks. He told me the warden wouldn't let any inmates read *your* books because they're all about murder. But you got him reading a little bit after all—mostly non-fiction about history. Especially black history in this country."

"You got him reading the Bible, too," Perwin added.

I laughed. "There were more murders, mass slaughter and

slavery in the Old Testament than in all my books put together. I guess the warden hasn't figured that one out yet."

Cassidy said to the assembled group, "I read all Russ's books before I ever met him. Sure, there were murders in all of them—graphic sex, too. But there was strong morality in each of them, and that's why I loved them so much." She looked down at the table and blushed a little. "And I loved him, too, before I even met him."

"What about now?" Kalinda asked, eyes sparkling.

"Now I'm learning slowly how to put up with him."

"That," I said to Cass, "means tonight you're washing the dishes."

"While I'm doing the dishes—which means with one click I just turn on the dishwasher—you'll get busy writing tonight?"

"Yeah," Perwin said, "I can't wait until you write another one."

His mother chimed in, "I'm going to send your next one to Denver so he can read it, too."

Suddenly my mouth dried up, and I used the last sip of Armagnac to allow me to talk. Everyone was jabbering about my next novel, and I hadn't the foggiest notion of what it's going to be about. "That'll be a while, Kalinda. I haven't started one yet."

Tana Phillips said, "You're joking! Haven't even started?"

"I haven't written a word since I walked out of Joliet."

"My god, Russ! You've been addicted to writing for your whole life. It's like someone who survived on bread and water for many years and then isn't even interested in a sausage and pepperoni pizza when he could eat one if he wanted it."

"It's my fault," Cassidy confessed. "I'm taking up too much of your time. I'll have to break up with you so you can start writing."

"If you do," I warned, "you'll get killed on the first page."

She couldn't avoid a teasing grin. "I die on the first page? What method? Shooting? Drowning? Poisoning?"

"Typed to death."

That got a laugh from everybody, but I must have been one of those stand-up comics who hate their own jokes. It bothered the hell out of me I hadn't been able to write after seven-plus years of not being allowed to. I tried to push it out of my mind since I was set free, and I even went over the notes I took in prison and sent to Tana for one of her people to type up.

About forty-five minutes later, after kisses and hugs and thank-yous and goodbyes, we were alone. Cassidy actually cleared the table and turned on the dishwasher as she'd planned. Then, the soft rumbling from the kitchen behind her, she re-entered the living room. I was working on another Armagnac—my third since dinner ended. She didn't sit down.

"Russ, I think I'll go home tonight."

"You don't have to leave. Besides, you have a toothbrush and nightgown right here."

"This may shock you, but I have another nightgown at home. Several. I also have a toothbrush in my own bathroom."

"Jesus," I almost whispered, "I've turned you off."

"Not at all. But you're halfway buzzed and you'll fall asleep in the middle."

"The middle of what?" I tried for a laugh, but didn't get one.

"I got thinking why you haven't started writing yet. That's what writers do—they write. That's who you are, Russ, and don't for one minute think it's not. You were an only child, which you talk a lot about—and sometimes whine about. Then you took a chunk of your life off from writing to hang out in Joliet Prison. Now you've got family of your own. Tana and Jack. Kalinda and Perwin. Even Denver Tolliver, even though you might never see him again, because he adores you every bit as much as I do.

"Remember," she continued, "I was in love with you before I ever said hello to you. I loved your writing—and it pisses me off thinking I might never get any more."

"I'll write," I said. "I promise."

"When? Next week? Next year? I loved the invisible you and waited seven years for you. I'm in my thirties now. I don't have another seven years."

"Cassidy, are you dumping me?"

"Not forever. Just for tonight. When we're making love, I want your complete attention. And when you're writing, I don't want you thinking about me at all."

She walked to the front closet by the door and took out her coat. "If you don't sober up, you'll have a hangover tomorrow—one more day you won't be able to write. And the day after that and the day after that. You've always thought you were another Dashiell Hammett, but eventually you won't even be you anymore."

She walked over to where I was sitting, bent down, and kissed me on the forehead. "Call me whenever you feel like it, Russ. You have my number—and goddammit, I have your number, too."

Then she was gone.

Who in their right mind brews a pot of coffee to drink at eleven o'clock at night?

But Cassidy was right. I haven't really been a writer for a quite a long time. I spent a hunk of my life in a lousy marriage, I got arrested and convicted for involuntary manslaughter, and spent seven years rubbing shoulders with a few thousand other guys who walked around with sharp knives in their pockets they'd made out of teaspoons from the prison cafeteria—and they would have used them on me if not for my cop-killing guardian angel.

When I finally got out on some sort of technicality, l learned my old acquaintances didn't give a shit about me anymore. I fell in love while gasping for breath on a lonely beach. Days later, I got sucked into a kidnapping and murder case, almost got killed before I lucked out with the help of a detached toilet seat and an oversized kid I'd only known for a few days.

Then the love-of-my-life of one month said good night and went away, leaving me with nothing but a forehead kiss when we both realized my typing fingers had forgotten how to write.

What the hell would I write about, anyway? Family scandals? There hadn't been any, unless my biological parents had turned out to be mass murderers or traitors working for Russia. I had no clue as to that.

Prison? No way—certainly not after reading Stephan King's "Rita Hayworth and the Shawshank Redemption," which is the best damn prison story ever written. The Aubrey kidnapping? No one's ever going to believe it; I hardly believe it myself. And somebody already wrote *'The Godfather.'*

I opened the file Tana's assistant put together for me, dug out the story notes I'd jotted down in Joliet and began thumbing through them. Not about my fellow convicts, naturally, but of those I remembered from earlier in my life, as a kid or a college student or even as a sort-of-famous writer of crime fiction—like my fucking agent and publisher who dumped me after I paid my debt to society—even if I hadn't owed that debt.

Maybe there were those faces I just imagined while lying on my cell cot, staring at the ceiling and waiting for that every-morning signal to wake up and go to breakfast. All interesting, I guess, maybe for another time. But the mood didn't strike me.

I got up for the fourth time to pee. Drinking an entire pot of coffee all by myself in the middle of the night just does that to the kidneys and bladder. But as I was tucking myself back into my pants, a bolt of lightning struck me from above. An idea, and I wouldn't have to do ten minutes' worth of research before I wrote it. It was all in my head. Cassidy Hammond and Denver Tolliver and Armagnac and coffee had loosed the bonds of forgetfulness.

I sat at my desk, switched my new gold-colored laptop to *Word*, tapped a few keys I remembered from seven years ago, looked up some more technical shit about MacBook Air that always threw me for a loop, and began to write.

Fearfully.

Joyfully.

Frightened to death.

Chapter One, I punched out carefully. I stared at those words for a long time. Then, at three o'clock in the morning, I began to write.

"I am an only child...."

ACKNOWLEDGMENTS

Each time I teach a writing class, I tell writer wannabes that no matter what fiction they are working on—comedy, drama, romance, Sci-Fi, Mystery, horror, Western—they are really writing a sort of autobiography without realizing it.

I am indeed an only child. I had an amazing father whose fascinating background I included in this book. I was born and raised in Chicago, like my protagonist. I am a mystery author, as is he, but not nearly as rich and successful. He is also in his late thirties—and I try hard to remember what being late thirties was like. But his life on pages, and mine which I actually lived were very different, too—and I never went to prison.

So I guess I consider this novel a fictional autobiography.

LES ROBERTS came to mystery writing by winning the very first "First Private Eye Novel" Contest, which gave him his literary start. Prior to that, he worked in Los Angeles for a quarter of a century, writing and/or producing more than 2500 half hours of network and syndicated television. A Chicago native, he has lived for the past 31 years in Northeast Ohio.

On the following pages are a few
more great titles from the
Down & Out Books publishing family.

For a complete list of books and to
sign up for our newsletter,
go to DownAndOutBooks.com.

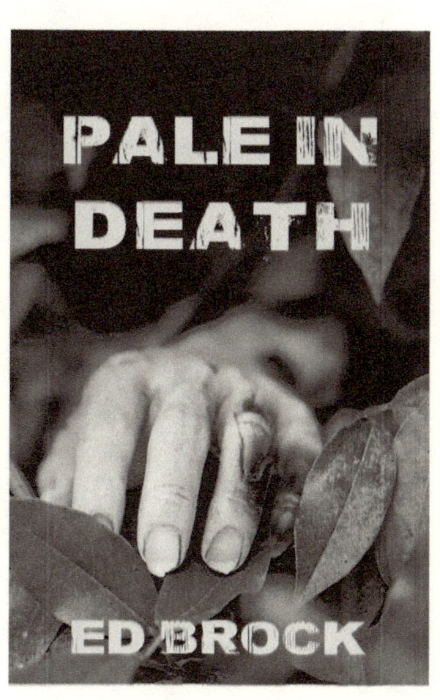

Pale in Death
Ed Brock

Down & Out Books
January 2024
978-1-64396-351-8

Reporter Mark Freer learns that the body of an old girlfriend has been found, beaten to death, in the county where he now lives and works south of Atlanta. He left the girl, Amanda, years before due to her drug addiction but feels guilty because he played a part in beginning that addiction.

Driven by that guilt, he begins to investigate Amanda's death.

The Price You Pay
Jim Fusilli

Down & Out Books
January 2024
978-1-64396-352-5

A crime thriller and coming-of-age story, *The Price You Pay* unravels in crumbling Jersey City where violence and coercion reign.

Young Mickey Wright is thrust by his father, a free-wheeling policeman well-known to politicians and drug dealers, into a world controlled by a powerful Teamster local associated with the Genovese crime syndicate.

The Jan Larkin Mysteries Volume 1
Stephen Burdick

Down & Out Books
January 2024
978-1-64396-353-2

Sergeant Jan Larkin is the best detective in the homicide division of the Pinellas County Sheriff's Office.

The murder of the district attorney's daughter, a serial killer with an unusual method of choosing his victims, and a revenge-minded assassin will put her reputation to the test.

Operation Snow Queen
A Jim Grant Thriller
Colin Campbell

Down & Out Books
February 2024
978-1-64396-354-9

Before Jim Grant was a cop, he was a soldier in the British Army. With only two years' service, he is posted to Germany after a runaway suitcase at Waterloo Station breaks a civilian passenger's leg. He replaces a Company Clerk who lost his head in an accident, and a smuggling ring that doesn't want him.

Following an explosion at the Ammunition Depot, and a court martial in Dusseldorf, Grant is assigned to *Operation Snow Queen,* a training exercise in Bavaria. A place where landslides and falling off a mountain are the least of his worries.